...us is the Son of God - one with ... ...

... Socinian makes Christ m...
...rianism makes him super human - intermediate God -
created for judge, Redeemer, King - but subject ...God.

Testimony of experience. 197-8 } not an impression
    For witness of spirit - 199 - ... } made on me but an ...
Unites one in a new sympathy with mankind } in me, on me, by me,

A religion of moral redemption can only be understood by morally redeemed - (219)

Christianity gives us life, God, - not forms - words only.
Christo power - omnipotence & retroactive, ...
concentrated into potentiality.

Grace came to destroy fatal disease, an infusion
of divine, incorruptible nature into corruptible nature

THE PERSON AND PLACE OF
JESUS CHRIST

THE PERSON AND PLACE OF JESUS CHRIST

The Congregational Union Lecture for 1909

BY

P. T. FORSYTH, M.A., D.D.

PRINCIPAL OF HACKNEY COLLEGE
HAMPSTEAD

"*Morality is the nature of things.*" — BUTLER

BOSTON
THE PILGRIM PRESS
NEW YORK   CHICAGO

ADVERTISEMENT

By the Committee of the Congregational Union of England and Wales.

The Congregational Union Lecture has been established with a view to the promotion of Biblical Science, and Theological and Ecclesiastical Literature.

It is intended that each Lecture shall consist of a course of Prelections delivered at the Memorial Hall, but when the convenience of the Lecturer shall so require, the oral delivery will be dispensed with.

The Committee promise to continue it only so long as it seems to be efficiently serving the end for which it was established, or as they have the necessary funds at their disposal.

For the opinions advanced in any of the Lectures, the Lecturer alone will be responsible.

Congregational Memorial Hall,
Farringdon Street, London.

PREFACE

I WILL beg leave to plead that these pages are lectures and not a treatise. The handling rests on a system, but it is less systematic than suggestive in form. Some repetition also may perhaps be tolerated on this ground. The same may, I hope, be borne in mind in regard to the style. Most of the discourses were in part delivered to an audience, which may account for features that would be less in place if only meant for the eye. The spoken style admits for instance of inflections and emphases which made sufficiently clear a sentence that may have to be read twice. It admits also of more ease and intimacy at times, of personal references and spiritual applications foreign to the remoter and more ambitious idea of a treatise. Moreover the position I take up makes the personal religion of the matter the base of the theology.

I cannot hope to have made every suggestion on such a theme as obvious as it should be in a press article. It is a subject in which the writer must rely much on the co-operative effort of the reader, and must chiefly court the student. The merchan of these goodly pearls must be seekers; and without even divers they cannot be had.

If it came to expressing obligations the foot of each page would bristle with notes and references. But that also is foreign to the lecture form, and especially to the form of lectures which made a certain effort to be as popular as the subject and its depth allowed. Besides, an apparatus of the kind would have given to the book an aspect of erudition which its author does not possess. It is not meant for scholars, but largely for ministers of the Word which it seeks in its own way to serve. It does not extend the frontiers of scientific knowledge or thought in its subject. One or two references I have given. But had they been multiplied there are some names that would have incessantly recurred. And especially those of Rothe, Kähler, Seeberg and Grützmacher—without whom these pages would have been lean indeed. In certain moods, as one traces back the origin of some lines of thought or even phrases of speech, the words come to mind, "What have I that I have not received?"

Those who read to the end will find that the writer agrees with the opinion that the British attitude to criticism must be above all critical. The service rendered to Christianity by the great critical movement is almost beyond words. And there is a vast amount of foreign work which duly and practically recognises the fact, without surrendering the note of a positive Gospel. But it is a misfortune to us, which is also almost beyond reckoning, that most of the translated works are those of a more or less destructive school. For extremes are always easier to grasp and to sell. It should also be added in fairness that many scholars of the negative side possess the art of putting things; in high contrast with the style of their deeper opponents, so amorphous often both in matter and mode. The misfortune to the partially educated in this subject, who only read English, is great; especially as the popular impression is produced (and sometimes pursued) that all the ability and knowledge are on one side. Certain nimble popular journals live on the delusion; and they have not so much as heard whether there be alongside of brilliants like Wernle or Schmiedel giants like Kähler or Zahn. It would not be too much to say that the latter two are among the most powerful minds of the world in the region—one of theology, and one of scholarship. Yet in this country, and certainly to our preachers, they are almost unknown.

It may be useful to add that the lectures were undertaken ten years ago, that the lines of treatment were being then laid down in the writer's mind, and that in the choice of his subject he took counsel with none, met no request, and even had to put aside suggestions of subjects which it would have been valuable to follow. The Congregational Union, under whose auspices the lecture stands, simply asked the present writer to be the next to deliver it. The Union neither prescribed nor suggested subject or point of view. And responsibility belongs entirely to the author to whom was given so free a hand.

SCHEME

___

SYNOPSIS

SYNOPSIS

LECTURE I

LAY RELIGION

Christianity is a theological religion or nothing. It centres in the person of Christ rather than in the Christian principle, and is the religion of His atoning Incarnation. How does this affect the fact that it is a lay religion? Our erroneous conception of lay religion—which is not opposed to a religion truly priestly, but to a theology mainly expert. Lay religion means the experimental religion of the conscience. What is meant by theological reaction. Theocentric Christianity and anthropocentric. Here lies the great religious issue of the hour—a God that serves Humanity or a Humanity that serves God?

LECTURE II

THE RELIGION OF JESUS AND THE GOSPEL OF CHRIST

What is meant by the 'religion of Jesus' which is offered as simple lay Christianity—the difficulties in the seemingly simple phrase—the great reserves of Jesus. The effect on a 'religion of Jesus' of the new religious-historical school is that there never was in actual history any such thing as is meant by the phrase. Christ was not the first Christian. The real conflict is not between an infallible Bible and a fallible, but between a New Testament Christianity and one which believes it knows better. It is not between inspiration and criticism, but between incarnation and evolution. It is not between *no* revelation in Christ and *a* revelation, but between *a* revelation and *the* revelation in Him. The great issue is the superhistoric finality of Christ. That is the true value of His Godhead. And finality is a matter neither of thought nor power but of life, eternal life in Christ for every age alike. Here the most recent philosophy and evangelical Christianity meet. Christianity is not believing *with* Christ, but *in* Christ. Christ does not impress us with a new sense of God, but God in Christ creates us anew.

LECTURE III

THE GREATNESS OF CHRIST AND THE INTERPRETATIONS THEREOF

The recent growth in our sense of Christ's greatness developed by critical and historical study. Does it still reach Godhead? Is Godhead necessary to explain the personality achieved in Jesus Christ? The real site of Christ's greatness is not in His character but in His action, *i.e.* in His cross. It is the cross that ethicises, universalises, and therefore laicises, Christianity. The historic attempts to explain Christ are mainly three—Socinian, Arian, and Athanasian—God's prophet, His plenipotentiary, and His very presence as Redeemer. The necessity for some form of the Athanasian answer, with the *finality* which it alone assigns to Christ.

LECTURE IV

THE TESTIMONY OF CHRIST'S SELF-CONSCIOUSNESS— WAS HE A PART OF HIS OWN GOSPEL?

The Christ of the New Testament as a whole certainly was. The issue of the hour is a choice between the New Testament Christ and the academic—between the Christ of the Apostles and of the critics. The " scrapping " of the New Testament. The Christ of the Synoptics with His claims requires a Christology—the Christ of the extreme critics calls only for a psychology—with a type of religion subjective and ineffectual. The extraneous bias in much criticism. Christ's great confession of Himself in Matthew xi. 27 and its exposition. Only by his Godhead does he offer himself to the whole lay and laden world. The critical argument and its fallacy. What is our authority for confining ourselves to the words of Jesus for His Christianity? Or even to the Synoptical record? Do we have there the whole Christ? We certainly have not the whole Christ of the first Church, of His Apostles. What is the ground for going behind them? Have we the means? Can the Christ of the New Testament be got out of the Synoptics? Or is the Synoptic Christ quite incompatible with the apostolic? In selecting critically from the Gospels, what is to be the standard? Christ the Character or Christ the Redeemer? The development of Christ in the gospels—was it ethical or evangelical? Herrmann's severe verdict on theological liberalism.

LECTURE V

THE TESTIMONY OF APOSTOLIC INSPIRATION—IN GENERAL

Was apostolic inspiration simply a high form of the common faith? Was it the mark of gifted laymen? Was it the truest of tentative explanations of Christ, or had it an element of special knowledge? Was it the continuation of Christ's testimony to himself? Its place in the evolution of belief, and its relation to Christ's finality. Distinction between the material and the formal element in revelation. Inspiration the necessary and integral close of revelation. The New Testament represents not the first stage of a new evolution, but the last phase of the revelationary fact. Illustration from the acts of a legislature.

LECTURE VI

THE TESTIMONY OF APOSTOLIC INSPIRATION—IN PARTICULAR

"The fact without the word is dumb; the word without the fact is empty." The Apostles' own view of their inspiration as condensed in 1 Cor. ii. and 1 Peter i. 11, 12. Their inspiration was the unique and final interpretation of the unique and final revelation—the thought about himself of a Christ living in them. Could the synoptic Christ have produced historic Christianity? Genius and inspiration. The Bible is the real successor of the Apostolate. The authority of the Bible and the authority in the Bible. A parable.

LECTURE VII

THE TESTIMONY OF EXPERIENCE IN THE SOUL AND IN THE CHURCH

The two streams in current Protestanism, Revelation and Illumination. The place of experience in Christianity. As nature is to science so is Christ to faith. The difference between our experience of a Saviour, and our experience of a Saint. Faith and impression. What we experience in Christ is a Saviour for the lay soul and not merely a presence for the mystic adept. That is, we have one whose action is deeper than the certainty of our self-consciousness. There is no rational certainty which has a right to challenge moral—and especially the moral certainty of being saved. The enlargement of personal evangelical experience to the historic scale of the Church. The first Church could never have included Christ in his own Gospel unless he had himself done so. We must take the whole New Testament's Christianity, as prolonged in the experience of an Apostolic Church. Otherwise we must think it was a poor Christ who could not protect his followers from idolatry of him.

LECTURE VIII

THE MORALISING OF DOGMA—ILLUSTRATED BY THE OMNIPOTENCE OF GOD

Dogma, the intellectual self-expression of a living Church. It does not exclude but demand criticism—on its own evangelical base. Melanchthons words. Early dogma was too little lay and moral in its nature, and too prominently metaphysical, especially in connexion with Christ's person. We begin here by examining the empirical ideas of divine greatness and omnipotence. In what sense God is not omnipotent. The union of two natures in this light and its unsatisfactory moral results.

LECTURE IX

THE SAME ILLUSTRATED BY THE ABSOLUTENESS OF CHRIST

Let us get at truth whatever happen to tradition. and let us be exact with terms. Neither common sense nor philosophy gives a basis for the Incarnation, but at most only points of attachment. It can only be proved religiously—by the experience of its own action. The true assent to it is the life-act of faith. Application to religion of the idea of the absolute. It is an experience—and one open to all. And an experience of the historic Christ. And of him as final judge and redeemer. The absoluteness of holy love has other methods than the philosophic absolute, however adjustable they may be. "Morality (*i.e.* experience) the soul of things."

LECTURE X

THE PRE-EXISTENCE OF CHRIST

As emphasis moves from the Virgin birth, we must go to explain Christ by His pre-existence. The paucity of allusion in the New Testament, and the two ways of explaining it. Was Christ at every hour conscious of all He was? His pre-existence and its kenotic renunciation are needful to explain the volume and finality of the Church's adoring faith. Had Christ an esoteric teaching, reflected in John? The pre-existence of Christ cannot be directly verified by experience as His present life may be. But experience, though the mode of faith, is not its measure. A Christ who existed for the first time on earth is not adequate to the classic experience of the New Creation, and especially to the regeneration of the race. The chief object of such a doctrine is not philosophical nor even theological, but religious—to give effect to the depths of the condescending love of God. Jesus the only man in whom the relation to God *constitutes* his personality. He embodied not simply the divine *idea*, nor the divine *purpose*, but God's *presence* with us. And this He did not by the acquisition of a divine personality, but by its redintegration through a moral process.

LECTURE XI

THE KENOSIS, OR SELF-EMPTYING OF CHRIST

Some doctrine of kenosis is called for if we hold the pre-existence. There are difficulties, but it is a choice of difficulties. And they are more scientific than religious, as they concern the *how* and not the *what*. A series of analogies in the experience of life. Must a complete self-emptying part with holiness and share our sin? Only temptation, and not sin, is truly human. True freedom possible only to the holy. What then was renounced? Omniscience, etc.? The attributes of God cannot be parted with; but they may be retracted into a different mode of being, and from actual become potential. Such a view leaves us untroubled by the limitations and ignorances of Christ. He consented not to know, and was mighty not to do.

LECTURE XII

THE PLEROSIS, OR THE SELF-FULFILMENT OF CHRIST

A Christ merely kenotic would be but negative. And we must be positive. In humbling Himself, Christ must realise Himself. And His self-realisation must mean our redemption. Failure to find this positivity in the Chalcedonian doctrine of the two natures. Persons now count for more than natures in an Ethical Faith. It profits more, therefore, to speak of the involution and fulfilment in Christ of two personal movements—the manward movement of God and the Godward movement of man, each personal, and both meeting and blending in the person of the Son. The growth of Christ's personality was the growth of human redemption. In His person the Agent of creation became such a soul as He was wont to make —for a purpose possible only to Godhead. He was creaturely, but uncreated—all men's creator in a true man's life. What we really mean by the Godhead and manhood of Christ.

LECTURE I

LAY RELIGION

THE GOOD NEWS

By J. EDGAR WILSON

Price, 25 cents per 100

Leaflet Department
Publishing House
Methodist Episcopal Church, South
Nashville, Tennessee

THE GOOD NEWS

"I am not ashamed of the gospel of Christ
Rom. 1: 16.

The word "gospel" means *good news*.

We would do well to remind ourselves
this every time we use, or hear, the word.

But what was "the good news of Christ,"
which Paul declared he was "not ashamed"?

1. The good news of *a risen and glorifi*
Lord.

The resurrection of Jesus from the dead pr
duced upon his disciples a sudden and very
markable change. They had been disappointe
discouraged, depressed. "We trusted," th
said, "it had been he that should have redeem
Israel." Note the past tense—a hope abandone

But when the conviction forced itself up
them that Jesus was indeed alive from the dea
what a marked change occurred in them.
is very evident to my mind that no mere ho
of Jesus had spiritually survived the physic
death that had overtaken him would have p
duced this change in his disciples. It was on
produced by the conviction that this personal
with whom they had repeated interviews, ta
ing with him, eating with him, touching him w
their hands, was the very same Jesus—chang
in some respects, no doubt, but identical nev
theless, whom they had seen expire upon t
cross, and buried in his tomb.

The amazing fact of his resurrection clarifi

2

LECTURE I

LAY RELIGION

THE root of all theology is real religion; of all Christian theology, and even apologetic, it is Christian religion, it is saving faith in Jesus Christ. It is justifying faith, in the sense of faith in a forgiving God through the cross of Jesus Christ. But this religion cannot be stated without theology. If theology can be shewn to be irrelevant to a living and evangelical faith, then the Church can afford to treat it with some indifference, and to leave its pursuit, like philosophy, to the Universities. But the Christian religion is theological or nothing. We are but vaguely and partially right in saying that Christ is the Gospel. Years ago to say that was the needful word; but it is now outgrown and inadequate. The Gospel is a certain interpretation of Christ which is given in the New Testament, a mystic interpretation of a historic fact. It is the loving, redeeming grace of a holy God in Christ and His salvation alone. Theology, it is true, does not deal with thoughts but with facts. That is the great note of modern theology. But the Christian fact is not an historic fact or figure simply; it is a superhistoric fact living on in the new experience which it creates. The fact on which Christian theology works is the Christ of

faith and not of history only, of inspiration and not
mere record, of experience and not of memory.   It is
the Christ of the Church's saving, justifying faith.

A Christianity without such faith is not Christianity.
Spiritual sensibility is not Christianity, nor is any degree
of refined unction.   A spirituality without positive, and
even dogmatic, content is not Christianity; nor are
gropings when stated as dogmas; nor is a faith in the
broad general truths of religion.   Christian faith must
surely dogmatise about the goodness of God in Christ, at
the least. (A conversion which is but a wave of spiritual
experience is not the passage from death to life.) *Religion*
can only be made more real by a deepened sense of the
reality of the *salvation*. (An access of religion which does
not mean, first or last, a deeper repentance and a more
personal faith in Christ's salvation may be sincere enough,
and it is certainly better than worldliness or unconcern;
but it is not believing unto life.) It is not New Testament Christianity.   And, tender as we should be to it as
a stage, we must be very explicit when it is offered as a
goal.   Gentle as we may be to it as a search, we must be
quite plain with those who proclaim it as the great find.
If Claverhouse had developed a mystical piety which
made him deeply sensitive to the devotions of his Church;
or, if Alva had retired into a monastery and spent his
time in sincere devotion on the exercises of Loyola and
beatific visions; if they forswore their old aggression,
and melted to their depths at the presence of the sacrament; and if it was all unmingled with a repentance still
more deep, because they had harried the Church of God,
wounded his faithful saints, and crucified Christ afresh,
what would there be in that to place them in the same
faith as Paul, or the same spiritual company? I remember

Bradlaugh and his violent iconoclastic days, so able,
ardent and ignorant. And he might stand for a type of
others. If such men developed one of those spiritual
reactions which lead some of the unbalanced to a religious-
ness as extreme as their aggression had been; had a
long-starved soul burst into an Indian summer of mystic
sensibility and abstract piety, which all the time was
little troubled about the old intellectualist arrogance and
ignorant insolence, the rending of Churches, the grief
caused to the old disciples, or the shipwreck made of
many a young faith; if the new sense of God brought no
humiliation, no crushing, and almost desperate, repentance, curable only by a very positive faith and new life of
forgiveness in Christ and His Cross; what were the
Christian value of such a piety? Would such a religion
have much more than subjective worth as a phase of
religious experience more interesting to the psychologist
than precious for the Gospel?

The essential thing in a new Testament Christianity
is that it came to settle in a final way the issue between
a holy God and the guilt of man. All else is secondary.
All criticism is a minor matter if that be secure. The
only deadly criticism is what makes that incredible; the
only mischievous criticism is what makes that less credible.
And all the beauties and charms of a temperamental
religion, like Francis Newman's, for instance, or Renan's,
or many a Buddhist's, are insignificant compared with a
man's living attitude to that work of God's grace for the
world once and for ever in Jesus Christ.

§   §   §

A faith whose object is not such a Christ is not
Christianity; at least it is not New Testament Christianity; and the great battle is now for a New Testament

C

Christianity. It is not faith in Christ when we rise no higher than "just a man, but what a man!" You cannot use the word faith in relation to a Christ like that. Faith is an attitude we can take only to God. God is the only correlate of faith, if we use words with any conscience. Faith in Christ involves the Godhead of Christ. Faith in Christ, in the positive Christian sense, means much more than a relation to God to which Christ supremely helps us. It is a communion possible not *through*, but only *in* Christ and Him crucified. It means that to be in Christ is to be in God. It means the experience that the action of Christ with us is God's action, that Christ does for us and in us what holy God alone can do, and that in meeting with Christ we meet with God. When it comes to revelation, only God could do justice to God. Theologically, faith in Christ means that the person of Christ must be interpreted by what that saving action of God in him requires, that Christ's work is the master key to His person, that His benefits interpret His nature. It means, when theologically put, that Christology is the corollary of Soteriology; for a Christology vanishes with the reduction of faith to mere religion. It means that the deity of Christ is at the centre of Christian truth for us because it is the postulate of the redemption which *is* Christianity, because it alone makes the classic Christian experience possible for thought. I am not judging individuals, I speak of types of religion; and I suggest that the Christian experience, for the Church if not for every individual maturing in it, is the evangelical experience, the new creation in atoning forgiveness. It is not mere love and admiration of Jesus, however passionate. It is not simply a hearty conviction of the Christian principle. Nor is it a temper of Christian

charity. When Paul said he had the mind of Christ
he did not mean the temper of Christ ; he meant the
theology of Christ. And by that he meant not the
theology held by the earthly Christ, but that taught
him by Christ in heaven. A reference to 1 Cor. ii. 16
will show this at once. "Who hath known (by a gnosis)
the mind of the Lord that he may *instruct* Him ? But
we have (by faith) the mind of Christ." That is, of the
Lord, the Spirit.

§   §   §

The theology that turns merely on the Christian
principle (taken as distinct from Christ's perennial person)
reduces Christ's character to a far too placid level, which
does not correspond to the passionate Christ of Synoptic
history. Perhaps a one-sided reading of the Johannine
Christ might mislead us to think thus of Him. But his
was no Phidian majesty. He was not calmly, massively,
and harmoniously filled by a principle of divine sonship,
whose peace was as a brimming river ; for a pious sage, a
Christian Goethe, might be that. The sinlessness of
Jesus was not of that natural, sweet, poised, remote, and
æsthetic type. It was not the harmonious development
of that principle of sonship through the quietly deepening experiences of life—just as His nightly communion
cannot have been simply a blessed and oblivious respite
from the task of each day, but its offering, outspreading,
and disentangling before the Father who prescribed it.
Gethsemane was not the first agony. Each great season
was a crisis, and sometimes a stormy crisis, in which the
next step became clear. There is much truth in Keim's
treatment of Christ's temperament as the choleric. The
sinless certainty of Jesus was the result of constant
thought, passion, and conflict as to his course and victory,

crowned by the crisis of all His crises in the decision and
triumph of His cross.   And His power was not quiescent, reserved strength alone.   It was not monumental.
But it was energy put forth in a positive conflict, in
mortal moral strife for the overthrow of God's enemy,
through the redemption of the race, the forgiveness of its
guilt, and its moral re-creation.

And to such a Christ Christian faith corresponds.   It
is not a warm sense of sonship as the crowning form of
natural religion or of a devout temperament.   It is not
a frame of reasonable views, benignant charity, patient
pity, and strong repose.   It is the experience of having
in Christ, His crisis, and His victory, that salvation,
that pardon, that new life which God alone can give.   It
is not looking up trustfully to a loving Father, but giving
one's self thankfully to a redeeming Saviour and *His*
Father.   Again I say I am not speaking of ripening
individuals, but of that corporate, central, and classic
experience which gives the type of every other, makes
the Church the Church, and carries the note of the Gospel.

§   §   §

One is tempted sometimes to speak to preachers in this
vein : " Yes, the incarnation is the centre of Christianity,
and you must convince people that it is so.   But it is an
intricate question.   Its true solution is beyond the
average man.   Perhaps you can best accommodate it to
your lay hearers if you take it on the experimental side,
and bid them believe that Christ was God because He
forgives and redeems as God only can.   But, of course,
for the real grounds of the belief more deep and philosophic considerations are involved.   And these are
beyond you; they must be left to the Church through
its theologians.   And lay faith in the incarnation must be

a *fides implicita*, or the acceptance of something which experience only indicates, but does not found."

The advice in its first part is good ; but in its second it is bad and dangerous, and it would put Christ at the mercy of theological Brahmans. It is quite true that the scientific treatment of the question leads into regions where the lay believer is not at home. But these regions are only the hinterland of that historic Christ within our personal experience—within an experience where the believer is not only at home, but has his birth and being as a Christian. All Christology exists in the interest of the evangelical faith of the layman who has in Jesus Christ the pardon of his sins and everlasting life. We are all laymen here. It is quite misplaced patronage to condescend to lay experience with the superiority of the academic theologian or the idealist philosopher, and to treat such lay experience of the Gospel as if it were good enough for most, and the only one they are yet fit for, but if they passed through the schools they would be able to put their belief on another and better footing. It is the evangelical experience of every saved soul that is the real foundation of Christological belief anywhere. For Christ was not the epiphany of an idea, nor the epitome of a race, nor the incarnation, the precipitate, of a metaphysic—whatever metaphysic he may imply. The theology of the incarnation is necessary to explain our Christian experience and not our rational nature, nor our religious psychology. It is not a philosophical necessity, nor a metaphysical, but an evangelical. Philosophy, on the whole, is perhaps against it. And the adoption of the tone I deprecate is but a survival of the bad old time when we had to begin with a belief in the incarnation (on the authority of the Church and its metaphysical theologians

as set out in the creeds) before we could have the benefit
of an evangelical faith. It is on the contrary an evangelical faith like a converted miner's that makes any
belief in the incarnation necessary or possible at last.
We begin with facts of experience, not with forms of
thought. First the Gospel then its theology, first
redemption then incarnation—that is the order of experience. That is positive Christianity; which is as distinct
from rational orthodoxy on the one hand as it is from
rational heresy on the other. The mighty thing in
Christ is his grace and not His constitution—the fact
that it is God's grace that we have in Him, and no mere
echo of it, no witness to it, or tribute to it. That is our
Christian faith. And that certainty of the saved experience is the one foundation of all theology in such
Churches as are not stifled in mediæval methods or bur-
dened by their unconscious survival.

§   §   §

It is this unique experience of a unique Saviour who is
the new Creator that we have to urge in the face of every
theory that makes it impossible and of every practice
that would make it nugatory. And at the present day
we have to make it good both in life and in thought—in
life against the mere bustle of progress, and in thought
against a mere procession of evolution that has no goal
already latent at its centre.

The evolutionary idea is certainly compatible with
Christianity; but not so long as it claims to be the supreme idea, to which Christianity must be shaped.
Evolution is within Christianity, but Christianity is not
within evolution. For evolution means the rule of a
levelling relativism, which takes from Christ His absolute
value and final place, reduces Him to be but a stage of

God's revelation, or a phase of it that can be outgrown, and makes Him the less of a Creator as it ranges Him vividly in the scale of the creature. There is no such foe to Christianity in thought to-day as this idea is ; and we can make no terms with it so long as it claims the throne. The danger is the greater as the theory grows more religious, as it becomes sympathetic with a Christ it does not worship, and praises a Christ to whom it does not pray. A book so devout as Bousset's Jesus does for the Saviour what the one-eyed Wotan did so tenderly for Brunnhilde within the touching *Feuerzauber*, "Ich küsse die Gottheit dir ab," "I kiss thy Godhead away." To say that evolution is God's supreme method with the world is to rule out Christ as His final revelation. It is to place Christ but at a point in the series, and to find Him most valuable when he casts our thoughts forward from himself to a greater revelation which is bound to come if evolution go on. But when Christ's finality is gone, Christianity is gone. Yea, and progress itself is gone. For there is no faith in progress permanently possible without that standard of progress which we have in Christ, the earnest of the inheritance, the proleptic goal of history, the foregone sum of the whole matter of man. Progress without any certainty of the goal is as impossible in practice as it is senseless in thought. It is mere motion, mere change. We need a standard to determine whether movement be progress. And the only standard is some prevenient form or action of the final goal itself. Our claim is that for religion the standard is God's destiny for man, presented in advance in Christ—presented there, and not merely pictured— presented to man, not achieved by him—given us as a pure present and gift of grace—and presented finally there.

Man has in Christ the reality of his destiny, and not a prophecy of it.

§   §   §

We are often adjured to go the whole length of our Protestant principle by insisting that Christianity is a lay religion, not a priestly, and by adjusting the form of our Gospel to the lay mind. But this adjustment is coming to mean something which provokes a little doubt whether we have any positive idea of what a lay religion means. It properly means an experienced religion of direct, individual, and forgiven faith, in which we are not at the mercy of a priestly order of men, a class of sacramental experts. It is certainty of Christ's salvation at first hand, by personal forgiveness through the cross of Christ in the Holy Ghost. It does not mean a non-mediatorial religion, a religion stripped of the priestly order of acts or ideas. New Testament Christianity is a priestly religion or it is nothing. It gathers about a priestly cross on earth and a Great High Priest Eternal in the heavens. It means also the equal priesthood of each believer. But it means much more. That by itself is ruinous individualism. It means the collective priesthood of the Church as one. The greatest function of the Church in full communion with Him is priestly. It is to confess, to sacrifice, to intercede for the whole human race in Him. The Church, and those who speak in its name, have power and commandment to declare to the world being penitent the absolution and remission of its sins in Him. The Church is to stand thus, with the world's sins for a load, but the word of the atoning cross for the lifting of it. That is apostolic Christianity. That is the Gospel. Evangelical Christianity is mediatorial both in faith and function.

But, in the name of a simplicity which is not Christ's, lay Christianity is ceasing to be even the priesthood of each believer in virtue of the priesthood of Christ. It is coming to be understood as the rejection of apostolic, mediatorial, atoning Christianity and the sanctification of natural piety—sometimes only its refinement. It is more preoccupied with ethical conduct than with moral malady, with the fundamental truths of religion than with the fontal truths of mercy. And whereas we used to be able to appeal to our laymen and their experience against a Socinian and undogmatic and non-mediatorial Christianity, we can now appeal to them only against a sacerdotal and clerical. We used to be able to take refuge from Arianism (to which the ministers of the Church might be tempted by certain philosophies), in the evangelical experience of its members. We used to think that the sense of sin which was lost from the intellectuals or the worldlings would be found among the Christian men who were in lay contact with the world, its temptations, its lapses, and its tragedies. But experience hardly now bears out this hope. Perhaps the general conscience has succumbed to the cheap comforts and varied interests of life; or the modern stress on the sympathies has muffled the moral note; or the decency of life has stifled the need of mercy; or Christian liberty has in the liberty lost the Christ. But, whatever the cause, the lay mind becomes only too ready to interpret sin in a softer light than God's, and to see it only under the pity of a Lord to whom judgment is quite a strange work, and who forgives all because He knows all. It is on a broken reed we too often lean when we turn from the theologian's "subtleties" to rely on the layman's faith. For the layman becomes slow to own a faith

which begins in repentance rather than benevolence.
He is slow to confess a sin that is more than backward-
ness, untowardness, or ignorance. The number grows
of high and clean-living youths who cherish an ideal
Christianity but feel no need for a historic and perennial
Christ. The tendency of the lay mind is backward
to the eighteenth century, to a wise, humane, and urbane
religion, only enlarged by all the ideality and fraternity
that enlarge Deism to modern Theism. It goes back
to a religion of belief in human nature, of spiritual
bonhommie, of vague and kindly optimism, of good
sense, well-doing, and such a sober estimate of the state
of things between God and man as avoids extreme ideas
like curse, perdition, mortal vigilance, or any eternally
perilous edge of life. It is the type of religion which
commends itself to the intelligent, sympathetic, active
and well-disposed young Christian, who would like, above
all things, for righteousness' sake, to be an active
politician, alderman, or member of Parliament. This is
an excellent Christian ambition. May it spread! But it
is often the ambition of a type of man who tends to
treat positive Christianity as theology, and to regard the
theologian of an Atonement as our fathers did the priest,
or as the Sicilians regard a sanitary officer — to treat
him, at the worst, as a gratuitous sophisticator of things
very ancient, simple, and elemental, or as a mere survival,
now useless or even mischievous. Or it views him, at
the best, as a harmless hobbyist, no better than a philosopher. Such lay religion is ceasing to regard the apostles
with their priestly Gospel of Christ as laymen. It treats
them as theologians, and in so far complicators. It
views them as confusing the lay issue. It would eliminate
the priestly and atoning element from the nature of the

Gospel, for a kind of religion which is but a spiritualising of the natural man, or a mystic devoutness. It regards Christ as the most inspired of the prophets of God's love, the most radical of social reformers, and the noblest of elder brothers. Whereas, the Church must stand on Christ the priest, His sacrifice, and His redemption ; and it could not stand, as it did not arise, upon Christ the beneficent prophet or noble martyr. And the condition of our Churches shows that this is so. With an ideal or a fraternal Christ they dwindle and the power goes out of them.

§		§		§

I am trying to avoid the dogmatism of dogma. But I am also striving concisely to sharpen the issue, to be explicit and clear, and to point the choice the Church *must* make or go under. And the Free Churches the first.

Revelation did not come in a statement, but in a person ; yet stated it must be. Faith must go on to specify. It must be capable of statement, else it could not be spread ; for it is not an ineffable, incommunicable mysticism. It has its truth, yet it is not a mere truth but a power ; its truth, its statement, its theology, is part of it. There is theology and "theology." There is the theology which is a part of the Word, and the theology which is a product of it. There is a theology which is sacramental and is the body of Christ, so to say ; and there is a theology which is but scientific and descriptive and memorial. There is a theology which quickens, and one which elucidates. There is a theology which is valuable because it is evangelical, and one which is valuable because it is scholastic. It is no Christianity which cannot say : " I believe in God the

Creator, who, in Christ, is my Almighty Father, Judge
and Redeemer." That is theology, but not " theology."
It is pure religion and undefiled. It is worlds more
precious than any freedom that forwandered spirits deify
in its place. But our laity has not yet learned to
distinguish between these two senses of Christian truth.
They are ghost-ridden. They are obsessed by a mere
tradition of the long gone days, when the theologians
made a hierarchy which only changed the form but not the
spirit of the Roman ; when the Reformation succumbed
to a theological hierarchy instead of a sacerdotal ; when
the laity, who were not professional theologians, had to
take an intricate system from the experts, with an
implicit faith like that of Rome in the old days, or, in
new days, like the implicit faith with which the inexpert
readers swallow the expert critics ; when the laity took
over this faith provided for them, and only made it their
business to see it accepted and carried through into
public life by others equally unable to judge it. What
the laity is suffering from is the feeble afterwash of the
long past days of tests. But the ministry in the main,
and the theologians in particular, have for some generations now moved forward into another world of things,
another habit of thought, and another kind of authority.
And our competent guides know this. But our laity to
a large extent do not know it, and they are played upon
by those who know just a little more. They are victims
to an anachronist suspicion of an obsolete " theology,"
when they should be confessors of personal faith and its
vital theology, if Christianity is not to be lost in the
sand. It would be a deadly calamity if we were to relapse
to that dogmatocracy, that rule of the professional
theologian, that Protestant Catholicism which half-ruined

Lutheran Protestantism in the seventeenth century.
How great a calamity it would be, we are able to mark,
when we observe the effects of our subjection to-day to
the negative dogmatocracy of the critics, evolutionists,
monists, and socialists who take Christianity in hand in
the interest of dogma which changes its spots but not
its spirit.

§ § §

Lay religion tends to be simple, easy, and domestic
religion, with a due suspicion not only of a priesthood
but even of a ministry. Some sections of it are more
interested in the children than in the ministry. They
believe in schools, hospitals, temperance, boys' brigades,
and all the excellent things the mayor can open; with
sometimes but small insight and distant respect for the
deeper things that dawn upon the experts of the Soul,
and do not go straight home to business or bosom. It
is preoccupied with righteousness as conduct more than
with faith as life indeed. It thinks the holiness of God
a theological term, because nothing but love appeals to
the young people who must be won. If it only knew
how the best of the young people turn from such
novelistic piety! And the view taken of sin corresponds.
Sin is an offence against righteousness or love instead of
against holiness; and it can be put straight by repentance
and amendment without such artifices as atonement. It
just means going wrong; it does not mean being guilty.
The cross is not a sacrifice for guilt, but a divine object-
lesson in self-sacrifice for people or principles. The lay
mind tends to associate a sense of sin with the morbid
side of human nature, or with the studies of men who
are in more contact with a theological past than with a
human present. Christ saves from misery, and wrong,

and bad habits, and self distrust; but not from guilt.
He reveals a Father who is but rarely a judge, and then
only for corrective purposes. The idea of a soul absolutely
forfeit, and of its salvation in a new creation, grows
foreign to the lay mind. And the deep root of it all is
the growing detachment of that mind from the Bible, and
its personal disuse.

And this lay religion the pulpit is occasionally tempted
to adopt, partly from wrong education, partly from
poverty of nature or belief, partly from a fear of seeming
to be behind date or out of touch with the pew. While
those preachers who do not thus part with the native
language of the Gospel, and to whom its specialities are
the true realities, are apt to be disheartened, benumbed,
and paralysed in the face of the spiritual self-satisfaction
that confronts them, the this-worldiness, the at-homeness
in human nature. They find no effective fulcrum in a laity
like that for any protest they may make against clerical
priestliness. They find but a platform impatience, and
irritation, and invective. And they begin to ask if clerical
priesthood deserves all the denunciation it gets. They
ask if the clerical priest, by the effect he does give to
the real and distinctive priestliness of Christianity, will
not always be stronger than a lay anti-priestliness of the
unspiritual sort. They would rather spend less time and
fury upon the denunciation of priesthood, and more upon
an effort to make the Churches realise the priestliness
they have all but lost. What shall it profit any Church
to commit suicide to save itself from slaughter.

§   §   §

It is probably impossible now to change the lay mentality of which I speak in those who are its victims.
But we can perhaps save the next generation for a true

Church. We can teach and act as men who really believe
that it is only a Church of true priests that can withstand
a Church of false ones.   It cannot be done by a Church
of no priests, which is indeed no Church.   A lay religion,
alien to apostolic and mediatorial belief, can never
make head against the evangelical apostolicity which
may lie deep but potent beneath the errors of sacerdotal
Catholicism.

We have laicised the idea of the ministry by treating
it simply as one of the departments of Christian work.
We have been told that all forms of Christian life are
equally sacred, and that just as good work can be done
for Christ in the Christian pursuit of other walks of life.
And the half-truth there has been so abused and over-
driven that the Churches send their most capable youth
to these other pursuits (often to make proof how false
the notion of their equal sanctity can become) ; and we
tend to a ministry of the mentally and spiritually inferior,
unable to command the strong and capable personalities.
That is one result of the laicising of belief, of the levelling of the Gospel to life instead of the lifting of life to
the Gospel.   It is the result of erasing the feature unique
in the Gospel, and consequently in the office which
preaches it.

§   §   §

In a word, as I say, lay religion is coming to be understood as the antithesis, not of sacerdotal religion, but
of theological, of atoning religion ; that is to say,
really of New Testament Christianity.   And so
understood, it has neither power nor future.   And
most thorough Christians will move in the end to join
that Church, free or bond, which has most of the

power, the future, the authority, and the liberty which are in the Christ of the Apostles, and of the Church.

The greatest of the human race is He who, as the Holy One that came out from the Father, was a priest before all else, and who has for His chief object with the world the ordination of all men in a Church as priests in Him. He was one to whose sacrifice, atonement, and prayer mankind owes, daily and for ever owes, its moral renovation and its divine destiny. Christianity is such priestly religion; it is not what tends to be known as lay religion, or the religion that arrests the well-disposed man in the street. It is the religion of the common man who lives on the sacrifice of Christ. If the belief in a priestly Christianity came to be confined to the ministry, then spiritual command and influence would, and should, remain with the ministry, amid whatever errors beside, amid the errors even of Rome. But lay religion, in the minimist sense of the word, affectional and ethical religion, will never save us from the perils of priestly rule. For it cannot give us our Great High Priest, eternal in the heavens. And it certainly cannot unite us with Him in the priesthood of a true Church. They are logical enough who say that Incarnation, Atonement, Priesthood, and a Church all hang together; so that having denounced an Atonement they must go on to denounce a Church. But it is more logical still to extend the chain and go on to say that a Church with all these beliefs is indissolubly bound up with the consummation of Humanity in a Kingdom of God.

§   §   §

There is a misunderstanding that is likely enough here. One might easily incur the charge of being a *laudator temporis acti*, and of lamenting the former days

that were better than these.   I would, on the contrary,
State my conviction that there never was a time in the
history of the world when there were so many souls bent
on seeing and doing the will of God.   There was never
a time when spiritual sympathies and appetites were so
quick and general as to-day, never an age when so
many were set upon the Kingdom of God, and certain
aspects of it were so clearly and widely seen.

A slight knowledge of the past can readily mislead us
here.   We too easily transfer the religious eminence of
the historic saints and heroes to the Christian public of
their time, which we view in the golden haze which
radiates from them.   But in the Middle Ages of Anselm
and Bernard personal piety was almost confined to the
monasteries and convents.   The rest were but institutional
Christians, and members of the Church without being,
or professing to be, members of Christ.   Men were religious in the lump, as tribes often are that are converted
with their chiefs but unchanged in their hearts.   And
even when the Reformation substituted personal faith for
wholesale religion the change was realised but by few
beyond the great leaders.   The passionate interest and
conflict of the hour was not for personal piety, but for
public liberties, for the right of Gospel preaching, for
freedom of Confession, or for a national Church.   And
in all these public ardours there was the greatest danger
of the Reformation burning out, and the old Church
flowing back over its ashes, as public Christianity is en-
dangering us to-day.   What saved the Reformation
religiously was the rise of Pietism, which rescued faith
both from the politicians and the theologians.   It was
not till then, and but partially then, that the religion of
the Reformation penetrated to masses of people.   Had

D

it done so before, the counter-Reformation would have been impossible. But before Pietism could fully reach the large Christian public as personal experience, the rationalism of the eighteenth century had begun to give off its widespread chill.

So I venture to say there are more spiritually-minded people in the world to-day than ever before; though I cannot stay to trace the renascence of spirituality from the century I have named. It is largely due, in this country at least, to the Evangelical movement, to the romantic or Tractarian movement, and to the idealist movement in philosophy, as these are represented by Low Church, High, and Broad.

But after this admission I also venture to repeat that Christianity means much more than spiritual appetite or sympathy. Personal faith means much more than ideal religion or romantic. These pieties are too subjective, and they do not contain that which makes Christianity Christian. The thing that marks Christianity is the objective gift of God in Jesus Christ. What is the nature of that gift? The difference between Catholicism and Protestantism is a very deep and real one, but it does not turn upon greater or less spirituality. It is hard to say on which side of the line you find more of that. They differ upon totally different conceptions of the gift of God in Christ. Both Rome and Reformation start from the supernatural gift in Christ, as every Church must do, else it does not remain a Church. No Church is possible on a basis of religion; it must be a basis of salvation. Both Churches knew that Christianity must be something more than religious sensibility, ideal aspiration, beautiful prayers, the great general truths of our spiritual nature, or even a passion for the Kingdom of God. Both knew that a

Church and a faith could rest only on a positive revelation
and not a subjective inspiration. They parted when
they came to describe the revelation, the gift, the way
by which the Kingdom must come. That was also what
parted Jesus and Judaism. Both of these lived for the
Kingdom. It was their life passion. But they were a
world apart in the way they believed it must come; and
the difference was fatal.

And to measure truly the Christianity of an age we
must ask how far it grasps God's true gift, and not how
eagerly or finely it seeks it. What is its conception of
salvation? What is it that makes it religious? What
is the object of its religion? Do not ask, What is its
dream? or, What is its programme or its piety? but,
What is its Gospel? Do not ask, What is its experience?
Ask what emerges in its experience? It is not the lack of
religiosity that ails the Church, it is the lack of a Gospel
and a faith, the lack of a spiritual authority and a
response to it.

For the leaders of the Reformation the gift was not an
institution, nor was it vaguely a Christian spirit, but the
Holy Spirit as personal life. It was direct personal
communion with a gracious and saving God in Jesus
Christ. It was direct obedience to his authority.
What they presented to us was a Kingdom finally
won in Christ, and not one yet to be won by any
faith or work of ours. It was what they called "the
finished work," and what is now called the absoluteness
or the finality of Christ. And it is here that, for the
hour, the Church is their inferior. It has fallen from
their evangelical height. The world has gone forward
in its religion, but the Church has gone back in its faith.
Unhappily, the thing in which the world has gone forward

is of less value than the thing in which the Church has
gone back. Religion is secondary, but positive faith is
primary. We have more religion than ever before—sometimes more than we know what to do with; do we find
more faith on the earth? We have more sensibility and
more seeking, but have we more strength, footing, and
command, in proportion? Have we the old heroes' grasp
of the sure and unspeakable gift? Have we their experience of it? Have we our fathers' experience of it? Is
it as hard as it should be for us to be patient with those
who deny and destroy it? Our religion understands
better some aspects of the Father; does it understand
the only guarantee of His fatherhood—the Redeemer?
The spread of religion has cost us the depth of it. Its
modern charm has cost us its power. We have vivid
religious interests, but no decisive experiences. We have
fine sympathies, but not a more fearless conscience; a
warmer ethic, but a poorer courage; eloquence about
morals, silence about holiness; much about criticism,
little sense of judgment. The religious crowd has little
discernment of the spirit of its prophets. Our religion
has more moral objects, but less moral interior. It wrestles
with many problems between man and man, class and
class, nation and nation; but it does not face the moral
problem between the guilty soul and God. It pursues a
high righteousness of its own, but it is too alien to the
righteousness which is of God by faith. It dwells upon
a growing moral adjustment, it does not centre on a
foregone and final moral judgment in which God has
come for our eternal salvation. In a word, as I have said,
we are more concerned with man's religion than with
God's salvation. We compare and classify religions
more than we grasp the massiveness of grace. And we

are more tender with the green shoots of the natural soul than we are passionate about the mighty fruits of the supernatural Spirit.

But all this means that a rich soil is forming for the great new word when it pleases God to send its Apostle. Only let us be sure that when he comes he will be an Apostle and not a Saviour, a preacher of the changeless word to the changed hour, and not a new Christ to make good something lacking in the old.

Our first business with the Gospel is to understand it. And our first business with the spiritual situation is to understand that. Let us go on to try to do both, to grasp the salvation of God in the religion of man. And here there is great hope. The critical challenge to Faith is drawing out the resources of faith.

§　§　§

An ultra-liberalism in a historic religion like Christianity has always this danger—that it advance so far from its base as to be cut off from supplies, and spiritually starved into surrender to the world. If it is not then exterminated it is interned in a region ruled entirely by the laws of the foreign country. Gradually it accommodates itself to the new population, and is slowly absorbed so as to forget the first principles of Christ. It comes to live in a religious syncretism which is too much at home with the natural man to bear the marks of the Lord Jesus. This is what happened to most of the Jews in the Exile.

But there a remnant remained, gathered the closer round the living word of the Lord, which is so exotic in the world and yet so charged with the true promise and life of the world's future. And this is also the effect of the ultra-liberalism of which I speak. It elicits a positive reaction which rallies the Israel of faith.

When we use the word reaction, let us note its two meanings. It may mean, passively, mere stampede. Or it may mean reacting positively; as a chemical reagent does, in the way of repelling the effect of something else, and even mastering it. It is often said that the effect of the reds and ultras of undogmatic religion is reaction in the passive sense of retreat, in the negative sense of merely throwing people back in panic to repristinate a stage which is really long outgrown. But what really happens with those who grasp the whole situation is not reaction in the sense of flight to cover; it is the deploying of reserves. It is a deeper evolution, under stress and crisis, of the resources latent in vital faith. It is a development, adjusted to the new situation, of wealth previously unrealized within our evangelical religion. Our depths are shaken to the top. We discover and work a gold-mine on our hereditary estate. The hidden riches of our secret power are brought to light. A new sense dawns on us of the depth, sweep, and solemnity of the trust God gave us in His Son. And we wake to feel anew, about the Gospel in which we slumbered, that God is in this place and we knew it not.

The heresy that creates the stampede is incompetent heresy. When the one thing comes lightly the other as lightly goes. But the beneficent function of competent heresy is to correct, nay, it is still more to elicit, to discover the higher truth to itself, and to enhance the Church's sense of power, even when the time is not ripe for scientific adjustment.

There is another effect—one of sifting and sobering

within the Church itself. Every crisis has this judging, separating, selective, steadying effect. It makes clearer and sharper the line between the real possessors of an evangelical, living, saving faith, and those who are merely spiritual. It clarifies. And it brings to their feet some who may have been but dabbling with belief and toying with negation.

When we write off entirely the worldly people who care for none of these things, and the light people who trifle with them, the real strife appears to be what it was in the first century of Christianity in the issue between Jew and Christian. It becomes the issue between the men of religion and the men of faith ; between those who reverence and those who worship Christ ; between those who beatify Him and those who deify Him ; between those who honour Him, with a certain discrimination and reserve, and those who trust their whole soul and world to him for ever and ever ; between those who treat Him with admiration or even affection, and those who give him faith—which (I have said) is a thing which can be given to no created being, even were he created before the worlds, but to God alone. It is an issue between those who regard him as the greatest contribution ever made to the human soul, and those who view Him as the one consummation and satisfaction of the holy will of God. We are driven to a vital choice, within Christianity itself, between an ego-centric and a theo-centric religion. It is not clear enough when we talk about a Christo-centric Christianity. Even with Christ in the centre we must go on to ask a question which divides Christianity into two streams, one of which ends in the eternal kingdom of holy God, and the other in the brief sovereignty of spiritual man. We have to ask, in the

Gospel's interest, whether Christ is central to a glorified Humanity or to a glorious God; whether man's chief end is to develop, by Christ's aid, the innate spiritual resource of a splendid race, or to let the development flow from its reconciliation, redemption, and subjection to God's holy will by Him. What we are developing at the moment is an anthropo-centric Christianity. God and Christ are practically treated as but the means to an end that is nearer to our enthusiasm than anything else—the consummation and perfecting of Humanity. The chief value of religion becomes then not its value to God, but its value for the completing and crowning of life, whether the great life of the race or the personal life of the individual. Love Christ, we are urged, if you would draw out all that is in you to be. Our eye is kept first upon our self-culture, our sanctification, in some form, by realising a divine presence or indwelling, with but a secondary reference to the divine purpose. God waits on man more than man waits on God. God is drawn into the circle of our spiritual interests, the interests of man's spiritual culture, as its mightiest ally and helper. We have many kinds of effort—some genial, some ascetic—for the development and deepening of the soul's life, in some of which the spiritual man is thought to be a stage higher than the Gospel man. Whereas, if we forgot our spiritual life after a wise and godly sort and lived more to God, His finished Gospel, and that purpose of a kingdom for which Christ died, He would take better care of our spiritual life than all our forced culture of it. In a subtle way this tendency is less Christo-centric than ego-centric. It is monastic. It is not theo-centric. For in any theo-centric faith man lives for the worship and glory of God and for

obedience to His revelation of Himself; which is not in
man, and not in spirituality, but in Christ, in the historic,
superhistoric, Christ. Christ is not the revelation of
man, but of God's will for man; not of the God
always in us, but of the God once and for all for us.
Christ did not come in the first instance to satisfy
the needs and instincts of our diviner self, but to
honour the claim of a holy God upon us, crush our guilt
into repentant faith, and create us anew in the act. He
did not come in the first instance to consecrate human
nature, but to hallow God's name in it. He came to
fulfil God's will in the first place, and to fulfil human
destiny only in the second place and by consequence.

These two streams may not seem far apart in their
origin, but they part widely as they flow on. And one
makes glad the City of God and His Kingdom, and the
other is lost at length in the desert. The latter makes
Christ and Christianity to culminate and be exhausted
in the service of man, the former makes their first work
always to be the honour and worship of God. In that
worship man grows to all his destiny, and warms, and
even melts, in perpetual brotherly love and service.
The one makes the centre of Christianity to be the
ideal or spirit of Christ, the other the Cross of
Christ. One makes the Cross the apotheosis of
sacrifice with a main effect on man, the other makes it
the Atonement with its first effect on God. The result
of the latter is a Church; of the former, a social State
more or less spiritualised, and more or less fleeting.
The latter postulates the deity of Christ, the other but
his relative divinity.

The Godhead of Christ is a faith that grows out of
that saved experience in the Cross which is not only the

mark but the being of a church ; so that undogmatic
Christianity is foreign, false, and fatal to any church.
The deity of Christ is the necessary expression of such a
church's sense of what God has done for the soul in
Christ.   It is the theological expression of the experience
which makes Christianity the experience that when we
commit ourselves in faith to Christ we enter actual
communion with God.   God is in us and we in God
when we are in Christ, when we are what Christ makes
us to be.   It is upon this experience that the Church
is thrown back in every challenge or crisis.   With all its
might the Christian Church repudiates the Unitarian
position of Wernle, that " there is much Christianity
without faith in Christ."   Christian men are thus made to
ask if they really have Christ in such a way as to have
God in Him and Him alone.   They are made to examine
their personal faith and that of their Church.   They are led
to ask if Christ has not been ceasing to be the sacrament
on earth of God's real presence, and becoming but the
prophet or saint of a God remote, however immanent.
They are roused to put such questions as these : Would
it make a real difference to me if Christ were not God, if
in Christ God were not in His world uniquely and once
and for all ?   Can the old faith live on its new phase ?
Can we sustain the old worship ?   Can we keep near to
a God who is only near to us in an immanent sense ?
Can a Christ who only ministers to the world by giving
it fresh hope and confidence in itself, cure the awful and
growing egoism of the world, or only sublimate it ?   Can
our souls find rest in a Christ who only says, " Come
unto Me, and behold what you may be if you are true
to your best self, and true to a divine Humanity, as I
am ? "   Such questions are forced on us by the hour ; and

we are driven, by God's grace, to repair a slackness that
was coming upon our communion with Christ, a shallow-
ness too easily exploited by the plausible; and we are
moved to reduce a distance that was growing between
us, and that failed to alarm us because we dreamily took
our sympathy with Him for our faith in Him.

LECTURE II

THE RELIGION OF JESUS AND THE GOSPEL OF CHRIST

LECTURE II

THE RELIGION OF JESUS AND THE GOSPEL OF CHRIST

THERE is nothing we are more often told by those who discard an evangelical faith than this—that we must now do what scholarship has only just enabled us to do and return to the religion of Jesus. We are bidden to go back to practise Jesus's own personal religion, as distinct from the Gospel of Christ, from a gospel which calls him its faith's object, and not its subject, founder, or classic only. We must learn to believe not *in* Christ, but *with* Christ, we are told.

But the innovator has always the burden of proof; and the first question we must ask our adviser here is, what is meant by the religion of Jesus? Have you in view his popular doctrine or his personal piety? Was it the religion he presented in his vocation, or that which he cherished in his most private soul? Do you mean that our religion should lie in following his popular teaching, or should it lie in reproducing his own personal faith? For the word religion is somewhat ambiguous. If you mean the doctrine he taught us, then you treat him as no more than a prophet of the most high and earnest kind. But he was more than teacher and preacher. He was a personality. However lofty that

treatment of Jesus as a prophet may be, it is, on the whole,
a lower spiritual level than is taken when we view him as
a saint, whose grand legacy is his inner self, with its personal and intimate faith lying behind the greatest things he
said to such audience as he had.   It is otherwise with us.
All the great Christian teachers impress us with the fact
that their teaching is far ahead of their experience,
and that they built better than they knew.   Even Paul
preached a Gospel greater than anything he attained in
his own soul.   He was apprehended of what he could but
imperfectly apprehend.   Whereas our impression from
Christ is just the converse.   His personal experience is
far greater than anything he said or could say to his
public.   All he said rose, indeed, from his own experience;
for he was no lecturer.   But also it is all less than his
experience.   He received from none the Gospel he spoke.
He found it in himself.   Indeed it was himself.   He only
preached the true relation between God and man because
he incarnated it, and because he established it.   But, as
we have his teaching, it is only a partial transcript of
himself, of his whole self as the Cross and its Apostles
revealed him.   And therefore you cannot treat him as
teacher alone.   You cannot do so even if you take his
teaching itself.   The doctrine carries you beyond a doctor.
He was a part of his own Gospel.   He could teach nothing
without indirectly teaching himself.   This is so, apart
from the fact that He did directly declare himself to be
our Judge, Redeemer and King, the sole determiner of our
relation to God?   So that the religion taught by Jesus
brings us face to face with his soul who taught it, as himself more momentous for our destiny than anything he
taught.   Jesus the saint, even if he go no higher, is more
for us than Jesus the prophet.

We are thus carried within the doctrine to the saint, from the public message to the private faith. We have to copy that faith, it is said, even more than we have to accept and obey those teachings, and the change represents the great difference between the old rationalism and the new.

But here, again, great difficulties arise. If by the religion of Jesus, which we are to reproduce in our degree, is meant his most private and intimate relation with the Father, two things must be said.

(1). We have few data.

(2). And the data that we have put it beyond us.

(1). We have few data. We have no information whatever about the form taken by the communion of Father and Son. How far it was what we call a revelation from soul to soul, or how far it was the thrill along the line, as it were of a common being—how far it was a God-consciousness and how far a self-consciousness of God—we are not informed. It was the secret of Jesus alone. And he kept it. Not by breaking that reserve must his religion act on men. His innermost experience was certainly engaged in our service, but the steps of the process are inaccessible to us. It is a mystery what took place on the nightly mountain tops, in the far interior of his soul, where his strength was perpetually renewed, his vision cleared, and his decisions made. The religion of Jesus in that sense was absolutely his own. What he *was* for God it was not for man intimately to know. We are blessed in what he *did*.

(2). And this is farther clear from the data we have. Especially from such a passage as Mat. 11, 27. "No man knoweth the son but the father, neither knoweth any man the father but the son, and he to whom the son

E

wills to reveal Him." This alone puts our faith, our
sonship through Jesus, on a quite different footing from
his, which was through none. The data we have put
the personal religion of Jesus beyond us, except in so far
as he might reveal it. And the only form in which he
revealed it was in the exercise of his public vocation.
He had esoterics, perhaps, but no confidants—not even in
Gethsemane, where we have but a corner of the veil lifted;
and that not in a confidence, but in a soliloquy indifferent
about being understood. Some even think the passage
in Matthew xi. 27 a soliloquy rather than an instruction.
His inmost experience was not a thing transferable in
itself. In so far as Fatherhood should come to us at all it
could only come by appropriating the Son, and not by cul-
tivating Sonship, not by repeating the Son's experience.
For he could not be repeated. " Me ye have not always."
Such was the nature of the revelation he had from God—
that it could only be man's according as man was in him—
not directly, as his own knowledge was, but only through
him. No one was for Jesus with the Father what he must
be for all, he had a relation with God, he had dealings with
God, which were not a part of his vocation with men,
but the ground of it, and its condition—just as we, his
preachers, have dealings with him which are no part of
our service of his church, and must not be flung before
our public.

§   §   §

It has been lightly said that there is no sin against God
but the sin we commit against our brother; which seems
to imply that for the soul there is no relation with God,
and no practical duty owed Him by the soul and refused,
except that of the love or service of man. It is surely
forgotten what is the first table of the Christian Law.

"Thou shalt love the Lord thy God with all thy heart, and soul, and will, and mind." That is the greatest of acts. And the love of our neighbour is but the second thing. Have there been no cases where God was defrauded of his first claim on man, while the second was even more than met? Have there been no men—are there none—who have loved, served, and helped man with the devotion of a lifetime, while they never were fired or lost in love of God, and never gathered strength from reposing in a complete trust in Him, and leaving men in His hands? Is our first duty to humanity not to commit it to God? Are there none to-day, blameless in all the service of their kind, for whom there can be waiting nothing but condemnation in respect of the love and communion they denied to a God Who sought that above all else, and Who had the first right to both trust and worship?

There is a devotion to God, and to God in Christ, which calls for the spikenard of our secret souls at the cost even of some oblivion of the obvious poor. And to refuse that claim, if the claim be good, is surely no light sin; for it defrauds God of the first of His rights over us, and of our response to His personal and private love. There is a life within the life of service, and within the fellowship of humanity, which is in the long run the condition of all the best human service and the most patient human pity. Without it the enthusiasm of humanity dies. Christianity becomes a fine and fading Positivism; and Positivism is unable to bear the strain of the world's grief and guilt. The fierce impatience of many who love men not wisely but too well, because they love them more than God, is proof how little the soul can be stayed upon public service, or its spiritual ritual exhausted in beneficence.

So also within the soul of Jesus at its centre, and throughout his whole life, there was an obedience and a communion which was a charge on him, and a joy, prior to all the blessing he shed on men.   His first and inmost relation was to his Holy Father whose name he had to hallow before all else.   That holiness in its love was his supreme revelation.   So much so that the one and only thing he could do at last, even for the men who refused him, was the hallowing of that name, and the perfect honouring and atoning of that supreme sanctity in his steadfast experience even unto death.   Nothing he did *on* man could do so much *for* man at last as his hallowing and satisfying, *as* man, of God's holy soul.

But about that whole region Christ was almost entirely silent.   We have it but indirectly.   He only said as much as lets us know it was there, and supremely there.   And it is so easy, therefore, for those who come to these records with but the critical or the humanitarian tact, to miss it; and to declare with great plausibility that it was not there, and was only imported by apostles who fixed it upon their master in a way that, had he lived, he would have lived to repel.   *The* secret of the Father was with the Son alone.   No man knew why the Father had chosen Jesus of Nazareth.   And Jesus believed in his sonship for reasons entirely between his Father and himself, for reasons quite past us.   We believe in the Father because of Christ ; why he believed in the Father he has not told us.   We are here at an ultimate.   We may gauge the meaning of his public Messiahship as we can never pierce the sonship that underlay that expression of it.   For that sonship there was an inner condition in his nature, a native and unique unity with God, which all Christology is but an imperfect attempt to pierce. He knew the Father's love, and he was himself pure love, without the alienation, the self-will, the sin, that not only removes us far from God but severs us.   For the peculiar revelation of his Father's ove there was in Christ a peculiar being.   But two things here are greatly dark.   We cannot trace either the steps by which the Son became incarnate, or those by which Jesus arrived at the consciousness of his unique sonship, and reached that perfect certainty and clarity of it which shines in all he said or did.   Neither history nor psychology gives us the means of sounding such mysteries.   The analogy of our own religious experience fails us here; and scientific inquiry is arrested for want of objective material.   But when we consider what he is to our practical faith; when we reflect on his Church's experience of him, and feel how far it is beyond either our analogy or our induction; when we remember, indeed, how far faith is from having a parallel in any other experience or process of the soul whatever; we are driven to conclude that that sense of himself, as one who could be neither paralleled or repeated, had a superhuman foundation.   The last roots of his unique experience lay in a nature as unique; from which it grew in an organic way, with the kind of free necessity which belongs to that spiritual region of things.

§   §   §

Let us observe what is the effect of the most recent views about the origin of Christianity upon this point, upon the plea that the first form of Christianity was the so-called religion of Jesus.   I refer to the new religious-historical school of Germany. At the present hour it is not the evolution of the biologists or the anthropologists that need give us much concern.   Any fear once entertained

of these is now outgrown. Our real concern begins when
the evolutionary principle is carried into the history of
religion ; when it is made to organise the new knowledge
drawn from psychology and comparative religion, and
to organise it with the same confidence with which, in
the levels of biology, the new knowledge was once
organised into an evolutionary doctrine declared to
be the world's explanation come at last. ⎩Religion,
it is now said, is evolution which has reached spiritual
pitch. ⎭ The various religions represent various stages
in the ascent. Each religion is the best for the social
stage it covers. No religion is final. And so, with
the end of any absolute or final religion, there is an end of
much that troubles the world, for instance of Missions at
least. ⎝For Christian Missions cannot live upon improving
the heathen, but only on passing them from death to life.⎠

But the crisis is concentrated when we come to the
religions that surrounded Israel, and especially Christ.
They really supplied, it is said, those ideal elements that
have done most to make Christianity so powerful in history. There is, of course, it is said, no denying the historic
reality of some prophetic Christ, of great ethical and spiritual power. But the Christ of Paul, of the New Testament
generally, the Christ of the first ages of the Church, the
incarnate, the atoning, the judging, the redeeming, the
adored, the glorified Christ, the Christ of the Apostles,
the Sacraments, and the Church is described as a syncretism. He is not the inner Christ revealed but a
compounded Christ put forward. He is a splendid column
of spray sent up by the collision of east and west, of
Judaism and the farther East, of prophetism and
gnosticism. It is impossible to believe, Relativism will
not allow us to believe, that " the Holy God was a con-

temporary of Augustus." The deification of a Roman Emperor or the worship of the Buddha is to religious psychology intelligible enough. We rate such things at their proper anthropological value. And in the like valuation we must now include the worship of Christ. There was a certain psychological necessity in it—men being what they are—but no theological reality. The dream of a Christ was afloat on the age in various forms. Spiritual history had been conceived by fantastic oriental mysticisms as a redemptive drama. Gnostic notions of strange and heavenly beings created a whole ascending and descending hierarchy of occult redemptive influences. These more or less naturalistic dreams and longings were drawn to Judaism for a stay, with its supernatural genius and its ethical salvation. And they found a fruitful point of attachment for the great æon in Jesus with his ethic, his healing, his love, his obedience, his religious insight, his spiritual genius, his powerful personality. And so we explain the rise of a whole religion of man's mediated union with the heavenly being; but so, also, we find such a creed impossible as a revelation, however explicable by the laws of historic development in the spiritual region of man's nature. Israel's national spirituality was hypostatised into a Christ decorated by pagan idealism with cosmic powers. For it is quite impossible, it is said, from the meagre relics about Jesus left us by criticism, to construct the kind of Christ that grew out of Jesus, without importations from other sources. Thus Christianity is really a religion of general spiritual truths, developed by man in aspiration, and not of special facts willed by God in revelation. It need hardly be said that such an explanation of Christianity is entirely fatal to its survival, except as an old phase of religious development which has its

uses still, and as a fine but passing product of the
spiritual genius of the race now essentially outgrown.

§   §   §

We shall, however, leave for the present the discussion
of these theories in order to exhibit their bearing on the
matter we have in hand—the first form of Christianity
to which we have access.   There is one great service
which this religious-historical school has rendered.   It
has destroyed the fiction of the 19th century that there
was ever a time in the earliest history of the Church
when it cultivated the religion of Jesus as distinct from
the Gospel of Christ.   The school, of course, may believe
itself able to insulate that religion of Jesus and cultivate it,
to disengage it from the Gospels by a critical process, and
preach it to a world pining for a simple creed rescued
from the Apostles.   That is another matter which I do
not here discuss.   But it is a great thing to have it
settled that, as far as the face value of our record goes,
and apart from elaborate critical ·constructions of
them, such imitation of the faith of Jesus never existed
in the very first Church; but that, as far back as
we can go, we find only the belief and worship of a
risen, redeeming, and glorified Christ, whom they could
wholly trust but only very poorly imitate; and in his
relation to God could not imitate at all.   It does not of
course follow that the first Church was right in this
respect.   That is not the point at present.   They might
have been doing Jesus an injustice in regarding him as
they did.   They might have been, the Apostles in particular
might have been, so misled by contact with him, that their
mystical enthusiasm could not be quite fair to his more
modest claims.   They might have been superstitious
hero-worshippers.   They might, through ·their very

There is another thing. The Gnostic systems which are regarded as providing the theological material of a supernatural Christ had this common feature. Their spiritual universe was an elaborate provision for an absentee God. Their object was to secure the supreme God as far as possible from contact with the world, or even proximity to it, by providing hosts of intermediary æons, emanations, and the like. That was the genius of their systems, among whatever variations in detail. I confess that in these systems, so far as I know anything about them, I find much that is attractive, much that is more congenial to the modern and idealist mind than the somewhat stiff mentality of the Apostolic Fathers, or the Christianised philosophy of the Apologists with their logism. The Gnostics had what these had not. They had *Geist*. They had spiritual imagination and subtlety. And it strikes a more modern, spiritual, and universal note than all the pagan philosophy which was discovered by the Apologists to underlie the Gospel of Christ. The Gnostics were really obsessed with the idea of Redemption—which always tends to vanish when it is the chief business of the Church to produce political apologists, or to commend itself to the State or the public by showing how long men have been Christians without knowing it, and how much more deeply Christian they have been and are than they feel. There is much in the old Gnosticism which comes home to the weary Titan of the modern mind. But one thing there is which does not appeal to us of these Christian days. And it is a thing that we should have expected to find repelling us in the New Testament if its theology had been constructed under gnostic influences. I mean that gnostic effort to keep the divinest in the divine as far as

Gnostics

possible from real contact with the world, while his agent at several removes fills the foreground. We find the tendency even in pre-Christian Judaism with its hosts of angels. But it is just the opposite that we discover in the New Testament, and especially in its Pauline and Johannine parts. Its Christ does not come between us and God, either as prophet, teacher, or saint. He brings God. God is in him. He does not darken deity, or push deity away. Whatever may be said of the crimes of some later theologians in that way, it cannot be said that the total effect either of the New Testament or its Christ has been to banish God from humanity. Quite the other way. The immanence of judgment in life (to take no more than that), the moral continuity and sequacity of life here and hereafter, the award for deeds done in the body—the Church's insistence on these things has neutralised the effect of a heaven or hell which it made too remote, and has kept God in man's life. The central object of the systems said to be syncretised into Christian theology has been not only ignored, but defeated by New Testament Christianity. God is brought near both theologically and experimentally. And He has been brought near to all. Christ did not enable certain promising classes of men, by escaping from their first gross and hylic condition, to rise to the supreme God and his far country. But this high God was in Christ, not creating Christ, and not emitting Christ at some removes, but present in Him, acting and suffering in him, reconciling the world, making men sons only in this His son, and giving them an intimacy of communion as far from their old alienation at the one end as from mere fusion of being at the other.

[margin note] Christ does not banish God from humanity.

And if it be said that Gnosticism was so modified and made innocuous by passing through the best Judaism on its way to Jesus as to produce this change, one asks whether any syncretism with the effect of a distinctive religion could possibly take place between the work of Jesus, viewed as the lofty ethical imperative of his grand individualism, and the myth of redemption as Gnosticism presents it.

§   §   §

Much that is of permanent value has been done by the religious-historical school. Criticism is our friend and not our enemy in its place. It is a good servant but a deadly master. It becomes our enemy only when it aspires from being an organ of Evangelical faith to be its controller. Now as of old the Church has to listen to the thought, the science, that grew up in it and around it; but it has to accept or reject it not according to its rational value, but according to its compatibility with the central life and experience of redemption which makes the Church. The school I name takes, indeed, too much on itself when it dissolves into syncretistic myth the version of Christ that has made the Church, and goes behind even the Jesus of the Gospels to reduce him to the limits of a spiritualised rationalism. If the extreme critics are right with the Jesus they construct scientifically from the records, then we know the real Jesus rather in spite of the New Testament than by it. But all the same they have done much fine and new work. They have greatly vivified the New Testament. They have helped to clear up some of the relations between Paul or John and the Gnostic influences these apostles had to deal with. They have made it more clear than before that influences which could not create Christ yet prepared for him and formed a calculus to express him; that he gave voice to much that was tongue-tied in the aspiring world, and revealed the thoughts of many hearts; that he came in a fulness of time to be the key of a world of which he was not the product, and to answer questions which if he do not answer he only aggravates. For it should be more clear than it is to many that by his fate he does aggravate *the* problem of life if he do not answer it.

But we should not avoid the real issue raised by the school—Did the New Testament faith, the apostolic faith, in Christ make Christianity, or was it made by Christianity? For the answer represents two distinct religions. The evolution, the relativism, that makes us to outgrow the New Testament Christ will also carry us beyond the religion of Jesus, and the cult of Fatherhood. Christianity itself will become but a stage, even on its ethical side. Its Fatherhood of God will be merely a spiritual idea of great but passing value. The Father will come to appear but a shimmering, fleeting, and perhaps credulous symbol of an unknown Hinterland capable of we know not what. It will be a symbol, also, not unmixed with an alloy of illusion for practical purposes. And as these purposes are effec-ted in the moral march of man out of old Judea, and as the illusion can be safely dropped, the idea may pass into another idea which supersedes it; but an idea which may also round upon it, and destroy it, as it, in its day, de-stroyed the passionate gods of the pagan pantheon. The Father God may go the way of the despot God when the paternal conception has worked out its happy moral effect; and it may yield its place to the monistic substi-tute which moves altogether if it move at all; which moves to pessimism, racial suicide, and finally the suicide of God ; and which meaning to move on the whole to righteousness, moves only to whatever righteousness may be made to mean in the absence of an absolutely righteous and Holy One who has given a revelation of Himself as final as the problem is universal.

§ § §

To imitate the religion of Jesus is to cultivate an order of piety absolutely different from the entire tradition of the Christendom created by the Gospel of Christ, a tradition which became most explicit in evangelical Protestantism. And though tradition may have less weight in systematic theology, (which is a branch of science, and so far progressive in its nature,) in the region of piety we are in the most conservative part of us, where tradition means and ought to mean most. In any faith the type of its religion is far more stable and continuous than its dogmatic form. And a real and great reformation is so much more than a reconstruction according as it affects this type. It is much easier to change a whole theology than to change the type of a religion, to change faith where it appeals to the most permanent elements of the soul. Now in the great Lutheran Reformation, which changed the religious type much more than the theological or even ecclesiastical, there was one thing that was not changed but only deepened, and that was the necessity of repentance for a truly Christian faith. It was on the matter of sin, repentance, confession and absolution that the whole Reformation movement turned. And its effect was to lay a stress unprecedented upon what had always been a central affair of Christianity—a religion of repentance and forgiveness. Roman, Greek and Protestant Christianity are here at one. And the declaration now that

Christianity consists in imitating at a reverent distance
the religion of Jesus only shows that we are in the
midst of a movement and an apostacy more serious
than anything that has occurred in the Church's history
since Gnosticism was overcome.

For if the religion of Jesus means the state of his own
consciousness there is there no trace of repentance, however far we go back in pursuit of his experience. On the
other hand, if we take the teaching of Jesus, he was upon
this matter of repentance most insistent. Without
it all must perish. Was he, then, practising one
type and prescribing another? Can it be doubted?
But if he prescribed a repentance he never
felt, and could not feel, then he was destroying
in advance any suggestion that our religion was his own
at several removes. He was destroying the idea that
ours could be a filial and uplooking piety as free of
repentance as his own. He was setting up for us a type
different from his own, though one which was made
possible for us by his own alone. And the whole faith of
the Church has recognised the deep and vital distinction.
Has there ever been an influential man in the Catholic
Church who could say that his type of religion has
more in common with that of Christ than with that of
Peter, Paul and John?

The tendency to ignore this distinction, and to make
classic for Christians a type of faith in which sin is
converted into immaturity or ignorance, and repentance
becomes but regret—that tendency is at the root of all
that does most to weaken and secularise the Churches
to-day; and its exponents are moral reactionaries.
They teach a paganism which, however refined in them,
will not remain refined for long in those they persuade.

Faith is ceasing among many of the religious to be penitential faith; and this is a lack that no mere spirituality can fill. It is a mere sympathetic faith, or a faith of heroics, like Peter's ignorant boast that he would never desert his Master. And it will have Peter's end. No mere faith in a Master can ensure that we shall not betray him under sufficient pressure. "Though all men forsake Thee yet will not I." "I know not the man." The boast was sincere enough, sympathetic and shallow enough. From a platform it would have swept the house. But Christ knew men. His deepest insight was into religious sophistication. And he put the avowal by him. He weighed it at its true worth. Then came the days of horror and humiliation, when Peter lay in a deeper grave than Christ. That is the kind of humiliation that is being prepared for a slight and facile faith. And the only hope for us then is in the Resurrection light upon the Cross. Our only hope is not simply in a deepened spirituality chastened by error. A chastened piety is not the Christian faith, else Martineau were its great modern prophet. Our only hope is to be rooted in repentance, grounded in forgiveness, established in a redemption. and quickened in a real regeneration. It is that we may be "regenerated to a living hope by the Resurrection of Christ from the dead" (1 Peter i. 3). I have used these words not as a mere quotation, but because they are Peter's own account of his experience of what made him a Christian for good. It was the word of the risen Saviour "Tell my disciples *and Peter*" that raised him from the lying and perdition of those awful days to a life he never lost. It was this that translated him into a confession deeper than that of his sin, that that same Jesus he had crucified was both

F

Messiah and God (Acts ii. 36).   It was no remembrance
of Christ's teaching and no emulation of Christ's
religion that brought that to pass.

Our talk of sin is palpably ceasing to be the talk of
broken and contrite men.   It has no note of humiliation in it.   Our pious heart does not meditate terror.
We are not frightened at ourselves.   We have a softness,
but not the sacred tenderness that comes from that
humiliation alone. It has not the patience, the love of
the brotherhood, the passion to serve the Church instead
of correcting and scourging it, which come over the
hearts of men taken from the jaws of death, nay
raised from its abyss.   Our speech of sin has not behind
it the note of "my sin, my sin!"   And in consequence
our thought and speech of Christ loses the authentic
note of "My Lord and My God."   We do not know an
"eternal sin" and an awful Redemption, and therefore
we do not know an Eternal Redeemer in the Christ we
praise.   That Redeemer must prevail; but his Kingdom
and its service may be taken from us and given to others.

§   §   §

But, it is said, this is the religion of judaised apostles;
it is not the religion of the gospels, which knows repentance, to be sure, but does not grow out of it as a native
soil.   Well, let us ask if that be so.   If we turn to
the Synoptics with their reflection of the apostles' religion
(which is the only religion we can copy) what do we
find the type to be?   It is a continuous confession of the
sinless Christ by sinful men.   Like all the deepest confession of Christ, it is a confession not of religion but of
sin and salvation.   Everything these narratives say is to
glorify such a Christ; and they miss no chance of confessing the stupidity and the wickedness of the men who

wrote them (or who were at the writer's ear), stupidity and wickedness not only continued up to the very end, but contributing to the crisis and the catastrophe. These gospels form an apostolic confession of unfaith to all time. They confess their Lord in a form which, like the epistles also, is a confession of faith carrying an unsparing confession of sin. (The apostles always denounce sin in the spirit of confessors of it—which is a very safe rule for denunciators.) It is the confession of men to whom their sin and its forgiveness by Christ was so serious and central that it was a new creation and passage from death to life. It is the confession of men so centrally changed by this forgiveness that, while their sin is blacker than ever, they can write of it almost as if it were not theirs; so thoroughly are they severed from it by their new Creator. To see in the apostolic expressions about the meaning of Christ's death nothing but dogma, and no tremendous witnesses of an unutterable new life—are we harsh if we say that that is a confession of spiritual trance, if not decadence.

At least it is no wonder that such eyes should fail to see in the Saviour the Incarnate God. For it is only on the experience of a Redeemer from eternal death into eternal life that the New Testament witness of Christ's Godhead rests. And it is only the same experience that has prolonged that witness in the Church. The Gospel of Jesus made the " Religion of Jesus," impossible. For it made the first Christians worship in the Holy One of God the very Holiness of God. And for the religion of to-day there is not hope till, by grace or judgment, by repentance or calamity, we get over the levity of modern liberalism, and restore repentance to the foundation of our faith. No faith born in true repentance could speak of our all being "sons of God" like Christ. Nor can we hear without fear and grief such words from Christian men.

§   §   §

We come, then, to our communion with God not along with Christ, and in like fashion with Christ, but *through* Christ, and *in* him. We do not believe *with* him, or by his help, but *in* him. We believe in *Him*; and *in Him* it is that we have our power to believe. He is not only faith's object but also faith's world. He becomes our universe that feels, and knows, and makes us what we are. (Deep as the thirst for God lies in the soul, nowhere but in Christ do we have the communion that stills it.) The communion, I say, and not merely the union, the fusion, the co-mingling, of which the high mystic dreams. Truly it is a mystic communion. The possession of God is sure for every age and soul only *in* Jesus Christ as its living ground, and not merely *by* Christ as its historic medium. The historic prophet is our Eternal priest. All other union is partial, occasional, not for life, but for moods and hours. To live in the love of God is, indeed, a passion, and from time to time an experience, perhaps, of high gifted souls. But only by faith in Christ does it cease to mark certain fitful seasons or favoured groups, and become a public possession and a constant life. It is impossible to live the religion of Jesus, because there are not in us the conditions there were in Jesus for God to reveal Himself directly, completely, and finally. He cannot do this mighty work because of our unbelief. But the belief which makes our sonship possible He gives us in the gift of Christ and Christ's action upon the soul. The superhistoric personality of Jesus was the only human personality to whom God could fully reveal himself as the Holy and absolute Father. Therefore that personality, condensed, realised, and pointed in his cross is our only way to the final certainty of such a Father. True, it is not the only thing that makes us crave for a Father in heaven; nor, perhaps, the only thing that fills us at times with the great surmise and voluminous intuition that it is so. For many experiences in fine lives may raise us to that conviction for the time. But Christ crucified is the only power that makes it for us a life-certainty, a new and sure life, a new life-principle, a new creation, with no more doubt and no more denial for ever. Whatever clouds may dim the radiance of our day from time to time there is no night there. And however the flush of elation may subside, and the sense of God's nearness abate, there is no more dividing and estranging sea. And why? Because in Christ God not only comes near to us but by an eternal act makes us His own. We hold for ever only because here we are seized and held by the Eternal. God *has*, by the resurrection of Christ, regenerated us into a living hope; He has not simply given us a living hope that we may one day be regenerate (1 P. i. 3). Any living hope we have is the action of Christ's resurrection in us. Prophets, and even men of genius, can by their message bring us near to God, but they cannot permanently keep us there, or cure that rebound and reversion in which our soul gravitates to earth and cleaves to the dust. Nothing can, till we are quickened by that unique, living, and Eternal word wherein God comes near to us in very presence and act, and not in message alone. He comes near and makes us His own. Others can impress us with God; in Christ God creates us anew. Others by their very purity may make us doubt whether we have any right to approach a Holy God who is only too sure to us for our peace; but in Christ such misgivings are submerged in the discovery that He has taken the matter out of our hands into His own, and Himself has come to us and made us His for ever. And then we not only draw near to God and not only have a new relation to Him, but we enter His communion, and share His life, and are marvellously made to partake of His Eternal Love to His Eternal Son. That is done in Christ ; where God did not send but came. Our life is hid with Christ in God. He is the ground, and not only the means, of our salvation. And the ground of our salvation must be the object of our faith, and of our faith in God. The godhead in a Redeemer is the only form of godhead we can bring to the test of experience. Godhead means finality ; and we can have no real God on the lines of either thought or power, because there we can have no finality. Finality is a matter of life, of the Eternal Life given by Christ alone. Here the newest philosophy and the oldest Christianity meet.

For personal and final union with the Father and His love there is no way for us but that faith in Jesus which his disciples found forced upon them by the compulsion of his grace. And the one compressed channel by which it came was the cross and its redemption. Jesus was for the Apostles and their Churches not the consummation of a God-consciousness, labouring up through creation, but the invasive source of forgiveness, new creation, and eternal life. In Christ God did not simply countersign the best intuitions of the heart but He created a new heart within us. There was for the New Testament no way to the communion of the Father but by the forgiveness which was Christ's grand and comprehensive gift— at once redemption and eternal life. It was in giving him up unsparingly to the death that God gave us all things, all our destiny, all Eternity. What, it has been asked in many tones of late, what is the essence of Christianity ? The best known answer that of Harnack, is too meagre. He is too much of a devout historian, and too little of a spiritual thinker. The essence of Christianity is Jesus Christ, the historic Redeemer and Lord and God, dwelling in his Church's faith. I have already said that there never was a time, even in the Church's earliest days, when Christianity was but the reproduction of the personal faith of Jesus, or the effort to live his ethic. It was always a faith in Jesus concentric with the Church's faith in God.

"The Christian religion begins," says Wobbermin, "historically viewed (*i.e.* apart from faith and so far as documents carry us) it begins, not with the religious self-consciousness of Jesus but with that of the first disciples. We can carry back the line of Christian faith straight to them, but not beyond them to Jesus himself. Beyond the whole chain he stands as the person who first made this form of faith and life possible. And it was not that he extended into his disciples his own religious self-consciousness. Not one of them ever said or thought that. None came to the Father but only the Son, and those to whom it was the Son's will to reveal Him."

In the first form in which we know it then, the religion of Jesus was the religion of which Jesus was the object and not the subject. (He was never regarded as the first Christian.) If we reject that objective faith in him, then, we start with something quite different from the religion of our only source of information, and if we start with a Jesus different from that of our New Testament sources, a saint rather than a Redeemer, we are beginning with a construction, a manufactured article. And not only is a construction no beginning, but, if it come to construction, why must we prefer the Jesus of critical or speculative construction to the Christ of theological and apostolic construction? Why prefer a Christ constructed from documents, without their experience, to a Christ constructed from documents whose experience we repeat, and which are themselves a part of the revelation (*See Lecture on Inspiration*). For upon the central things the apostolic documents are the prolongation of the message of Jesus. They are Christ himself interpreting his finished work, through men in whom not they lived but he lived in them. Christ in the Apostles interpreted his finished work as truly as in his lifetime he interpreted his unfinished work. In both cases he interpreted it as the hour shaped it and as a growing faith could bear it. Many things which they were not able to bear during his life he said, through select lips, to those in whom the finished work had created the soul of insight and understanding. It is men broken by his cross and healed by his Spirit that have the secret of the Lord.

LECTURE III

THE GREATNESS OF CHRIST AND THE INTERPRETATIONS THEREOF

LECTURE III

THE GREATNESS OF CHRIST AND THE INTERPRETATIONS THEREOF

THE sense of the greatness of Christ's character and of his historic influence is higher to-day than ever. What does that mean in regard to his person? We may note one or two points at the outset.

1. As to his antecedents in Israel and the Old Testament it must be admitted gratefully to modern scholarship that Israel began by sharing with the whole Semitic East, and the nearer East generally, the same religious ideas, ethics, and customs, allowing for their development by each nation on its own lines. So far God was working in them all. Yet only in one people, only in Israel, did God Himself open out, and reveal Himself by a special and redeeming word   ... this word for this people gradually revolutionised all, renovated it, surmounted it, and either neutralised a great part of the Oriental   ...acy, or rejected it. So that the difference, on the whole, submerges the affinities between Israel and the Semitic East, between the revelation which finds in Israel and that which seeks in all the rest of Humanity.

2. So, also, when it came to a point, in regard to Christ. A deeper knowledge of the Judaism of Christ's

time forces on us the conviction that there was in his mere thought or precept little that was new and original. It can mostly be gathered from contemporary Judaic ideas on such subjects as the Kingdom of Heaven and its ethic, God, Father, Messiah, Resurrection, and the conflict between God and Satan. But the power of Jesus still grows, both in the way of drawing men, subduing them, and uniting them; and no less in the way of dividing them, Where does it lie? It is something gained to recognise that it does not lie in novel truth (and that heresy, therefore, is not necessarily loyalty); but that it lies in the new divine personality, and the redeeming, consummating act of God effected in it. The religious power of the world is not ideas or truths, powerful as these are, but personalities and their deeds.

3. And this impression of Christ's greatness is deepened as we turn to account the fine results of recent scholarship upon his life; especially if we were to follow those who reduce his public activity to a year. We remark that he entered on life with anything but a passionless simplicity of nature; yet it was as a complete and finished character, with entire moral adultness and adequacy to each deepening situation. He was perfectly sure and self-sure, knowing his mind and carrying it through with an energy of will unparalleled in the history of the great. The concentration and unity of his character and purpose is the more amazing as he had not a long life, like Goethe's, in which to work out the tremendous contradictions and collisions in his vast soul. "The spiritual power which broke up the old pagan world and founded a new is here compressed into a single volcanic point." What a man! What a maker of men! What a master of men and of events! What

a sovereignty was the mien of his self-consciousness! Lord of himself and all besides; with an irresistible power to force, and even hurry, events on a world scale; and yet with the soul that sat among children, and the heart in which children sat. He had an intense reverence for a past that was yet too small for him. It rent him to rend it; and yet he had to break it up, to the breaking of his own heart, in the greatest revolution the world ever saw. (He was an austere man, a severe critic, a born fighter, of choleric wrath and fiery scorn, so that the people thought that he was Elijah or the Baptist; yet he was gentle to the last degree, especially with those ignorant and out of the way.) In the thick of life and love he yet stood detached, sympathetic yet aloof, cleaving at once both to men and to solitude. He spoke with such power because he loved silence. With an almost sacramental idea of human relations, especially the central relation of marriage, he yet avoided for himself every bond of property, vocation, or family; and he cut these bonds when they stood between men and himself. Full of biting irony upon men he yet was their healer and Saviour. Of a quick understanding which tore through the pedantry of the Scribes, with a sure dialectic which never failed him, and never left him at the mercy of his hecklers, he had yet a naïve nature and a pictorial speech which brought him very near to the simplest—whom next moment some deep paradox would confound, and even wound. Clear, calm, determined, and sure of his mark, he was next hour roused to such impulsive passion as if he were beside himself. But if he let himself go he always knew where he was going. With a royal, and almost proud, sense of himself, he poured out his soul unto God and unto death, and was the friend of publicans and sinners. With a superhuman sense of authority he had a superhuman humility. When he emptied himself it was done in the fulness of God. He could be bitter, and almost rough in his virility, yet he could pity, obey and sacrifice like a woman. The mightiest of all individual powers, he has yet set on foot the greatest Socialism and Fraternity the world has known, which is still but in its dawn. " King and beggar, Hero and Child, Prophet and Reformer, Polemist and Prince of Peace, Ruler and Servant, Revolutionist and Sage, man of action, man of ideas, and man of the Word—he was all these strange things, and more, in one person." *

And he was all that without being torn asunder as a common man would have been ; for, if his heart broke, his soul never did, nor his will. He was all that, in a unity greater than the unity of the most uncommon men, a unity ruled by his tremendous will. Dwell on the wealth of his person more than its mystery, on his irresistibility rather than his gentleness, on his steadfast energy of concentration upon his one work more even than his elemental force of passion or his depth of suffering—dwell on such things if you would come near the centre and secret of this personality and its root in coequal God. His effect on the human soul is greater than any human cause can explain, whether you think of the extent of his effect in history, or, still more, of the nature of his effect in a Church and its experience.

§   §   §

We may, perhaps, put the matter thus. If we say there is no limit to the greatness of Christ's personality, where, then, did his limitation lie?

* For this sentence, and more in this paragraph, cf. Weidel, Jesu Persönlichkeit, 1908.

It is not relevant to point to the limitation of his knowledge, the absence of political or æsthetic sympathies, or any other result of his being the true son of his age and servant of his special vocation. These things do not constitute moral personality. They are only some of the conditions within which moral personality may reveal or approve itself. Personality is not limitation, nor the negation of limitation, but the surmounting of it. Determination here is not negation, but power. For it is self-determination. Christ, as the moral result of his life's humbled action in death and resurrection, was determined as the Son of God in power. Rom. i. 4. The personality is shown not *by* the limitations but *in* them— in their conquest and exploitation. *In der Beschränkung zeigt sich erst der Meister.* Mere individuality may be defined by limitations, but personality is expressed within them, by transcending, overflowing, and utilising them. The individual may be a circle or plot walled off from others, but the person is a bubbling spring among them that overflows them. The one is an area, the other is a centre of power The sun is not a measurable round hole in the sky, but a power-centre so active that when we feel him most we cannot see his rim and limit, which we yet know to be there. It is overflowed and irradiated. The limitation is lost in the power. So with the limitations on the glory of Christ. They give it feature and enhance it. On the other hand we may often observe that an excess of such powers as Christ lacked may go along with great poverty of moral power or greatness. Napoleon was one of the greatest elemental geniuses the world has ever seen, yet under his very shadow Wordsworth could still deplore in France the absence of a "master spirit." Greatness of personality is quite compatible with absence of genius; while consummate genius may go with great moral poverty in the personality, and a total lack of personal greatness—as a case like Turner's shows.

But it will be said that however we magnify the greatness of Christ's personality we yet cannot reach a Godhead for him. For that is a qualitative difference, and we cannot cross the bar of deity by any mere expansion of human greatness. The remark might be true if by the greatness of personality we meant but its wide vision, its elemental force or its demonic genius. But we are concerned in Christ with something much more than the area, the force, or the velocity of a personality. As the person of Christ is much more than his character, so it is also more than his personality. He was a personality, to be sure, whatever we think of his person. He was a very great personage. But he could never have been for history what he is had he been but a colossal and magnetic personage. The mystery of his person resides in its nature from the beginning, in its quality and not its amount, in its native finality and not its volume or passion. It is in its divine nature and moral quality : in its holy quality more than its infinite compass; in such a way that we say, if God be not thus He is less than the God we crave for and the world needs, the last reality of soul and conscience. This is the holy love that deserves to be almighty and infinite. Nay, this is the holy love that is infinite. For it is a greatness of love, not only an intensity but an intrinsic greatness of love, a kind and not a degree of love, which shows itself invincible by all the world and all its worst. It is holy, sacrificing, saving love to the uttermost.

It is infinite love not finite, God's love not man's. God *so* loved; not so intensely but so holily. God is in Christ, loving to the uttermost there, and not merely saying or showing by an agent that He loved. There is a qualitative difference from any natural passion or affection in the love that loves the Holy with entire holiness, loves a world in arms against it, and loves it so invincibly as to save, loves it from death into life eternal. Love that was not overcome of such evil overcame evil as God— overcame it absolutely, finally, with the grace of an infinite holy God. To extend what is given us in Christ, therefore, is not to pass into another genus when we are driven to call him God.

§ § §

But granting the tremendous differences, and contradictions even, between man and God, it is not impossible to find in the reality of a person a union of them which is impossible in a rational scheme. And in this respect modern, philosophical thought is totally different from Hellenic or medieval. It has come to realise the inadequacy of thought for reality. It has therefore given more room and rank to faith as an organ of knowledge. It has admitted that all real knowledge is not scientific in its form. Indeed it sees that science cannot give us reality (but only method), whereas faith can. And a formula which logic might call contradictory, such as the Godman, becomes less an absurdity than an indication of adequate thought on the greatest matters. It is in the region of moral personality that we find the truth that lies in *credo quia absurdum*. The absolute claim of pure and logical thought has been reduced. It is not equal to modern life—and especially to the growth of the personal idea, and the pricelessness of the soul. Scholasticism, medieval and modern, has been dethroned. No dogma is adequate to spiritual reality. Things have to be

G

reckoned with as real which are quite irrational, and life's whole destiny is risked on them. Those who use rationality as the test of reality, however modernist they may be, are not yet out of the medieval ban; and when they apply the rational principle destructively they are only the victims of an inverted scholasticism. They are the dogmatists of negation. And in the end they form a bitter disappointment to those who once hoped to find through them an escape from traditional dogma into a grander plerophory of truth, but who really find only that they have exchanged a rich dogma for a lean. Some things irreducible to proof or logic, and some vulnerable to the critic, are among our mightiest forces; and on the other hand some things logically irresistible are for life totally inapplicable and absurd. The greatest things we believe we cannot comprehend, not only in religion, but in practical life. Nor is it fatal if our statements about them are in flat contradiction. The greatest of realities is the greatest of paradoxes. This is true even of the final quantities handled by science itself, like the atom; which is extended and yet indivisible for thought; yet in the paradox we have the most fruitful of beliefs for the development of modern physics.

But we can rise higher than that. We have the most obstinate of antinomies, we have the most intractable of paradoxes, when a belief so essential to society, action, and character as human freedom and responsibility is conjoined, as it must be, with its incompatibles—scientific causation or divine grace. There is a series of facts explicable only on the one line, and a parallel series, inseparable from it, explicable only on the other. We have to accept both, and to believe for our life that reality is too great to be covered by one of the formulæ alone, but equally needs the other and opposite. We can daily observe that these two contradictory things have their practical and fruitful union in many a character, which they unite to sustain, develop, and adorn in the maze of life. And we are well aware that human society and history would be impossible without belief in both; as the government of a free country is carried on only by two irreconcilable yet cooperant parties.

Kant revealed a whole series of these rational antimonies. And it was thus that he broke the reign of dogma; it was by no direct criticism of theological *loci*. For the essence of authoritative dogma is to make faith depend on rational consistency for its being; and the essence of negative dogma is to think belief can be destroyed by being shewn to be rationally inconsistent. Beware of clearness, consistency, and simplicity, especially about Christ. The higher we go the more polygonal the truth is. Thesis and antithesis are both true. But their reconciliation lies, not as Hegel said, with a superfined rationalism, in a higher truth which is also of the reason, but in a supreme and absolute personality, in whom the antinomies *work*. *Ils marchont.* It is the category of personality that adjusts the contradictions of reason; which, after all, is not abstract thought but a person thinking.

[marginal note: Faith cannot be destroyed by dogma or Rationalism]

[marginal note: The great truth of christ can't be confined to words — logic]

§ § §

The application to the Godhead of Christ may be clear. God and man seem to exclude each other; and the difference certainly is very deep. But to realise the depth of the difference is only the more to realise the greatness of Christ as the Godman. Theology is peculiarly vulnerable to the rationalist, because it is engrossed with the last, and therefore the most alogical, realities. And its central doctrine in particular seems offensive to a rapacious logic, to a common sense with an insatiable thirst for empire. But none the less, as the kind of greatness grows on us which exists in Christ's person, we grow also to feel that the categories of critical thought which are so useful below are no more competent there than feet for the air. To express this greatness we need not two truths lying in a third, but two great powers at least, two personal movements, and these in a surmounted collision within a person. We need man and God, and we need them in a Godman and in a cross. How inadequate it must be to rationalise as doctrine, in even the most constructive way, a revelation which was only possible by the act of the Son of God in the Cross. So true is it that the wisdom of God is folly with men, and the foolishness of men is God's wisdom. Theory indeed we must prosecute. The effort to adjust the great paradox could only cease with the paralysis of thought. But we shall theorise more successfully and modestly on our living and justifying faith if we realise that our theories are but "thrown out." They are but projected at the reality from our experience of it ; they are faith codifying itself; they are not reality, nor competent to reality. After all the centuries of toil upon this doctrine, even with our kenotic efforts, we sometimes ask, have we really done what was not done at Chalcedon, where the two sides were stated against their heresies but not adjusted, and left lying parallel but not organised ? Only some heresies were repudiated as being incompatible not with logic so much as with the evangelical experience. They were repudiated, but no real solution could be put in their place. And no theories, and no clash of theories,

no mere truths, or the incompatibility of truths, can destroy
our confidence of faith that the Christ who gave and
gives us our redemption is the rock of any reality
possible to life at its deepest, to life as one whole, to life
eternal, and that he is the human presence of Eternal
God. But most of the failure to recognise the divine
greatness of Christ arises in the end from a moral failure
to appreciate him as personal saviour; and that failure
rises from a defect in the estimate of the sin from which he
saves. A lofty ideal is not mighty to save.

§ § §

For where is the true site of the greatness of Christ?
Is it in the mere force and volume of the historic figure,
or in the nature of his historic work?

If we take but two features alone in Christ we find ourselves before elements which it is impossible to combine
in any conception except that of personality with its
alogical and inconsistent unity; and in this case it is a
personality great and contradictory beyond the mould of
any other. Unity of personality does not always go with
harmony of qualities. Unity of purpose need not imply
æsthetic symmetry of character. And the artists, and
æsthetic Christianity generally, have misled us about the
harmony and balance of Christ's character. There is
something too Mendelssohnian in their moral music,
something too well-groomed and habited in their mental
type, in their carriage something too much of the
Christian gentleman. In Christ there are two features
which are to be unified in no fair picture but only in one
mighty person. The severity of judgment in Christ and
the tenderness of the pity form a contradiction which
seems as final in its own region as the antinomy of the
divine sovereignty and human freedom is in another

plane. So much so that between these two elements some can never find themselves in Christ, never come to rest in him, so long as they view him as a teacher, a character, or a personality alone. At one time they are drawn to his mercy, at another they are crushed by his severity. Now they run into his shelter, now they are chilled in his austere shadow. Now he is all sympathy, now all judgment. And their whole life in relation to him is an alternation of moods, now trust, now fear—until the personality is consummated for them, and perfectly expressed in his " finished work." It is expressed and consummated in no symmetrical scheme or conception of his character, and in no psychological harmony of his history, but in the deed unspeakable and full of glory, in the final act of the cross, where all is gathered in one for our peace, where the whole Jesus at last takes effect, with the judgment, indeed, there, but the grace uppermost, as he bears in himself his own judgment on us. What the cross is for the soul and the race can be put into no theology, adjusted in no philosophy. No thought or form can contain the greatness of the personality which it took the eternal act of cross and resurrection fully to express.

It is the work of the cross that crowns and carries home the greatness of Christ. There the Master becomes our Lord and our God. Impression there becomes faith. And as faith can only have God for its object it is bound to pass, in the cultus at least, into the worship of Christ; and in theology it passes into the belief in his real deity, however expressed. It cannot be too often recalled that the article of Christ's deity is the theological expression of the evangelical experience of his salvation, apart from which it is little less than absurd, and no wonder it is incredible.

§   §   §

Some unity of a Christ so great with God is not denied by any with whom we are here concerned. The problem is, how we are to construe it.

When Jesus says, " I and the Father are one," he uttered an experience which the author of the Fourth Gospel cannot have merely imagined. To think he did is pure pyrrhonism; it is not criticism. If anything is sure to us about the mind of Christ we are sure that such was the relation he cherished and expressed towards his Father. The only question is, what did it mean for him?

Now, in asking what was the exact content of Christ's consciousness on such a point we are barred at the outset not merely by the meagreness of our data but by a consideration still more serious, It is a psychological impossibility for us to go very far in reconstituting the consciousness of Christ. To say we can is to beg the question by placing him on a human and penetrable level at the start. He knew what was in man and needed no telling; but does not his own chief account of himself say that no man knoweth the Son but the Father? The intimate relationship between them is not accessible to us. We can only say, with Lotze, that it is impossible for us to exaggerate that intimacy. And the most subtle speculations of the Church, when they are interpreted with the insight of a sympathetic intelligence instead of sealed up by the dulness of a scornful, are but the finest efforts of human thought to feel its way into that divinest mystery.

But yet we do not easily consent to be entirely Agnostic on such a matter. Nor do we believe that such entire ignorance is the decree of Him who wills to be inquired

of. And Christian effort to advance, to grow in the
knowledge of the Son of God has taken three historic
stages, all of which survive in modern forms. These we
may describe, in ecclesiastical language, as the Ebionite
(or Socinian), the Arian, and the Athanasian. Of these
the Ebionite or Socinian stage we may perhaps consider
to have been outgrown in principle as the result of the
more competent and sympathetic attention given by
modern thought both to the nature of religion and to the
self-consciousness of Jesus. The Athanasian stage, at
the other end, is bound up with the existence of a
Church, and is alone compatible with that experience of
final Redemption in Christ which makes the Church·
The Arian stage is that which still fascinates those who
have abandoned the lower extreme without having
reached the higher, and who, having lost faith, or never
having had the historic mind, sit loose to the Church
and its experience. It is the conflict of Arianism and
Athanasianism, under modern conditions, ideas, and
methods, which must engage the concern of Christian
people for at least the next generation.

§   §   §

1. The first or Socinian stage represents what is true
enough if it be not called final—the individual saintliness
and moral supereminence of Christ. For it is individualist. When he spoke of his unity with the
Father, and said they were one, he only meant (it is
said) that they were entirely at one. It was an ethical
unity. The one will was tuned completely to his vis-à-
vis in the other and gave back his note. The son of
man had an insight into the Father's will which was
only matched by his absorbing desire and moral power
to do it. Father and Son confront each other. The

idea is harmony or congruity rather than condignity; and the conception of Christ involved is no more than prophetic. He is our religious hero, a religious genius unsurpassed; but not "My Lord and my God." The advantage of such a conception is, first, that, as far as it goes, it is true. And second, that everyone who need be considered is agreed about it. If Christ was no more than moral hero and prophet of the Lord he was that at least. So that if the essence of Christianity were its lowest common denominator, if it were (as it is not), what divides us least, we need go no further than this position to gather the greatest possible number into the Christian pale. But the genius of Christianity is not minimist. And the object of Christianity is not majorities, not the gathering in or as many people as possible in a given time on the simplest base; which would be setting the great pyramid on its moral apex. But it is the glorifying of the Father, the hallowing of his name; and then the enfolding of as many as seek first such a Kingdom as the cross founded in doing so. It is peace among men of such good-will. The Socinian position has attractions for the lay stage or type of mind, which is religious, and rational, and nothing more. But it abolishes certain finite difficulties only to create infinite. It places Christ as it places all the prophets whose series he crowns, among the men to whom God but spake, and who could not but obey that word. And the deep difference, among those who are interested in Christ at all, is that between those who call him "Lord and God" with his first believers, and those who call him hero with his latest admirers— admirers who are yet able to judge him more searchingly than they were ever judged by him, or expect to be.

I cannot regard as other than Socinian the idea that in Christ we have the greatest of created personalities completely filled with the Spirit of God. For the centre of gravity must always be where the personality is; and in this case it is in the created humanity alone. The person concerned is a person in the same created sense as the rest of us, however magnificent in his scale and range, and however filled with the Holy Ghost. His communion with God is in principle the same as ours. He is, like the Church, the habitation of the Spirit, and neither the giver of the Spirit nor his eternal correlate. The Lord is not the Spirit. Such a Christ does not indeed offer to the Spirit the opposition presented by the rest of us, but that is a matter of relative perfection. Like us, he is a creature, only created *ad hoc*, for a special function, and as a special organ of the Spirit. And he is not even created before the world; but he is the classic instance of created man. The notion of Jesus as the grand and perfect *receptacle* of the spirit, its most glorious tenement, the most fine and adequate of all its human instruments in history, however generously you construe that notion, does not really rise above the Socinian level. It is certainly below the New Testament idea, whatever countenance it may find in certain inchoate New Testament phrases. For we must often remark that in the New Testament we find no complete theory or explicit theology of either Trinity or Incarnation; but we have the faith and the principle which are impossible otherwise, and which, under the heat of conflict and the growth of Christian mind, revealed at last the invisible writing on its heart of a perfectly triune God.

2. The second or Arian stage is represented by those who see in Christ not merely the perfect prophet, but a

personality unique in his supramundane nature, and not merely in his function and the way he discharged it. They do lay stress not on his message but on his divine person, and the position he took toward men. They recognise not only his spotlessness before men, but his sinlessness before his own conscience and God, rising to such a height that he knows and proclaims himself to be the final judge of mankind. He is not only man's moral model and his spiritual king; and he is so related to God that he declares man's final standing before God to be identical with man's relation to himself.* They own tha Christ has not only a special function but a unique position. He stands with God facing man much more than with man facing God. He is a secondary God. So that our highest possible development of human communion with God could never reach that of Christ. Yet he is not of one nature with God. He is a creation—an intermediary creation. If he is not of Humanity, neither is he of Deity. He was too humble before God to be of God. His subordination is that of a creature, after all, though created before the worlds for a unique task. And it carried with it inferiority.† It is admitted that the highest claims which we find in the

* That Christ did make that claim to the divine function of judging and determining the world for eternity is to me so indubitable that I should make the point decisive of sound and guiding criticism. And, in my humble opinion, a scholar so able and sympathetic in many ways as Bousset is here discredited for the higher ranges of the subject as the victim of criticism rather than its master. And this estimate is confirmed by his treatment of the Messianic idea, and the part it played in the mind of Christ.

† This is a moral position which it is the whole business of the Athanasian position to deny : and it is a position which, from its urgent ethical mischief to-day, might alone condemn it as the theology most fitting to the chaotic time. Service and obedience are not undivine, and not a badge of inferiority.

mouth and the mien of Jesus are claims that he really made.
And he was justified in making them.   He was sinless.
He was, and is, man's Judge, Redeemer, and King.   But
these functions were conferred and delegated by God,
who will one day resume them from His sublime servant.
All that is held is an Arian idea of Christ's person, its
origin, and nature.   He was not a man, but he shared
creatureship with man.   He was a created being;
fashioned before the foundation of the world, indeed, and
equipped by his Maker with especial power and place,
which took him out of individual Humanity, made him
God's corporate representative of Humanity, perhaps the
agent of its creation, and enabled him for the exercise of
the one grand divine purpose with Humanity; but still a
creation, with less than eternity in his own nature,
with no more than such endowment as made him the
efficient organ for carrying out what was more eternal
than himself, namely, God's purpose of self-revelation.
Even were he regarded as a personality created for the
special purpose of being filled with the Spirit uniquely
and entirely—he would still be a created being and
therefore more man than God.   What he had from God
was a plenary commission, in virtue of which he redeemed,
judged, and ruled as King.   But as a Satrap King still,
with a Suzerain who conceivably could dethrone him; a
tributary King, who one day would render his royalty
up.   He was God's plenipotentiary, His superhuman
chancellor, the most private secretary of his eternal
praise, and so far invested with His power and prestige.

They draw this conception of Christ especially from
his own consciousness of himself, so far as we can reach
it, especially from his humility and sense of dependence.   But they exclude almost entirely the one

decisive factor in the modern strife between a lay liberalism and positive faith — his consummatory and final work of the cross, and all that that meant for the soul's destiny in the apostolic gospel. With that exclusion there is no poor case for such an interpretation of Jesus. It is, in some form, the view of most of those who treat the cross as otiose and yet cannot settle to a thin Unitarianism. It is the crypto-unitarianism of many who feed themselves and others on Christian sympathies and Christian ethic without Christian redemption. With that omission there is no little to be said for an Arian Jesus. He seems at home in our lay reading of the Synoptics—which forgets the space they give to his priestly passion. Many of his *express* statements about himself, during that fragment of his existence which was covered by the kenosis of his earthly life, and was engaged with the national prolegomena of his universal work, are compatible with such a view. What he knew of his work and Kingdom was taught him of God (Mat. xi. 27). "It is all taught me of my Father." In John he speaks but what he hears from the Father, and does but what he sees the Father do. His miracles, even in the Synoptics, he often does as the organ of the Father, and often also as the result of answered prayer, and not out of a parallel and autonomous power. John xi. 41, 42, "Father, I know that thou hearest me now as always," said just before calling Lazarus forth, and said in a voice whose loudness revealed the spiritual tension which for him was prevailing prayer. In Luke xi. 20, he casts out devils with the finger of God, or, as Matthew says, by the Spirit of God. And a phrase I used a moment ago, about the surrender of his kingship at last, will recall, by its echo of 1 Cor. xv. 24-28, how much could be said for this Arian stage from other parts of the New Testament. It is a matter of fair discussion whether the *express* and formal theology of the New Testament, as distinct from its gospel, faith and worship, is always beyond the Arian stage. I mean what is called the Biblical stage of theology; remembering that the New Testament has faith and not dogma for its first concern, and that the expressly theological passages are incidental to a pastoral purpose and an evangelical effect. They are incidental to the epistle though fundamental to the subject. Such truth is distinct from the theology latent and necessary to the New Testament *gospel*, and waiting there to be revealed by the Spirit to the Church's soul, when it became tense in the strain of a mortal crisis, and when its last spiritual reserves had to be called out in the battle for its existence in a pagan world. It is one thing to see but an Arian Christ while the theology of the gospel was but in the making. That is the morning twilight. It is another thing to stand arrested there and denounce an Athanasian Christ now that the providence of the Spirit has revealed, in the tremendous experience of the historic Church, a gospel which is possible on that profound base alone. That is the evening twilight. And when it claims to be the advanced and primitive view it can only be advanced in the sense of being at eventide and verging to sheer oblivion.

But even if the reported and express statements of Christ carried us no farther than this stage the matter is not closed. Could Christ teach the disciples what he taught Paul? For if on earth he was always fully conscious of all he was, where were his real humiliation and his true humanity? We ourselves are at no moment conscious of all we are or have been, and certainly not of what we shall be (1 Jn. iii. 2). Would even a Christ created before the worlds be conscious on earth of all the power and glory that the greatest Arianism would postulate for him in his antenatal life? I speak of the greatest Arianism, as distinct from the trivial Arianism to which the public mind is apt to turn.

§   §   §

We may perhaps put it thus. If in the first, or Socinian, stage Christ appeared as God's perfect *prophet*, in this second, or Arian, stage he appears as God's *plenipotentiary*. What more do we want? Have we not explained the greatness of Christ? No, not yet. We want in Christ God's real *presence*.

In the first stage Christ is the *man*; in the second he is the *superman*. We must still ascend to the *supernal* man, the *Lord* from heaven.

§   §   §

I spoke of a fatal exclusion and renunciation of the work of the cross made by those who hold this Arian view on the basis of one part of Christ's self-consciousness alone. I call it fatal because it displaces the centre of gravity, because the last secret of the Saviour is not in his earthly self-consciousness as we know it but in his salvation. They ignore not only other parts of Christ's self-consciousness as I hope to show later (Lect. XI.) but, still more, the Christianity of the Epistles, the Christianity of Redemption, the crisis and crown of Christ and his salvation in the cross. In so doing they raise what is the question of the hour in this subject. It is a question that rose also upon the apostles. And the Epistles are the first stage of the answer, religiously normative, though not theologically finished. It is this

question; could God's plenipotentiary, for the last purposes
of the soul and the last destiny of the race, be a creature?
Could man's King, Judge, and Saviour be other than
Godhead itself?   Could God's commission, however
superhuman, do, for such as we, the work of his presence?
Could God delegate his divinest work of redemption to
even the greatest of his creatures, or commit all judgment
to one with less than the Godhead of the Eternal Son?

This, at least, is the great question within the Church
to-day.   It is not the question between the Church and
the world, which is whether there was in Christ a real
revelation.   We have settled that, wherever Agnosticism
is surmounted.   And what is crucial is the farther inquiry
whether that revelation in Christ was final; whether in
Christ God sent or went to the world; whether in Christ
He announced himself or gave Himself; whether Jesus,
who spoke in God's name, *really* stood in God's place,
where the first Church, by its worship of him, put him.
The greatest issue for the moment is within the Christian
pale; it is not between Christianity and the world.   It
is the issue between theological liberalism (which is practically unitarian) and a free but positive theology, which
is essentially evangelical.

§   §   §

3. It is a question that demands at last the Athanasian
answer.   Christ is too great for any smaller answer.   For
greatness is in the nature of Athanasianism.   The first
Athanasianism was a grand escape for the soul.   And
the passion for amplitude and plerophory to the measure
of Christ will always send the human mind to some form
of Athanasianism, with such metaphysic, whether in the
Bible or not, as makes that answer possible, according
to the state of contemporary thought at any specified

time. The question I have described as so crucial in the Church demands the answer of the cross, when the cross is taken as redemption from guilt, and not mere martyr-dom for principle, or sacrifice for love. It demands the faith of such a cross, and the metaphysic arising out of that faith. The sinner's reconcilement with a holy God could only be effected by God. And I press the *effectuation* of it. The cross did not mean news that God was willing to receive us on terms which another than God should meet ; nor that God sat at home, like the prodigal's father, waiting to be gracious when we came. But with God to will is to do ; and the God who willed man's salvation must himself effect it—not accept it, and not contrive it, but effect it. Only he who had lost us could find us, only he who was wronged could forgive, only the Holy One satisfy His own holiness. To forgive he must redeem. Fully to forgive the guilt he must redeem from the curse. And only the creator knew the creature so as to redeem. And to know mankind He must live in mankind. To offer for man he must be man. Only God Himself with us, and no creature of His, could meet the soul's last need, and restore a creation undone. Christ, the source of the race's new creation, is as divine and as truly creator as the God of the world's beginning. (So with the Spirit, as the source of the new birth of the individual). For the great work needed was to recreate, which is what mere liberalism and its humanism denies. The great task was not to re-inforce but to re-create, and to set us on Eternal rock. But if the Saviour was but an emissary of God and not very God, we are not on rock, even if we are off the sand. There is then no absolute certainty of salvation for the race. And we must have that certainty for faith. For Christian faith

H

is much more than the sense of a spiritual God : it is the trust of an absolute God. And the note of an Apostle is not spirituality, but the power of a Gospel which passes us from death to life ; passes us not merely through a stage, but through the mortal crisis. This power and certainty of the race's salvation we can only have from God Himself as Saviour. God could not depute redemption. We could not take eternal pardon from a demigod, or commit the soul to him for ever as we do to Christ. No half-God could redeem the soul which it took the whole God to create. God himself must be the immediate doer in what Christ did to save. I shall have to point out, nearer the close of this series, that the effect of Christ upon history could not be explained by any greatness which a created soul could achieve on earth ; and certainly not by the moral action cognisable by us during his brief public life. It is explicable only by an eternal act in Godhead which was the ground of all on earth—only by God acting in him. On any lower ground God but accepted Christ's work, or even commissioned it ; he did not do it. And does it need a God to accept another's sacrifice ? Are not all egoists masters in the un-divine art of arranging for the sacrifice of others and accepting it ? Mere acceptance of sacrifice by God means that He was really reconciled by a third person neither God nor man. And what is the effect of that on free grace? Ruinous. There is then no such thing. If a created being, however much of a personal splendour, was the real agent either of revelation or redemption, then grace was procured from God, and not given—which is a contradiction in terms. For then the effectual thing was not done by God but by another. And God was not reconciling in Christ, but at most through him. It all impairs the freedom and

[handwritten marginal note: Nothing less than God could satisfy—could redeem the soul, ue created]

monopoly of the jealous God Himself in our salvation. And remember the first charge upon any theology which has gone beyond the rationalist stage of an egotist concern for its own liberty—the first charge on a true and positive theology is regard for the freedom of God. That is the only source and condition of man's freedom. The prime condition of human freedom is a free God, and such faith as seeks first his freedom, and has all other things added unto it. And especially we must regard the freedom of God's grace and of his salvation. If a created will effected our salvation, God's reality in it is one vast stage removed, and His sole grace is impaired. The only real representative or plenipotentiary of a God whose grace is free and all his own must be God. He must be of God not merely from God. He could be no creature, whether that creature had his power as a gift from God, or acquired it by moral effort under God. The absolute nature of the salvation brought to our faith can only be secured by the absolute nature of him who brought it. If it is an eternal salvation, and the gates of hell cannot prevail against it, he who gives it is an eternal saviour. If we have God for our eternal portion, then he is God *in* whom we have it, and not only *through* whom. In him, and not through him! The Christianity which denies that is less "advanced" than that which confesses it—less advanced at least as Christianity, less forward in the faith that makes theology, however it may stand with the rationalist theology that claims to licence faith from some source above it. A salvation only *through* Christ leaves us with a religion too subjective for use. And the excessive religious subjectivity of the hour is the nemesis of a mere liberalism whose next stage is the destruction of religion altogether.

§   §   §

And this consideration may be added here. Will
many not be driven to the alternative of either praying
to Christ or praying *for* him? Many of those who lean
to a positive and liberal theology, and who retain belief
in intercessory prayer at all, both believe in prayer
for the dead and practise it. And when they pray for
the whole of mankind they cannot ignore its majority in
the unseen, including both our benefactors and our beloved,
We may pray, we do pray, for the whole creation. If
that may include the dead, can it exclude a created and
departed Christ? May we, must we, not, if we have
leave to pray for the blessed dead at all, pray for the
greatest lover and benefactor in our race? Should not
the collective Church pray for its founder? If he was
but a created Christ, *to* whom we may not pray, would
the gratitude of a Church he created not move it to a
great bidding prayer *for* him? And on great commemor-
ative occasions at least, as the sense grows of our spiritual
obligations to such a Christ, should we not be driven to
lift our soul as *Parsifal* ends "Redeemed be the
Redeemer."

> Lord God, who savest men, save most
> Of men Christ Jesus who saved me.

§   §   §

The two lines of inquiry converge, I said—the work of
Christ and the consciousness of Christ; and they converge here. He was conscious of himself *as Redeemer*.
This was a part of his Messianic sense, no less than was
his action as Judge and King. He knew he was there
not only with God's judgment, but with God's final
salvation. And for Israel that had always meant the

presence of God Himself as man's refuge, righteousness, and redeemer. Each of these three features, God's judgment, His salvation, and His presence, is equally prominent in the Messianic idea of the Old Testament and its great good time. The closing era should be so rich in good because God himself would dwell in it. And when Christ knew Himself as the Messiah of man and of God, when he translated the Messianic idea in terms of his own sonship, he lost no one of these features. If the judgment and the salvation of God were incorporated in him, so also, and no less directly, was God's *presence*. The great Messianic time, like the history it crowned, was God's coming, it was not His sending. God was no more remote. He did not begin where his messenger, his creature ended. He was not removed by the measure of Christ's very existence, nor distant by the diameter of that vast personality. He *was* that messenger. That greatness was God's greatness. That love was God's love. That grace was God's immediate grace, and no echo, report, or image of it; it was God's grace as surely as that judgment, or that forgiveness, was God's.

Jesus did not indeed put all this into words. He did not lecture about his person. He spoke and acted as only such a God with us could. But if he was not theologically express about his Godhead was he not conscious of it? Surely he was at least subconscious. It was fundamental to his manner of life, and work, even if we thought a full sense of it was but occasional and incidental. Our greatest truths, perhaps, escape from us rather than are preached. If his deity be not express always in the preaching of his lips, it is essential in the gospel of his person and cross. If it is not unmistakable in everything he said it is inevitable in the thing he did.

Had he no sense of that? How could one of his insight miss all such latent significance as I have indicated in the claims he made? He knew himself to be among men for certain universal purposes, to be final king, judge, and redeemer. Could it escape him that these were functions which in Israel's ideal were reserved for God alone? He calls himself king in God's kingdom. He is the bridegroom of the true Israel, whose husband, in all the Old Testament, was God alone. He is to sit on the throne of glory, where no Jew could place any but God. The angels he sends forth as *his* angels. The blessed of the father are *his* elect. The omnipotence of God is given him in a passage (Mat. xxviii. 18) which it is much easier, with all the tremendous demand it makes on us, to assign to him than to ascribe to the daring of a Church which put it in his mouth. How could disciples of his have made him say anything like that (whether the words are stenographically correct or not) unless it was in tune with his own claim for himself? He knows himself to be the final judge, and there is no appeal, and no revision of his sentence. He takes, in many ways, God's place to the faithful. And all the while he is not obscuring God, or displacing Him, but revealing, mediating, conveying Him; yet doing it not as a mere transparency, a mere exhibition of God, but as a mighty will and living personality, with a real agency in things. Either in such a case we have the incarnation of God, or we have the deification, and the self-deification, of a man. If we are to talk of mythology, which of these is more mythological? And the latter was especially alien to Israel, with its awful gulf between God and man.

§   §   §

The tendency of the hour among the more piquant

expositors of such matters is to regard the greatness of Christ as the incarnation of Humanity rather than of God. On this two remarks only may be made. First, if we use Saxon, and say, for the incarnation of Humanity, the enfleshment of flesh, we perceive that there is something wrong. And we go on to see that it is not an incarnation of Humanity that is meant, but only a condensation, or epitome. And second, if we speak of the incarnation of Humanity in any sense that leaves room for God at all, one of two things follows, which are both wrong. (1) Either Christ incarnates a created Humanity dwelling with God in the recesses of premundane time—in which case we are back upon one of the many shades of Arianism. (2) Or he incarnates an increate Humanity; which is therefore an eternal integer or factor in Godhead. This gives us not so much an incarnation of God as a deification and idolatry of man, ending practically in his debasement. The finitude, and therefore the reality, of man is gone.

The Eternal Son of God is then but the Humanity eternal in God. This is a view which is much in keeping with the modern man's keen self-consciousness and his dull ethic which takes no measure of either his race's sin or a holy God. It gives to Humanity what belongs to the only begotten Son. It gives to the Humanity that the Son came to redeem the position which belongs to the Son alone, and alone made redemption possible. Humanism is then simply the old ethnicism, gentilism, or heathenism made universal. It is an enlargement of what is both to Old Testament and New Testament the supreme heresy, that man is enough for himself and has a right in God. Man is referred to his divine self for his destiny. It is paganism with a Christian facing.

Humanity is safe in its own innate resources, its immanent inalienable deity. If redeemed at all it is self-redeemed, to its own endless praise and glory; which is surely another religion from Christ's. Positivism has been described as Catholicism with the bottom knocked out; but this is a Positivism with a Trinity forced in. The old beliefs, cults, and phrases are first deflated, and then twisted into modern arabesques. As history goes on the burden of the old ceremonialism is replaced by the officialism of the social state. A church of faith becomes a fraternity of comfort. Theology becomes anthropology. And religion hardens into a service without a trust or a loyalty. Worship vanishes for work, and work descends into an Egyptian corvee.

§   §   §

Throughout all, the impressive thing about Christ's vast self-consciousness is his sense of finality. It is upon this that so much turns—not on his being *a* revelation of God but *the* revelation, the final revelation. It was with Christ's world that God had henceforth to do. There is no thought in Christ (or in the New Testament at all!) of another coming from God to complete his work. The Spirit only applied it—especially to individuals. In him God said his last word, and took his inmost and final attitude to men. The Father has only now to do with a kingdom created by the Son. But if the Son were a creature that means that God had to do with a kingdom secured by an inferior, and only presented to Him. And how could God's kingdom be the work of another than God, or only indirectly of God? Christ's sense of finality we must recognise; which is his faith, however implicit, in his own Godhead. We must acknowledge his sense of his own finality in the last moral issue of the world, the supreme human issue, the issue between God and man, life and death. He knew he was decisive in that issue. And who could be final or decisive there but God? The final revelation could only be God revealing Himself, in the sense of God bestowing Himself, and Himself coming to men to restore communion. What remains to be done for finality after that? A message could never be a final revelation, nor could a messenger. We should then infer God, surmise God, take Him on trust from another, or otherwise have him at one remove, but we should not possess him. He might be God *for* us, but not God *with* us, or *in* us. And unless he were God finally with and in us we should doubt often if he was for us. But we possess God in a Christ who does, and knows he does, things reserved always for God to do. His love was not an echo of God's love; or a declaration of it by one who might have exaggerated by temperament. No depth of conviction on the part of a created and prophetic Christ however holy could give us final certainty as to the Grace of God. "God only knows the love of God." God alone can forgive, who is the holiness offended; God alone judge who is the living law. Was the Great Saviour so dull as not to realise that? As he felt his own mission alone among all men to save, how did he feel as he read in his Bible words like these:—"I am God, and besides me there is no Saviour"? How would that strike him as he knew himself to be not the mere herald of salvation but the Saviour, when he not only forgave particular cases but knew that he was there to ransom the world by an offering for its sin? Could he have said "indirectly it is God, but directly it is I"? Is there any trace of such theologising with him? Must he not have known himself for the incarnation of the Eternal saving Will of God, the Eternal agent of the Eternal purpose?

§   §   §

If it be said that he must have showed his consciousness of his divine nature (and not merely of his divine vocation), by a position of more independence and initiative over against God, the answer is this: His sense of unity with God was too great and intimate for that. It was the unity of the Son—of a perfect obedience; which is just as divine as perfect authority is. It was not the unity of a second God, a joint God, a God in perpetual alliance with God. I keep asking, is the principle of obedience, which is man's very salvation, not divine, not in Godhead at all?

§   §   §

At least, we have seen and shall see, there is nothing in the consciousness of Christ, however reserved about it he had reason to be, which is incompatible with the postulate of his deity as that is demanded by the nature of his work in our saved experience. And it is only to that personal and final faith that it really comes home. The deity of Christ cannot be proved to either the lower or the higher rationalism, either to the deistic or the idealist, the Wolffian or the Hegelian. It cannot be proved either to the man in the street or the sage in the chair—but only to the evangelical experience. It is our pardon that is the foundation of our theology—our eternal pardon for an "eternal sin" (Mark iii. 29). Did Jesus connect this saving effect of his with his person or with his message? With the work he did, or with the idea he brought? We are here at a most crucial question—indeed *the* question. He can only be understood by those who hold the right relation to him. I suppose we are all agreed about that. What is that right relation ? Is it our critical relation to an idealist, or our subject relation to a Saviour ? Are we but an *aided* Church, or are we a *purchased* people ? Do we chiefly learn from his words, and admire at his character, or do we worship at his feet—which ? It is really the choice between a religion finally cosmic and rational and one finally personal, ethical, and evangelical. The great conflict to-day must be settled in the personal religion of each inquirer. It really is not a question of our conclusions but of our faith. It calls for decision rather than arbitration, for choice rather than compromise ; because it is the finest form of the deep dilemma between Christianity and the world. And it is this. Is saving faith a Rationalism, *i.e.* a faith in universal ideas, intuitions, or processes, which have no exclusive relation to a fixed point in history ? Or is it gathered to such a fixed point, in the historic Christ, where God, in presence, actually offers himself *to* man in judgment and *for* man in Grace ? Do we start from the World or the Word ? Are we to demand that Christ shall submit to the standard of certain principles or ideals which we bring to him from our human nature at its heart's highest and its thought's best ? Or as our new creator is he his own standard, and not only so but both judge, king, and redeemer of human nature, and the fountain of a new life, autonomous in him, and for all the rest derived ? Is he our spiritual hero, or our Eternal Lord and God ? Is he the prophet and champion of man's magnificent resource, or is he the redeemer of man's spiritual poverty and moral wreck ? Did he come to transfigure before men the great religious and ethical ideas, or to infuse into men new power, in the thorough, final, and godlike

sense of endowing them with a new and ransomed life?
Did he refurbish Humanity, or redeem it? Did he
release its best powers, or bestow them? That is the
last issue, however we may blunt its edge, or soften its
exigency in particular cases. It is between a rational
Christianity and a redemptive. And it is not to be
obscured by extenuations which plead that the function
of ideas is redemptive, or that redemption is the pro-
foundest rationality in the world, the "passion which is
highest reason in a soul divine." That was a line that
nearly lost Christianity to the pagan public in the old
apologists, whose great object was to make their religion
stand well with the Universities and the State—a perilous
attempt for Christianity. The crisis of society and of the
Church is at present such that a clear issue is the first
necessity, a clear issue for a final choice. When we are
dealing with the last things it is from the lack of choice
that we suffer most, not from the lack of compromise.
It is lack of decision, it is not lack of an ideal ethic, that
is our moral disease at this hour. We avoid decision in
a languid liberalism, or in a gentle, genial spirituality. But
though we may compromise on measures we may not on
faith. We need more of the spirit of compromise in
affairs, but we have too much of it in the soul's faith.
The real object of Christian research is not the purely
historic Christ, the historic residuum, nor is it
Humanity's spiritual ideal; but within the historic
Christ it is the living God, the Saviour, who chose
us to choose Him, and whom we find here, in his history,
or not at all. It is not the ideal man we seek,
who verifies and glorifies our noblest Humanity, con-
vincing us of its inalienable place in God in spite of all
our sin; but it is the redeeming God who sets Humanity

in heavenly places in Christ Jesus. It is not a theological difference which troubles us but a religious. It is lack of personal and positive religion. And it is the attempt to cover with one vague Christian name two different religions, and two distinct and incompatible gods. And when it comes to a choice of religions, what we need is more religion, more searching religion, and not advanced knowledge. And more religion among the religious is the chief need of the hour.

LECTURE IV

*THE TESTIMONY OF CHRIST'S SELF-
CONSCIOUSNESS—WAS HE A PART OF HIS
OWN GOSPEL?*

LECTURE IV

THE TESTIMONY OF CHRIST'S SELF-CONSCIOUSNESS— WAS HE A PART OF HIS OWN GOSPEL?

THIS is a question that has been stirred into extraordinary vitality by Dr. Harnack. And that I may be just to Harnack, and dissever him from the extreme critics who have exploited his phrase, let me quote his words. He says: "What belongs to the Gospel *as Jesus preached it*, is not the Son but the Father alone." In quoting these words it is common to overlook the important qualification, "As Jesus preached it." Now what Jesus preached was but part of the whole Gospel. The whole claim of Jesus for himself is not to be determined by the explicit words he uses about himself, but also, and even more, by the claims set up on us by the whole gospel of his person and work when these had been perfected. The claim of Jesus in his cross and resurrection is even greater than the claim explicit in his mouth. His redemption has been a greater power than his doctrine. In respect of Harnack's meaning, the author puts himself right in the sentence following that I have quoted, where so many stop and do him wrong: He goes on "Jesus belongs to his gospel not as a part of it, but as its embodiment. He is its personal realization and its power. And such he will always be felt to be." Moreover, adds Harnack in a subsequent publication (*Reden und Aufsätze* II. 364), "There is no generic category under which Christ can be placed, whether it be Reformer, Prophet or Founder." Harnack's meaning, therefore, would seem to be that Christ was no part of his own gospel but the whole. He declared a Father who was only to be known in the Son. He did not belong to God's great gift; he was that Gift. God gave Himself in Christ. Such a belief would seem to be more just to Harnack than the use too often made of his isolated phrase.

The answer to the question does not lie on the surface if we confine ourselves to the Synoptics. But there is no doubt about it if we go by the whole apostolic teaching. From Paul to John it is declared that Jesus was the gospel, and offered himself as such, and that none come to the Father but by him and in him. For the New Testament, taken as a whole, the historical Christ is the Messiah that was coming through the Old Testament; who appeared in Jesus as the word made flesh, full of grace, and truth, and power, and signs, and wonders; who was crucified and rose, making atonement for the sins of the whole world; who ascended up to heaven, where he now and forever represents us with the Father, sends his Spirit, and rules his Church. He was not a mere Rabbi of the law, but the Messiah of the final promise, and, since his death, the Saviour of the whole world. He was not the Nazarene, the most illustrious figure of the New Testament, and, indeed, of religious history; but he was the Christ who underlies and carries the whole history of salvation, and therefore the history of the world. He was a Christ with a premundane history of his own. For

the New Testament, as a whole, he was the Christ of the
gospel—of something which is indeed within the Bible—
but of something which is its soul and not its residuum.
He was the Christ of a Gospel within the Bible, and not
simply the Jesus of a Bible within the Bible, not simply
the Jesus of a Bible reduced by criticism alone to a
historical remnant. He was not the Jesus left us by the
extreme critics, one whose great action must be wholly
compressed between his baptism and his death; but
he was the Eternal Son of God, preached by a cloud
of witnesses, many nameless, of whom Paul was the
chief. He was the Son " with a prologue of eternal
history and an epilogue of the same," throned not on
the world's history simply, but at God's right hand where
all history is judged; the Son whose earthly life is only
intelligible on that background.

That is the New Testament Christ. And if we repudiate that we should be clear what we do. We are
making a choice between the New Testament and the
modern critical school. It is not as if the whole New Testament when critically handled were on their side. They do
not now claim that. What they claim is that the history
behind the New Testament is. They claim that apostolic
Christianity, being what I have said, misunderstood Jesus.
They do not attempt to read modern interpretations into
Pauline passages, as our Broad Churchism was apt to do.
We should be clear and frank that in adopting the most
modern view we repudiate the New Testament as Christ's
expositor, in favour of an exposition totally different,
offered by modern criticism working entirely on the
Synoptics, or on what is left of them by a certain
philosophy of religion. We reduce the New Testament
to a piece of tradition; and in so doing we surrender the

protestant position to the catholic, as so much modern
culture does in effect.

The question of the hour then, is this—if we
keep critically to the Synoptics can the Christ of the
New Testament be retained? The inquiry has changed
since the Tübingen days. The historical reality of Jesus
is not much challenged. What is challenged is the
dogmatic Christ in his finality and absoluteness, which
is the apostolic interpretation of his history. And of
late the question is even more narrowed. Criticism is
being driven to grant that even the Synoptics are
written in the interest of this final and apostolic Christ.
Can we, may we, go behind that Christ? Can we shed the
apostolic theologisms which are said to distort even the
Synoptics, and construct a simple human Jesus to be the
delight of the lay type of mind everywhere? You perceive
that such teaching does not repudiate evangelical Protestantism merely, but the New Testament. And thus the
question of the right of such teaching in the Church is
more serious than ever. Undogmatic Christianity repudiates the New Testament interpretation of Christ. It is
one thing to claim the right to a free handling of the
New Testament, it is another to repudiate the New
Testament version of Christ for the critical. One is
lawful in a Church, and one is illicit.

Of course it must at once be recognised that if
Christ did preach himself he did not do it in the
way of a blunt or naïve egotism. That is not how
he convinced the disciples that he was the Messiah,
yet he made the belief irresistible in them. It is not the
way he convinced the apostles of the divinity in him; yet
he so impressed it that they could do no other than
worship him. We shall have gained much from questions

[handwritten margin note:] Fight not against the historical reality of Jesus but against the N. Tes.

like Harnack's if they cure us of the habit of looking for
a revelation in statements, for brusque dogmatisms of
the kind that satisfies the plain man, with the muzzle of
his ' Yes or No ' at our head.   Christ always refused
satisfaction to the demand that he would tell his critics
plainly if he were the Messiah or not.   He is not the
Christ of the plain-dealer.   He always did refuse to
be coerced, or have his methods prescribed.   There he
was masterful and impracticable.   He was the sole
judge of the situation, as he is of the world.   It was for
him, as the revealer, both to read the moment and to take
the only way in it consistent with the revelation.   And
that some people should perish upon his refusals concerned him less than that he should compromise his
Father's way and will for his work—which was not, after
all, to save men the trouble of judging and choosing, nor to
gather the largest possible number of believers in a
given time.

§   §   §

Let us look at his teaching in the Synoptics then and
see where it carries us.   Let us see if it do not carry us far
beyond a teacher of truth, or even a preacher of the Father;
if we have not in his synoptical proclamation of the
Kingdom sufficient points of attachment for the Johannine
preaching of himself.

Surely he preached himself as the Messiah of the
Kingdom.   It was a Messiahship of burden much more
than of elation—even if we do not interpret the burden
of it in the sense of Bousset, who reads there not the
burden of the Cross but the burden of a misconception in
which he was hopelessly entangled.   Is it not equally
true that he thought of himself as in a category distinct
from other men, whether we regard his relation to God

or to the world ?   Where he came salvation came—as to
Zaccheus by his very presence.   He stood between men
and God, not with men before God.   A word spoken
against him was comparable, however different, to a sin
against God's Holy Spirit.   For both were against God.
They were not like sins against men.   That is to say, he
has to make his historic personality parallel with the Holy
Spirit before he can set up the contrast, which is only
effectual between beings *ejusdem generis*.   He was greater
than the temple, he said—as no prophet could be.   In
the parable of the vineyard he is the only son, the
beloved, distinct from all the messengers besides.   He
never prays with his disciples, much as he prays for
them; and the Lord's prayer was given by him but not
used by him.   There is a line between him and them,
delicate but firm, "often as fine as a hair but always as
hard as a diamond."   What he asks is devotion to his
person and not simply to his doings, to his soul and not
to his words.   To trust him is more even than to do his
commands.   To love God and man in obedience to a
commandment is better than to be the slave of ritual, but
it is still to be outside the Kingdom of his Gospel.   (Mark
xii. 34).   He has nothing to say about martyrdom for a
cause, even for the Gospel ; but he has a supreme blessing
for those who lose life *for his sake* and the Gospel's.
There is not a relation of life, however deep or tender,
that must not be sacrificed to his claim upon due occasion.   Here he assumes a right comparable only to that
of death, which claims and snatches us from every relation of duty, passion, or interest.   He assumes the right
belonging to a God who masters us in death if He never
did before.   Perhaps no age has ever been so qualified to
measure the tremendous nature of this claim as our own ;

when the natural and family affections are prized and praised as they never were before; when the whole of literature is dominated by them, through minor poets and novelists; and when the whole of Christianity is often expressed, and taken to be exhaustively expressed, in their terms as a pitiful fatherhood and a loving sonship. Again, what does he say has the blessing at the last? It is not kindness to children (or to childlike believers), nor to the poor, but their treatment in his name. Philanthropy, indeed, means much in the great judgment; but not for itself, not as humanity, but because it was done to him really, however unwittingly. His reward was to those who made themselves hated, not for their religion but for him. Men's final relation to God would depend not on moral conduct but on whether Jesus owned or disowned them as true confessors of him. But this is surely justification by faith. Or can Jesus have forgotten himself for a moment in the interest of theology? Or has some Pauline editor put the words into Christ's mouth? I have never heard that this has been suggested. But I do note that even Johannes Weiss, in his commentary, is carried by such a passage beyond the human personality to its divine content. Such an identification by Jesus of his own work with God's one business with history, of his own world-role with God's, leads Weiss to say that " Jesus is here thinking no longer of his human personality but of the divine content whose vessel he is " (on Mark viii. 38). We recall the other well known passages where Jesus considers himself the Judge of the world. While his promise of his presence in the midst of any group met in His name was something that a Jew associated only with God. His exercise of forgiveness, again, all the by-

standers understood, and resented, as infringing the
prerogative of God. If it be said that forgiveness for
Christ's sake is not in the Gospels, but only a direct forgiveness from God, it must be answered that that is not
so. It is true that forgiveness for the sake of Christ
crucified is not expressed in the Gospels; but, apart
from all disputes about the meaning of 'Thy sins are
forgiven thee,' it is not disputable that it is always forgiveness conditioned by faith in Jesus, and repentance
before his great and condescending personality, whose
mighty humility the cross did but gather up and consummate. It was a forgiveness he knew to be guaranteed
by something peculiar to himself. The kingdom, moreover, is promised only to those that attach themselves
to his person. If it is not expressly forgiveness for
the cross's sake, it is forgiveness for Christ's sake.
But in the light of after events and experiences we
see what that meant. We see the whole Christ. It
meant for the sake of one who had the cross latent in his
very nature, and that not only as his fate but as his con
summation (for the cross did not simply befall Christ).
It was for the sake of one whose person never came to
its full self, or took full effect, but in the cross—even as
he came to earth altogether by a supramundane sacrifice,
and in the exercise of a cross assumed before the foundation of the world.* Further, He repeals at will parts of the
divinest thing they knew—the Mosaic Law (Mat. xix. 3).
He declares that the supreme organ of God's will on
earth, Israel,—God's Son Israel, will be wrecked upon
its attitude to him, and replaced by foreigners. In
regard to the Pharisees, again, he uses not so much the

* See the closing lectures.

fierce bitterness of the mere Carlylese critic as the awful
severity of the supreme Judge. In the whole region of
revelation, indeed, he carries himself in a sovereign and
final way. And if it be said that even he always treated
his sovereignty as conferred, what is that so long as it was
eternally conferred ?   What is it but the principle of an
Eternal Son in eternal generation from the Father.
Neither he nor his have claimed that he was an independent and rival potentate in heaven, but that he was
and is a personal and eternal pole in Godhead. Is it a
misuse of the Great Invitation, 'Come unto me, etc.'
(Mat. xi. 28) to treat it, in the way Christendom has
done, as opening for every age alike an eternal refuge
in him, and not merely as an appeal to the harassed
contemporaries of his earthly life ?   Or did he mean,
not 'I am the secret,' but only 'the secret is with me' ?
Could any man keep himself out of his Gospel of a
Father if he had that consciousness of moral and spiritual
perfection, of absolute holiness, of room for the race, which
never deserted Jesus in his darkest hour ?   He never did,
or felt he did, anything but the will of the Father, which
will indeed he was. And he looked forward to his life
and all its ministry being consummated in a death which
was to open a new relation between God and man, and
to set up the new and universal covenant, whose day had
long ago been foreseen by Jeremiah, his nearest counterpart in the Old Testament, and the culmination of its
content. I venture to think that these are all features
which, though they have not all been unchallenged, yet
are challenged by a criticism which is not purely historic,
but which has made up its mind before on other grounds,
on grounds of philosophic, dogmatic, or anti-dogmatic
dogmatism.

§   §   §

But can you possibly explain such a Christ except by
some Christology? Can a mere psychology with its
subjective type of Christianity explain such a Christ? Is
the absence of a Christology in the Synoptics not the
assumption of much 'advanced' criticism, instead of its
result? Can it be that advanced criticism means criticism in advance of the facts? Is it pure historicism that
is at work here? Is it strict evidential science? Is it
not the philosopher in the historian that does the criticism
when we are told that Christ was not essential to his
own Gospel? Not that I object on principle to a *parti
pris*. Pure historical criticism is impossible in the case
of Jesus. I would only urge that the prejudice should be
faith and not dogma, personal faith and not negative
dogma. I would urge that the prejudice should be
positive religion and not negative theology. Can such
a record be adequately, sympathetically handled without faith in the person? Must you not trust him
ere he shall seem worthy of your trust? Can you
sift and win the essential thing out of these documents by scientific research alone? Criticism of such a
story is not possible without a side taken, consciously or
unconsciously, either in faith, unfaith, or philosophy? Is
not every estimate of Jesus a confession of faith, rich or
poor? Does he not reveal every man, judge him, and
place him? In the case of a figure like Jesus, with
such an appeal to the soul, does an absolutely scientific
critic exist, one perfectly disinterested, who has
completely succeeded in excluding every ray of light
likely to discolour a portrait wholly and solely historical? If the belief of Christendom has been
deflected by the apostolic version of Christ, is there

nothing which deflects, to right or left, the version
of the modern critic ? The mischievous work of the
apostles on the genuine human Christ has been compared
by some critics to that of those speculative monks who
thought nothing of covering a priceless Greek classic
with a palimpsest of medieval dreams. Is it quite absurd,
when we see the work of some of the critics, to recall the
treatment of Shakespeare by Colley Cibber, or of
" Paradise Lost " by Bentley ?

§   §   §

I have asked if Jesus was in his own doctrine of God,
in his supreme revelation of God as Father ?   Now it is
not well to stake any great doctrine upon a single text,
or, indeed, on several.   But, nevertheless, there are texts
and texts.   And a well-assured saying of Christ himself
about himself is more than a proof text.   As the expression of his own experience it is one of those documents,
like an imperial rescript, which are no mere documents,
but are themselves part of the history.   They are instruments and not mere evidences.   And there is one text
which every critical effort has failed to shake, except for
those who come to it with their minds made up so to
think of Christ that it could not be true on any
evidence. Harnack accepts it in the main. I allude to the
familiar passage already named, Mat. xi. 27 : " No man
knoweth the son but the father, neither knoweth any
man the Father but the son, and he to whom the Son
willeth to reveal him." Upon this passage alone I should
be ready to base my own conviction that Christ believed
his sonship to be unique in kind. And I am driven farther
by it—to his pre-existence.   I do believe that that idea
was in Christ's consciousness here ; though it may be
hard, on the one hand, to adjust it to other phases of

that consciousness, and though we cannot, on the other hand, suppose he had in his thought later trinitarian categories.

I make no direct use in this connexion of the prior phrase, about all things having been delivered to him of the Father; because I agree with Wellhausen and others who interpret it not of all power but of all the knowledge, the revelation, needful for his task. "All I need to know for my task has been taught me by the Father." But I would make this use of the words—to show that when he said the unique knowledge of the Father was the great gift that was directly his, his for his Father's work, he believed that it was his alone; that no one was for him with the Father what he was for all; and that, therefore, his own word must be the last word on his relation to the Father. Whatever he thought of his relation to the Father and the Father's work with men was, in his judgment, given him of God, and there was no more to be said.

What, then, did he think of that relation? What was taught him by the Father about his Sonship? Surely the Father and the Son here are both absolute terms. Certainly it is so with the Father. The phrases are "*the* Father" and "*the* Son." It is not *my* father. *The* Father in his holy Eternity is meant. And with such a Father the Son is *correlative*. Whatever is meant by the Father has its counterpart in the Son. If the one is an eternal Father the other is a co-eternal Son. There is all the fulness in the expression, "the Son," that there is in "the Father." Moreover, it is said here that our human knowledge of the Father, as distinct from surmises, analogies, or deductions about a Father—any knowledge which is comparable in certainty to

Christ's own—is derived from Christ, and is entirely
dependent on his will and nature. If we are sons we
are sons only in him. There is nothing absolute about
our sonship. Is it reading in Paulinism here, except in
phrase, when I say we are sons only if we are adopted
into sonship; which Christ does in the Father's name,
the passage says, and in no arbitrary way, but on the
principles which control his own filial relation to God,
and make him the one incarnation of God's holy saving
will. The Son is determined in his choice of his illuminates by the same principle as guided the Father (v. 25)
in his own case. The captain of the elect is the grand
Elector. There was an election of men by Christ as
of Christ by God; and Christ's election of men was
God's; and some were taught and some left, at Christ's
royal choice. He chose the seekers and left the
self-contented, filled the hungry with his good things
and sent the self-satisfied empty away. He had nothing
to teach those who knew all about it, any more than he
had healing for those who felt whole. He passed by the
philosophers and the healthy-minded, and spoke to the
sick waiters for Israel's salvation. And he is himself a
like mystery to men with the Father. His person is
beyond all psychology, and its key is in God's hands
alone. The Son is lighted up, is revealed only by the
Father, as the Father by the Son (Mat. xvi. 17). Flesh
and blood does not reveal the truth about him, but only
the Father in heaven. The son is so unique in his kind
that only God's revelation can read him or teach him.
At his inmost he is as much of a mystery as the Father
is. Yet he gives himself to be known. And this knowledge of him is a new religion. To know the God in Christ
is another religion from that which knows God only

through Christ. It is the new and only way to know God as religion must know him. With the person of Jesus comes a new religion, of which he is the object, and not simply the subject as its saint or sage.

The son, then, knows the Father with the same knowledge as the Father has of himself. And it was a knowledge which was not transferable. The power that Christ gave was the power to know the Father in him; it was not the power to know the Father as he did. It was the power to know the Godhead of the Father by the incarnate Godhead of the Son.

§   §   §

Do you complain that to speak of the son knowing the father with the Father's own knowledge of himself is to introduce theological intricacy into a matter of filial faith? Let me venture to answer (after reminding you that the words are Christ's), first, that if filial faith comes to possess our whole being the theological intelligence on such matters will no longer slumber. A filial faith is a theological faith. Second, that it is Christian teachers that we have in view; who, for the sake of their own certainty and the powerful simplicity that goes with certainty, might well be less afraid of faith's mental Hinterland than they are. And, third, that they should be ready with some answer to those of their flock who ask for an interpretation of passages like 1 Cor. ii., or who raise the question of two Gods, Father and Son. The chapter I have just named is classic for the psychology of inspiration and its value. I have more to say about its authority in the next lecture. But I point out here that Paul makes a tremendous claim for the Church's knowledge of God as concentrated in the knowledge of the apostles. He says it does not rest on human thought—neither upon logical inference, the divination of genius, nor the impressive speculation of philosophy. All these are more or less "thrown out" at God. What we have, he says, is the very truth given of God. Nay, we share in the self certainty of God. It was an immense thing to say—a thing as vast as when it is preached that God by His Grace and His Spirit includes us in His love for His eternal and holy Son. And if it was not true it was a huge and fantastic delusion which must discredit all apostolic witness. How could Paul possibly rise to such a statement? He did not rise; he was lifted. He was entered and seized by the Spirit. On these great central matters of faith not he spoke but Christ spoke in him—as, at his height, he knew it was not he that lived his life of faith but Christ that lived in him.* "We have the mind of Christ," the theology of Christ, Christ's theology. We think and know, on these things, as Christ did and does. And Christ? Christ is a part of the consciousness of God. Follow the passage up. Paul uses the psychological analogy of our self-consciousness. Man, he says, made in God's image, has the marvellous power of being at once the thinker and the object of thought, of facing himself, of observing himself, of understanding his own understanding, of reporting on himself. And this because he is a living Spirit. Who knoweth a man but the Spirit, the consciousness of a man which is in him.† His consciousness is a self-consciousness, which is also the only

* This no more implied infallibility in every statement than it did impeccability in every act. But it did imply central truth as it did central and subduing righteousness

† Spirit is here used as what makes man man, quite differently from its usual sense with Paul as the specific gift of new life which makes a Christian a Christian.

means of our knowing him. So also God knows himself—by his Spirit. Now the Lord Christ is that Spirit. Christ is part of the consciousness of Godhead. And as no man can read our interior till we utter ourselves, till our own spirit report, so we cannot know God except by his own Spirit—His Word (as John calls it), His Christ (as Paul calls it). God knows Himself by the Spirit. We know God by that Spirit issuing as a Word. We know Him by the Spirit by which he knows himself—by that Spirit living in Christ as its Word, knowing God by God's self-knowledge, and entering us, by Christ, with the same supernatural knowledge. The rest may reason, and welcome; but we of the Spirit know. Christ witnesses in us of his unity of being with the Father, when we pursue the faith that changes us from death to life.

So the great passage of Paul must be expounded. So he and his believed. We must then make a choice between the belief that he was profoundly, superhumanly right, or that he was learnedly and speculatively mad, as Festus decided before us. The theology of the extreme critics goes with Festus. So little is it "new."

I put it, then, that Christ uttered these words of Matthew, and that what they mean is what I have said.

This is, perhaps, the nearest approach made by Jesus in the synoptics to calling himself directly the Son of God in the special sense. It is the 4th Gospel *in nuce*. The idea of an Eternal Father is unthinkable without an Eternal Son of equal personal reality and finality. And, little as Jesus troubled himself with what was thinkable or unthinkable, how can we deny that that idea underlies his words and gives their full meaning. An Eternal Father must have an Eternal Son. The Father from before the foundation of the world has his *vis-a-vis* in a co-eternal Son. And Jesus believed himself to be that Son; else surely he would have confessed some religious relation to him. If he was not that Son, a relation to such a Son would have been part of his religion. But no Son, apart from himself, had any place in his religious world. So that the passage in Matthew is almost as clear as if Christ had said in words, what he did say in effect often, but never so nearly as here, " I am that Son." He was thus central to his own Gospel. But his was never the egoist's way of saying so. He never said, for instance, in so many words that he was the Messiah; but he spoke and acted as only Messiah could. And so he taught the one Father as only the one Son could. He taught a Son as unique as the Father. To acknowledge that Christ taught the Eternal Father is, in the presence of such a passage as this, to acknowledge also that he knew himself, in that hour at least, to be the Eternal Son that a real Fatherhood in Eternity demands. In recognising the substantial force of this passage Harnack is far separated from the extreme critics, whom he describes as the victims of their own subjectivity.

Yet the object of life is not to strive for a belief in the co-eternity of the Son, but to find in Christ, as the living Saviour, that which makes nothing less than such a belief a need, a refuge, and a joy of the soul.

§ § §

Observe at another angle the argument that is so freely used by many who carry Harnack whither he would not.

Jesus came chiefly to preach. What he left on earth was doctrine of an impressive kind. It is not made out that he was in his own doctrine. Therefore, the apostles

K

who, without question, put his person in front of his doctrine misrepresented him; and in their teaching they gave us too little of his speech and too much of himself (or their version of him).   They gave too little of his historic principles and too much of his super-historic self.   That is to say, Jesus was a preacher; He did not put himself in front of his doctrine ; His apostles did put him there; and in so far they are wrong, and they misrepresent him.   That is the argument.

There is a fallacy somewhere. And it is here. You say that the one legacy of Jesus was a doctrine of the Father, reinforced by the powerful personality of the prophet. *Why* do you say that ? What entitles you to say that the great thing Jesus brought the world was a doctrine, a doctrine rather than a deed, and that he left as his achievement his principle rather than his person ? You admit that this was not the view of the apostles, nor of the first Church; it was not the view of those who received whatever legacy he did leave. You are coming to admit that it was not the view of the Synoptists. Why do you say they were all of them wrong ? You take your stand on certain words of Jesus alone. But what entitles you to do that ? You make a huge assumption very silently. You *assume* that the words were his final or only expression of himself, and gave effect to all that was in him.   Does that go without saying?   *Was* it by his recorded words that his life took chief or sole effect ? Were they not, though expressions of his real self, yet of his unfinished self? His work was not half done till he died.   Why insulate the words, whose direct reference was but to an incomplete situation, a raw audience, and an inchoate context of events?   The synoptics are an apostolic product; why detach them so absolutely from the other apostolic products in the New Testament? Why say that in these you have no commentary from the completed Christ on his own words and work? When his life was over, and its net action on his world came to be realised, then the apostles had the full expression of the personality, in whose light all that precedes must be read. And in that light it was not his doctrine but his deed that arrested his circle, changed them, and sent them out to change the world. His words are so precious because they are the words of one who proved himself by his work alone to be the great authority on himself. Is it not the issue of his life that gives weight to his words about himself? With your emphasis upon his statements alone, are you not in bondage to the bad old idea of revelation, namely, that it consists of a teaching rather than a person, of statement or precept rather than act, of a complete truth rather than a finished deed, of truth about God rather than of God as truth? How ineradicable, how subtle, that pagan, catholic orthodox fallacy is! Have we not learned how much greater a person is than a principle or a truth, and by how much Christ's total work was his greatest word, in whose light we read all his words. In the light of his cross we see the most wondrous depths in his law. For instance, "I am not sent but unto the lost sheep of the house of Israel." When the cross broke open Christ's universality these words contain not a final truth but a great providential scheme at a penultimate stage. Do we not yet understand that the nature of true revelation is that it should come by historic facts and deeds rather than by truths, even the truths uttered at a stage by the chief actors in the deed? Whether Christ taught himself or not he *gave* himself, in a lifelong act as great as his person and ascending to his cross. He left this gift as his legacy to his Church and world. And what was the greatest effect of his gift to the Church? It was to open their eyes to see that his gift of himself to man was so great because of his prior and greater gift of himself to God, his offering of himself for men to God, which was always the supreme giving with him. And hence he was treated by those who first received the complete gift as no mere impressive personality to be remembered with reverence, but as a Saviour to be received by faith, and duly honoured by nothing less than worship. God alone could duly hallow God in man. It was only after his death that the full truth could be told because only then did the full truth exist, because his death was its creation. Only in the completion of the cross did Christ become the object of Gospel preaching, because only there was he perfected and final as Redeemer. It was not till then that his disciples came to worship him. And what one observes is this, that those who have found themselves in his death cannot hear enough about his life; but those who find their account only in his life are soon satiated with interpretations of his death. And they even sink to the level of Pfleiderer, and those who dilute his statement that, "The permanent thing in the Christian faith of redemption is the moral ideal of the self-redemption of society through the solidarity of the helpful and exalting love of its members." That is, all kind and helpful people are redeemers in the same sense as Christ. But for us it is his death that makes Christ unique. His death gives us command of the whole Christ as is not given us by his life or his words. He was perfected only in his conquest of death ; and only in that consummation do we see him clear and see him whole. And only when the deed was done was it of any use to talk of it, even to his own. His consummation there released the spirit by which alone he could be understood. Like the greatest geniuses, he had to create the spirit that understood him. The Spirit was released for men by the same act as released men for the Spirit.

§   §   §

We should take more seriously the growth of Jesus. We are all agreed that Jesus grew in obedience, learning it by the things that he suffered. He was not simply an event in history; he had himself a history, which is the moral marrow of all history. His natural consciousness grew, and the content of it grew, as he grew from child to man, and came to know the world. His spiritual consciousness, his *sense* of sonship, also grew, as he settled the conflicts that beset him about his Messiahship. Is it too much to press into the deeper meaning and condition of such growing obedience, and to say that as he did the deeper will he knew the deeper doctrine, his *grasp* of sonship also grew. The growing form of his obedience must have had for its concomitant a growth in the power of reading the meaning of his experiences; yea, a growth not only of his consciousness but of his personality, (his subjective personality, not his objective relation to God) a growth in which his deepening will met his deepening fate ? And must we not go forward on that line to say that it was only by death that he himself took the full measure of his death, and conveyed that interpretation to his disciples ? It was only in victorious death, (with its obverse of resurrection,) that he was perfected, found himself, 'arrived,' ripened, and was determined not as Son but as Son in power (Rom. i. 4). It was not till he died that he possessed his whole soul, came to his own, entered on all he really was, was exalted to his true heaven, and could teach about himself things impossible before His teaching during life was the teaching appropriate to the national stage of his universal work, to the provisional stage of his personal task. It is immaterial at this point to ask whether this great interpretation through death was conveyed by him to his disciples in a "gospel of the 40 days," or by his inspiration, from behind the veil, of men like Paul, in whom he lived more really than they did in themselves.

The question is often asked, why the idea of the kingdom of God disappears outside the Synoptics? Have we not here one answer? Is it not because of the essential change created in the whole situation by the finished work, by the perfecting of Christ, by his coming into his kingdom, by his identification with the kingdom, and its real establishment in his redemptive triumph? The King is the Kingdom. To be " in Christ " is to be in the Kingdom. The historic idea becomes the mystic reality. The future becomes the present. The apostolic preaching of Christ therefore took the place of Christ's own preaching of the kingdom. He was now identified with the Kingdom. How could that have happened if his teaching or memory had been his real legacy, if he was not more than all he said, and his manner of death more than all his method of address? Nothing in his life served the kingdom like his manner of leaving it. The Gospel of Christ replaced the Gospel of the Kingdom, because by his death he became the kingdom, because he became all that the kingdom contained, he was the "truth" of the Kingdom, and his personal perfecting was *ipso facto* and *pari passu* the securing of the Kingdom. Like "Messiah," the Kingdom was an Old Testament phrase, which served to enclose what he brought in himself; and the pitcher, the phrase, was broken as the true light shone. The testimony of Jesus is the Spirit of the Kingdom. The Kingdom was great with him. The Gospel of the Kingdom was Christ in essence; Christ was the Gospel of the Kingdom in power. The Kingdom was Christ in a mystery; Christ was the publication, the establishment of the Kingdom. To bring the kingdom preach the King. He was the truth of his own greatest Gospel. It is wherever he is. To have him is to ensure it. He sparkles in his Gospel of the Kingdom; but the Kingdom shines out full and final in his perfecting, in his finished soul and eternal whole.

§ § §

There is another way of putting the matter (suggested by Kähler) which does not always have due attention. Why should we insulate the Synoptics as the sole source of our knowledge of what Jesus wished taught as his gospel? He left some bequest; was it his teaching? If it was, did he make the careful provision he ought to have done for the preservation in purity of a gift so supreme? Or for any correct record of his life's story? Was it either his life or teaching that was understood to be his grand bequest by those he left? Did he think of leaving with them anything but himself, as cross and resurrection had made him—himself and his speedy return? If his words were the treasure, what foresight did he use to anticipate and avert that huge misrepresentation of him and his doctrine which, we are told, began almost at once, and which he would have been very dull as a teacher not to think possible in ordinary conditions? Did *he* ever erect

Jesus was bigger than what he said.

the Galilean ministry which fills the Synoptics into the
touchstone? If he did, where is it so said? And why
was it not at once put into fixed and authoritative shape
to meet the Apostolic doctrine that was doing his memory
such mischief? If he did mean the matter of his ministry
to be the test, why was the memory of it such a failure for
the purpose of arresting its perversion? Why did not
the very earliest Church in its mission work confine itself
to carrying on his sententious style, his moral precepts,
and his parabolic form? Why did they not adhere
closely to comment on his words and deeds, as all the
pupils of a great master did with his παράδοσις, or tradition, at that day? Even James, it is remarked, the
nearest in tone to the Synoptics, does not repeat their
teaching, but he calls for faith in the Lord of Glory, and
a life accordingly. What ground have we for saying that
if the Apostles had been true to the intention of Jesus
they would have prolonged and expanded his teaching
and beneficence, instead of going off upon a theological
Gospel? It is more than ever wonderful that they did
not prolong his mode of instruction if we follow the view
of so many and hold that there was little original in his
teaching, little beyond what could be drawn, and was
drawn, from the Old Testament, or Judaic tradition.
To Jews brought up like the Apostles that fact would
only have given the more weight to Christ's words, and
deepened their obligation to continue the new impulse he
had infused into the old truths.

Does it not all point to this, that the real legacy of
Jesus was himself—the impression of the personality
which gave to his ' occasional ', and sometimes transitory,
teaching its real worth. Nay, impression is not the
word. His great legacy was an achievement. The mere

impression evaporated as disciples forsook him and fled.
It was a new life, a new creation, that he effected. Something happened which rallied them, and converted the
fading impression into living and justifying faith—something which had the real gospel, and the real gospel power,
in it. Christ rose. A new master made of them new men.
A new Christ turned them from disciples into apostles.
The Spirit came. The cross opened. These things
were what made the Church, and not the teaching of
Jesus. That teaching was only preserved from oblivion
by the existence of a Church founded on another base,
on an atoning salvation which alone gave the Church its
living interest in the records of the Saviour, and gave to
his words their authority. (The gospels were written by
and for people who were made Christian by Christ's
death and resurrection and their theological meaning.
They were written to edify the converts of the Cross, and
not to challenge or correct a theology of incarnation and
redemption.)

§   §   §

The inadequacy of the Synoptics alone is shown from
another point of view, which I suggested a moment
ago. It is recognised by most that there was a development of some kind in the course of Christ's public
ministry. And it is admitted by most that such
an idea was not in the mind of the Evangelists, that
in the gospels it is not set out, and, if it is to be
traced, it must be picked out. It is more or less of a
construction. It does not lie on the face of the documents. So much so that within my own memory it was
thought a heretical and somewhat hazardous suggestion,
due to wits more sharp than sound. The Synoptics do
not offer it, though they may be made to yield it. But

how are we to trace it? I mean, what are we to look for
in that way? What kind of development shall we seek?
What is the ideal scheme of growth which the Gospel
material is to fill in, perhaps by some re-arrangement?
The Gospels themselves, I say, offer no such scheme.
We must get it elsewhere, and then the Gospels will
illustrate it. Where shall we get it? To what, in what
respect, are we to suppose Jesus developed?

Now, to these questions the apostles give a certain
answer. He grew as Saviour. He developed as Redeemer. He grew in his vocation rather than in his
position, more even than in character. He did not
become either the Son or the sinless. As the situation
became more vast, grave, and tense, there grew in him
not only knowledge but force and grasp in his one work.
He learned a redemptive obedience—not indeed to acquire
its nature, but to unfold its form as the crisis deepened.
Because he *was* a son (his Sonship he did not learn) he
learned obedience. It is not the acquisition of Sonship
but the growth of an incarnated *Redeemer* that the
Epistles teach us to look for in the Gospels, the process
of Redemption rather than incarnation. The idea is condensed in Hebrews ii. 10, "to perfect the captain
of salvation by sufferings." Not the man Jesus was
perfected but the Saviour, not the moral character so
much as the work possible only to that character. Here
we certainly have moral development, but it is not the
increase of a moral nature so much as the deepening
mastery of a moral vocation. It is not the aesthetic
development of a moral character of symmetry and
balance, but the dynamic development of a Redeemer,
of a Son of God in power which was at last determined
in his resurrection. It is not so much a perfect product

of sanctification that we have, but a perfect agent of justification; not perfection of the admirable personality — but perfection of the finished work; not

> "A soul by force of sorrows high,
>   Uplifted to the purest sky
>   Of undisturbed Humanity"

(which is a stoic ideal after all, as Wordsworth's always was a chastened spirituality) but one who was always equal to cope with each mounting antagonism that a Redeemer had to meet. This, of course, could only be done by an ethical personality and its victory; but it is not the ethical idea that is uppermost, but the evangelical, the theological, the functional, the evolution of the Saviour, rather than the man, in so far as they are separable. And it is not I who say they are, but those who take the man and leave the Saviour.

But the growth that is traced by those who reject the idea of redemption as being something foisted by the apostles on Jesus, is the growth of such ethical character as a saintly modern man would be expected to achieve by a sympathetic and scholarly biographer. If the Gospel material is to fill up some conception of development, and the development is not that of a redeemer, it must be that of an ethical character of the modern type. Is it hard to choose between the value and authority of the two ideals? If each is an importation into the Synoptics, which is the more likely to do justice to them—that favoured by the founders and heads of the Churches that produced and used them, or that imposed by laborious scholars living at a date so remote as our own, working often with more psychological acumen than personal faith, and working under a bias against apostolic interpretation. Development is meaningless without a

standard or principle.   And my contention would be that
the apostles represent the atmosphere of the evangelists ;
that the apostolic ideal is the principle of any development
which the evangelists may imply but do not set themselves to press; and that any construction of the evangelists other than this must be more alien and more
artificial.   To set forth Christ as Redeemer is at least
more germane to our data than to exhibit him as the
flower of spiritual character, which certainly was not the
interest of our sources at all.

§   §   §

Those who select the Gospels out of the New Testament, and the Synoptics out of the Gospels, you perceive
then, do not stop there.   They sift the Synoptics and
select from them a putative primitive Gospel.   They
select the essential thing, as they deem it.   I have
asked what is their test of the essential ?   The rest
of the New Testament, we have seen, does offer a
standard for those narratives.   It is the evangelical,
the dogmatic, Christ, whom the critics reject ;   the
Christ who is much more the object of faith than
the subject of it.   And that is the test that the
Church has used throughout its deeply experienced
history.   Even when the Bible was not accepted *en bloc*,
this was so.   It was Luther's test for a canon within the
canon.   He took what made for that apostolic, saving
Christ.   And we all do as Luther did, so far.   We all
make our own canon within the canon.   We do not find
every part of the Bible equally authoritative or equally
valuable.   We each select the passages which do most
for us, which come most home to our chief need, and
the need we find unmet elsewhere.   We have many
individual ways of making that selection, varying up-

wards from literary taste to evangelical experience. But
when it has to be done on the scale of a Church, or a
science, it must be done under some common guiding principle. Now for the Church's selection of the canon, the
guiding principle was the evangelical principle of
Redemption, the apostolic note. It was the witness,
direct or indirect, to Christ the Redeemer, and not
Christ the personage, the hero, saint, or prophet. And
it was the same redemptive principle that the Church
applied, in the evolution of its theology, to test the
heresies of the right or of the left. All its metaphysics
were so many inadequate efforts made, in the greatest
language of the period, to secure that substantial and
final interest of a real redemption—as our social efforts
are made to-day. These are efforts to express redemption
in the inadequate forms of social re-arrangement when
what we need is social re-generation. We need a reformed Church more than a re-adjusted state.

But if that redemptive and apostolic principle be
discarded in selecting from the select books the essential
Christ, what is to take its place? What is the guiding
principle to be? What is the ultimate thing, whose
witness in the Synoptics is their permanent thing? You
say it is just spirituality, a deeply humane spirituality?
What do you mean by that? Is it the simple, rational,
natural, continuous relation that we can now discern
between God and Man, the last conditions in thought of
God, man, and the world? But is that not Metaphysics?
At any rate, is it not religious psychology? It is not a
historical test pure and simple that you are making the
norm. It is often a metaphysical test, a monistic test,
in which we measure religion by its transfiguration of
our deep, natural, immanent relation to God and the

world based on identity of being and nature. Yet we were given to understand that it was just the metaphysic in the old creeds that made the worst burden of them. Can it be that the critic who sends in his card as the representative of the new scientific firm is really the agent of the old metaphysical house, who, after ruining it, is starting the same industry under entirely new management, in a fresh place of business? Is the test for the essential thing in the Gospels composed of certain ideas, movements, or sympathies, rising out of the continuity of rational process in God and man, and either springing up in the human mind as its natural nexus with God, or generalised from the various faiths into a universal philosophy of religion? Is general religiosity the test of positive religion? Is the amorphous the standard of the organic? Is the nebula the measure of the world, or the protoplast of the paragon? Is what we should naturally expect God to do to be the measure of faith in what he has done? Is that old apriorism not dead yet? Are we to begin by admitting only what we consider worthy of Him? Is that what we are to put in the centre of Christianity, that and not the invasive Word, the spiritual enclave, the actual revelation, the pure gift and person of Christ in its originality and finality, welling up in the soul's history like a quenchless spring of living water in the bottom of the Dead Sea? Is nothing to be credited to the Father of spirits but what is allowed by the instincts of nature's sweetest child? Everywhere (it is said) you find that a good God forgives upon mere repentance and confession, that he comes in aid to his worshipper's cry. Our hearts say that, the spiritual summary of the world's faiths says that. If there be anything said about Christ, even in the New Testament itself, which contradicts that, it must out. If a holy judge affright our dreams when we had gone to rest on a kind Father's kiss, it is the nightmare of a stale and indigestible creed. If a mediator, an atonement, is preached, it is a sophistication. If anything in the Gospels points that way, disallow it. It is a dishonour to the great and ready heart of God. "But then the textual or other evidence?" "O, that is lower "criticism. The passage has spoken blasphemy. What "further need have we of witnesses? It is worthy of "death." Is there anything in the Godhead of Christ which is forbidden by modern monism, modern evolution? "Delendum! Such a Christ is a foreign body intruded "between God and the Soul. Forgiveness is but a "rudimentary way of speaking about the relation of "absolute to finite being; or it is but 'a religious "expression for a psychological process,' a divine way of "speaking of the healing and softening effect of spiritual "time and its genial process upon the disturbed moral "consciousness. God is not angry. Ritschl has settled "that. It was all our ignorance. Salvation means "getting rid of the idea that he is angry; it is escaping "from a misconception of him, clearing up a misunder- "standing. Sanctification is the art of learning to soothe "the excessive pertinacity and philistinism of conscience, "putting that bore into his place, and acquiring the "*cachet* of the cultivated suburbs of the devout soul." O, it is all so able, so genteel, so dull, so morally ordinary, so spiritually banal! I must allow myself to quote here what one of the noblest Germans of them all, and the most religious, says about the liberal theologians and critics of the hour. Nobody will accuse Herrmann of orthodoxy. He has been pointing out that the liberal

theologian (what we call the advanced) lacks one thing
that orthodoxy had and still has—power.   If liberalism,
he says, could acquire this it would be far superior to the
old creed—if it could meet as effectively as the old did
man's need of power and life.   It would be better because
it would cut adrift much wreckage that the old still
drags with it and should lose.   And he associates this
element of power with the central and supernatural place
given to Christ, both in history and in our private experience—Christ as the sole being to whom the soul can and
must absolutely submit as unto God.   " But," he says,
" this is just what in the liberal theology you do not
have.   Its representatives are accomplished experts in
the appreciation of piety outside them, but a piety of
their own, a religion of decision, seldom emerges into the
light of their consciousness.   They are masters in the art
of presenting to us the way in which the prophets
received the word of God, or the way an apostle's soul
was filled with conflict first and then with peace.   They
can wipe the dust of centuries from the words of Jesus.
Nay, they can trace for you, with a high ardour, his
incomparable spiritual style.   But they seldom show a
sign of concern about what Christ means for themselves.
They do not betray that a personal life bears down on
them out of the page of Scripture, and, full and warm,
conquers them for his own.   If that were their concern
they would at least be silent when others adore him as
Lord because he alone compels the worship from their
soul.   So long as they do not feel that, they cannot do
the work of theology, nor lay for ever the ghost of dogmatic controversy when the old creed claims that there is
no theology but itself.   But in the Churches of the Reformation the sleeping sense will yet wake that religion is

the veracity of the inmost life to the actual situation of his soul, and that Christian religion can only grow from what a man himself experiences of the present reality of the person of Christ."   (Kultur d. Gegenwart I, 630.)

The final tendency of " advanced theology " is backwards.   Like Molière's ghost, it has improved very much for the worse.   It relapses to the outgrown Deism of the eighteenth century.   That was a rationalism which ignored history ; this is a rationalism which deforces it. And its great act of violence is the driving of a fatal wedge between the Synoptics and the Epistles, between the message of Jesus and the Gospel of his Apostles.

§   §   §

I should like to add a point which has often arrested me, and one whose development would carry us far. Jesus loved the Father in entire obedience, humility, and trust. He trusted Him when every human and rational reason for trust was gone.   But yet neither from himself nor his apostles do we hear any reference to his faith—though faith is the one link between him and them.   The evangelists have a rich store of phrases for his relation to God, whom he heard, saw, knew, etc., but they never say he believed in God.   And never does he say " Believe in me as I in the Father."   The reason is that our faith has to make its way over darkness and distance, both in thought and will, which never troubled him.   He no more confesses his faith than his sin.   The religious problem for him and us was not the same.   He possessed the certainty and communion of the Father in himself.   And we believe in the Only Son as he believed in none.

L

LECTURE V

THE TESTIMONY OF APOSTOLIC INSPIRATION—IN GENERAL

LECTURE V

THE TESTIMONY OF APOSTOLIC INSPIRATION—
IN GENERAL

THE line of proof we follow (if we may call it proof, if it is more than movement) is threefold. We began by interrogating the self-consciousness of Christ. But we may have had occasion to find that for some this is bound to be incomplete. For, first, we are exposed to the challenge of the Higher Criticism on the passages concerned. And second, on a kenotic theory, the self-consciousness of the earthly Christ is in comparative occultation. Hence, we push forward the second line of works—the New Testament, its reflection of Christ, and especially its inspiration by him. We are driven to what might be called his self-consciousness in his apostles. And beyond that we have the third line, the line of experience in the soul of the individual or the Church.

It is with the second parallel of advance that we come now to be concerned—with the value for our subject of the New Testament testimony and its inspiration, meaning by that the apostolic testimony. I do not refer here to the general faith of the first Church, to the faith that wrung from it the confession and worship of Jesus as Christ and Lord. I have more in view than the

impression Jesus produced on men in numbers.   I do
not speak of the New Testament as the *mirror* in which
we see the reflected image that Christ made in the
Church.   I speak now of it as his *mouthpiece*.   I speak
of the apostles in chief, and of that special exercise of
faith which in them is called inspiration.   And I go to
ask what is the value of the apostolic inspiration, in
order that we may assess the value of the apostles' view
of the person and work of Christ.   Was their view of
him a passing impression, a personal opinion, perhaps an
early extravagance that we must leave behind ?   The
religious-historical school have virtually recognised that
views of Incarnation, Atonement, Redemption and
Sacrament are not to be explained away out of the New
Testament however they may be explained into it.   It is
an immense admission which I shall often use ; for it
concedes that the views developed by the later Church
on such subjects are really rooted in the apostolic creed,
whether that creed was rooted in the mind of Jesus or
not.   If the apostles were right about Christ, the Gospel
of the whole Catholic and Evangelical Church is right.
It is of prime moment, therefore, that we should know if
the inspiration of the apostles was anything which gives
to their teaching on these heads more than a personal,
temporary, or deflected worth.

§   §   §

Must everything in the New Testament be true ?   Is
everything we find in Jesus revelation ?   Was his
geocentric view of the world, was his view of the author-
ship of a psalm, was his every precept—were these
permanent revelation ?   Again was everything equally
revelation that was believed about Jesus by an apostle ?
Or was there not rather a proportion and perspective of

faith? Do such things not stand at varying distances from the vital centre, and are they not vital accordingly?

Again, were there any extraneous ideas at work from other religions on Judaism, on the Church, on the Apostles, shaping the form of some of their beliefs? If so, have we not to go on to ask, what in the New Testament is of faith, and what comes either from the mental world of the time or from the idiosyncracy or the education of the writer—like his mode of argument? What is mere impression, and what is speculative explanation, and what is in the nature of miraculous supernatural insight by special action of the Spirit? These distinctions and questions are inevitable.

§   §   §

The Church made a great step forward when it was led to think less of the inspiration of a book and more of the inspiration of the men that wrote it and of the nation that bred them. We learned last century that inspiration was something too warm and vital to belong to a book; it could only be the state of a living soul. It was personal inspiration and not book inspiration. That is valuable, but it does not end the matter. We must take account, as of the Old Testament nation, so of the corporate consciousness of the Church as a site of inspiration. And not only so but about the man we must ask questions. If it was the man that was inspired, and not the book, was everything the man said or did inspired? Or did the inspiration only come when he had to speak in public, or take the pen in hand? It is no necessary guarantee of truth to say it came from an inspired man. Was he inspired when he saw it? Was he equally inspired when he said it, so that we may be sure that what he said is exactly what he saw? Which

acts of apostles were inspired? Was it inspiration (it
has been asked) when Peter decided to take his wife with
him on a missionary journey, or when Paul discouraged
marriage? Were such things in inspired men also
inspired? Or had these men but the potentiality of
inspiration for use on due occasions; and did it need
some particular historic situation, especially in the
consciousness of the Church, or some special divine
intervention, to produce the inspired state and insight?

§   §   §

Of course, to begin, they had at least such a personal
relation to history as is implied in saving faith in a
historic Saviour. Inspiration had faith for a base. And
it was faith positive, faith at a certain practical juncture.
Accordingly the New Testament books were mostly
occasional, applying fundamental Christianity to particular situations in the believing Church. But how
much is to be allowed for the situation? And where is
the permanent element independent of situation, and not
only good for all time but creative? Surely if we ask the
writers, the apostles in particular, their answer is that
there is such an element, and that it centres about the
person, place, and work of Christ, involving a real
incarnation and atonement. We escape thereby from
Rationalism, orthodox or heterodox ; there is a historic
authority claimed. But we cannot remain in mere
Biblicism. We cannot believe a certain thing just because
it is in the Bible. And our city of refuge is Evangelism.
What we really believe is the Gospel which, with the new
soul, called the Bible also into being, and for whose sake
it exists. It is not the Church. For the books of
the Bible were given *to* the Church, more than *by* it, and
they descended on it rather than rose from it. The canon

of the Bible rose from the Church, but not its contents.
Bible and Church were collateral products of the Gospel.

But we go on.   Having fixed in the New Testament
on what was held to be of faith and central to faith, we
must ask, was it true ?   How far is that theological faith
a true interpretation of the historical Jesus Christ ?
Does it assign to Jesus Christ what he himself claimed,
or wished claimed, when we read him as a whole ?   Does
it express what he compels from us by an examination of
his self-consciousness, or, still more, by an experience of
his work ?

§   §   §

Now this last, his work, contains the greatest claim of
all so far as the New Testament is concerned.   It is
what the apostles operate with almost entirely.   For
them Christians are not people who have a Christian
character, whatever their beliefs, nor those who cherish
ethical ideas about dying to self and living in a larger
whole.   But Christians are those who partake by
experience in Christ's death, resurrection, and eternal
life.   The apostles do not take our modern line and
interpret the self-consciousness of Jesus.   If they had,
we should have more data in our hands for doing it.
The apostolic method was to stake all upon Christ's
person and the cross (with its obverse of the Resurrection), upon the cross and Christ's work there, appropriated by the Church's faith and experience of the New
Creation.

The question then, is, Is the apostolic method right
in this respect ?   Is it a true interpretation of Jesus to do
as it did, and fix on the cross (with the resurrection) as
the key to him and his meaning ?   Is this the authentic
word in the Bible ?   It is now generally felt how true

was the selective insight of Jesus in respect to the Old
Testament, when for his teaching he seized on the
prophetic element in it rather than the legal as the fertile
core of its revelation and the red line of God's coming.
Can we be as sure that the apostles were equally right
when, in the prophets, they concentrated on Is. 53,
and seized on Christ's atoning death and resurrection
among all the features of his activity, as the site of
the consummatory and illuminative Word about himself ?
Were they wrong when they found the two lines, the
prophetic and the priestly, meeting there ?

§   §   §

In approaching the answer to such questions, and
assessing the value of New Testament inspiration as real
insight into the person and work of Christ, we might
clear the ground with a few more interrogatories.

Could the doctrine of the Atonement, or of the
Incarnation, be established for a Church, for the race,
on the synoptics alone, historically and critically
searched ? I do not think they could. But then neither
could the doctrine of the Holy Spirit, or the Church, to
say nothing of others. Indeed it is only constructively
that we can find there the modern idea of a development
of Christ's public character and purpose. I am sure that
the Church at least, which was founded on the apostles'
atoning interpretation of the cross, could not live upon
the Synoptics alone. It could not find itself in them.

But perhaps these doctrines then are compatible with
the Synoptics and latent there, if they are not palpable.
Are they ? Yes, some would say ; no, would be said by
others. I believe they are. And that is the real
question. It is not whether the Synoptics would yield
the doctrines, but whether the doctrines, and the doctrines

alone, explain them. And I think critical opinion is
growing that the doctrines do explain them; because
the Evangelists wrote in the atmosphere and interest
of such doctrines, though not to prove them. They knew
nothing of our undogmatic Christianity, however we
may revise and edit down what they wrote. They may
have, of course, been taking a liberty with the historic
Jesus in doing so. They may have been importing
the doctrines and imposing them on Jesus. That is
not here the question. But critical opinion is on the
point of outgrowing the idea that the Synoptics represent
undogmatic Christianity. So much the religious
historical school has done for us.

And if it be asked farther whether the apostles,
whether Paul, saw these doctrines in the historic Jesus,
and were forced on them by his revolutionary action on
themselves, of course we must recognise that they did
so see them. We are long past any twisting of their
meaning which would go to show that they did not,
that they meant less than the Reformers thought, and
were really Broad Church theologians or ideologues
born out of due time. We may treat their views as we
think proper once we settle what they were, but the
scientific, the purely historic version of their views is as
I say. For them the theological interest is fundamental.
On such a point Pfleiderer's *Paulinism* is very valuable.
They did believe they found such doctrines, the doctrines
of grace, at the centre of the historic Christ, whether
you think them fantastics or not for doing so. That is
another question. And it is one that we must go on
to discuss.

§   §   §

The apostles believed Jesus to be the eternal, atoning

and redeeming Son of God; what is the value of their belief? They did not reason it out on a speculative basis, however they may have sometimes used speculative ideas as a calculus in the attempt to convey it. It was a matter of their regenerate experience of Christ's historic work, and of their insight into its postulates in terms of current ideas. What is the worth of the apostolic insight? (Was Christ valuable for the sake of certain spiritual ideas, or were the ideas valuable as expositions of Christ?) Was the apostolic insight on the same footing as ours? Take the insight of reason, what Hegel calls the intuition of thought. Has modern reason as good a right over our faith as the interpretation of Christ which the apostles offered for revelation? Take faith. Has modern faith an equal validity with theirs, or one even greater by all the long experience through which the Church has since passed? Can modern Christianity, therefore, correct the apostles upon fundamental truths like the deity or atonement of Christ?

The answer to this question will depend on the place we assign to the apostles in the economy of revelation; on their place as uniquely inspired—inspired as much above the ordinary level of Christian faith as that is supernatural to the reason or vision of the world. Let us examine this.

§   §   §

If we start with Christ as giving the revelation of God *in nuce*, and say that Christendom and Christianity form the evolution of that infinite germ, we take a line which is very welcome to many among us to-day. But they do not measure, perhaps, all it carries. It carries this, that, as in the evolutionary progress we come to know better, the Apostles' Creed is worth more than the

Epistles, the Athanasian Creed worth more than the Nicene, the Augsburg Confession greater than them all, and the modern Christian consciousness the court of final appeal beyond that. Or the Vatican decrees, perhaps, may be the summit—unless you say offhand that the Roman Church is not a Church at all, but totally outside the evolutionary area.

This is, however, a result which, welcome as it may be to the masterless subjectivity of the time, gives no finality, but makes each age its own spiritual authority. It gives but Protestant Liberalism or Roman Modernism. And it is chiefly due to the error of thinking that a simple conception of evolution, evolution deploying, under spiritual law, in one direction, with a steady swell, will suit history, and especially religious history, as well as it does biology. If that were true, however, I am afraid we should have to reduce Christ to a position no higher essentially than one of his own apostles. He would be Master and they disciples, of course, but they would be *ejusdem generis*, like Socrates and his circle; and he could no longer be viewed as the revelationary fact but as its discoverer only—like Darwin. Nay he could discover but a stage of it. For the grand revelation, on such a theory, could only be at the end, and not at the beginning of the series, if it ever were attainable at all.

But if we are dealing with those who do believe in a past fact really revelationary, and no mere germ, the question is, what was that fact? What was the revelation? Where did it begin? And above all where did it end? For the kind of revelation here concerned is one that does not go on unrolling indefinitely, but it has an end. It has *a* finality, even if *the* finality were not allowed.

§   §   §

May I invite you a little way into the philosophy of the case. Consider the long evolutionary series. The whole process of creation did not develop at large, but developed in man to an end, an interpreting end, an end of infinite value. Man is a close for all the evolution that preceded him in nature. That is true even when we recognise the evolution within man himself. The evolution *in* man is a sublimation of the evolution *to* man. Nature evolves to a close, which is none the less a real close because it has within itself an evolving history. Such closes are what every soul is— ends in themselves (though with a career), and with a value more absolute than any mere stepping-stone to a sequel. When evolution reaches personality and history, it becomes more than simple and onward merely. Its nature and method change. It becomes another thing when it has to do with freedom and purpose—with souls. In the soul we have a spiritual world that does not simply arise and crown the past but invades it and stands over it as the earnest and surety of its future. The end emerges in the means. Evolution becomes quite another thing when it rises to be teleological in this way. It then becomes a "kingdom of ends." Each soul is an end in itself, and not a mere cell, or a mere link. Each great soul stands for a permanent value. And so with each historic crisis. History moves to ends; and even if these again move to higher ends, they are not mere points of transition. We have a rising series of peaks not of links—peaks of single and standing value against the infinite sky. We progress by a progression of crises, which close, or harvest, each a movement or age, and

garner its permanent value not only to be carried over to
the next age but also registered and credited in Eternity.
For we grow laterally, vertically, spherically, outward
into Eternity as surely as onward into the future. And
these peaks make an ascending range.   These real
closes again postulate a grand end of all ends and
crisis of all crises, a harvest of the world and all
its ages, and even of eternity; and one, too, not
awaiting history far off, but invading it, pervading it,
and mastering it always.   For the spiritual world, as
Eucken reiterates upon us in all his system, not only
accompanies this world but faces it, addresses it, inter-
feres with it, dictates to it, judges it and cannot
rest till it subdue it.   There is a fundamental inroad of
a final and autonomous power into the plexus of causal
evolution—a repeated and incessant miracle.   And the
Christian plea is that the nature and reality of this
supreme end for the whole soul of man is not only
anticipated or asserted but it is secured in advance by
revelation; which is not the process, but something in
the process yet not of it, and something that determines
it.   And it is this final thing that we have in Jesus
Christ and his crucial redemption.   We have in him a
close which is incompatible with a simple evolution, or
mere crescendo, of being. We have, midway, a creator, a
finality, an authority which no evolution can give.   That
is what we mean by starting from the revelation in
Christ.*

§   §   §

The question then becomes this; what is the place of
apostolic inspiration in this finality which we have in

---

*I must deal elsewhere more fully with the question whether in Christ
we have *a* revelation or *the* revelation, an interim report of God or a final.

Christ? If Christ was final what finality or authority over us is left for his Apostles and their inspiration? Have we in them but the first crude guesses in the evolution of thought about him, guesses raw in the ore of contemporary notions, which recent thought has smelted down to a small residuum? Was Christ the whole of the Christian revelation, body and soul of it, its matter and form? Did Israel, did revelation rise slowly to its full and final height in Jesus only to drop suddenly and sharply to the amateur and tentative level of Paul? Was Christ removed from the groping thought of Peter, Paul, and John by a greater gulf than that which parted him from the Judaism so fatal to him? Was the thought of his devotees about him more of a perversion of him than the thought of the foes he hated so well? Wernle says it was so. And it is an idea which acts on many who never formulate it, never express it, and do not realise how deeply it affects and depresses them. The whole stress is laid upon the historic act or person of Christ. The whole revelation is held to be exhausted there. That is the history as fact; the writing of the history is a quite secondary matter, and belongs to a much inferior stage. It is a product diluted by reflection and distorted by artificiality—at most a bad photograph of the revelation, and not a part of it; or it is light turned on Christ instead of issuing from him. In the actual history (it is said) God was at work revealing; but in the record, or commentary, it was man construing. In the transfer to writing much of the reality has vanished; and the living plant is even dried between the leaves of the book. So it is said. And thus our very exaltation of the personal revelation in Christ has led to a fatal depreciation and neglect of the Bible, as being a mere record, which we may use for our satisfaction but need not for our life.

§   §   §

Now on that head there is this to say. Christ certainly was the final and complete revelation of God, in every *material* sense. In him the great transaction was done, the great Word said. In him we have history's final cause and final crown. In him we have the great close. All evolution up to him now goes on in him. In Christ creation " arrived," attained for good. In every material sense that is so. But in a formal sense it is not so. The material revelation and consummation in Christ is not complete without a formal consummation in its *interpretation*. The finished work of Christ was not finished till it was got home. A lesson is not taught, say our educationalists, till it is learned. He made the victory real, but he had yet to make it actual. He had not to gain another victory, but he had to follow up the victory he had won, and enter on the kingdom it secured. The great close in Christ had itself to be closed, or at least clinched, in a close of its own.

§   §   §

I have spoken of one error that misleads us—the treatment of historic and moral development as if it were a case of simple and continuous evolution ; marred, indeed, by occasional fits of degeneration and reversion, but devoid of those great consummations or " harvests " which truly end one age and begin another, but are also permanent acts and conquests of the Absolute and Eternal. There is, however, another analogy from nature which is as misleading as it mostly is to carry natural law into the moral world. It is the analogy of the germ. The germ in nature unfolds

M

by absorbing the forces of its environment and exploiting them for its own individual growth.   It is more concerned to assert and develop its own individuality, or that of its species, than to create a new order and establish a new world.   But a germ, a source, in a revelation of grace, is different.   Its object is not to absorb the world but to act on it.   It has to unfold not within itself so much as within an intelligence of itself. Its purpose is not to be but to be understood, to be answered ; it is not to live on its environment but to bless it.   A germ of life is one thing, and a germ of revelation or redemption is another.   In the one case we have to do with a created fact, in the other with a creative.   In the one case we have the fact insulated and self-sufficient, in the other the fact is inert apart from its being understood and interpreted.   You have not the whole fact without its interpretation.   If human evolution closed in Christ it did not close in a mere Superman, whose genius it was to thrive on a merely tributary race. A gracious close like Christ is one that takes effect in human response and communion, and not in mere contribution.   His value is not in himself all unknown, but in himself interpreted and assimilated by the race in which he rises.   The fact Christ, however complete materially, is not complete formally, or in effect, till he is understood and answered, till he is explained and realised in a Church.   That he is complete materially is shown by the fact that his explanation proceeds from himself.   He is his own interpreter.   It is very properly asked concerning the synoptic Christ, Why did he not explain himself ?   And the answer is that he did, as soon as the whole work was done, and the whole fact accomplished which had to be explained.   He interpreted himself in his

Create new order

Bless its surroundings

Apostles, in the New Testament. If Paul's view of
Christ was but a guess, and can now be seen to be a
wrong one, the revelation was left by Christ incomplete,
and therewith the redemption. The great close, therefore, ends in bearing witness of itself, and coming to
its own in man's soul. And this happened in the
Apostles. To close this great close is the work of the
New Testament, as something formally, uniquely, integral
to the revelation in Christ.

§   §   §

When we say the revelation is Christ we must
take the whole Christ, the whole New Testament Christ,
the Christ as his Spirit interpreted him, and not only
the Christ as an annalist, a reporter, might record him.
To say vaguely that the revelation is Christ, or that
Christ is the centre, is the source of most of our
confusion. The manifestation had to be closed by the
interpretation or inspiration to complete the revelation.
The material revelation had to take effect in a formal inspiration before it could start on the career of its own
evolution. It took this formal effect in the New Testament, which is not the mere product of the revelation but
part of it, the formal element of it, as Christ was the
material. If the only legacy of Christ was the impression he left on his followers, of course this could
not be so. But impression was not all. Christianity
is not an impressionist creed. The faith of the
Church, being an act of life's self-committal and
worship, is more than the posthumous impression
left by Jesus. Had it not been more, like all impressions it would have worn off. As an act it
answered an act—an eternal act, which gives it its own
depth and permanency. It was a new life, a new

creation.   And still greater than the Church's faith is the
apostles' inspiration, a life even within the new life.   It
is not only a response, but that part of Christ's great and
final act which is continued by him from the unseen ;
it is not a mere echo of it in his survivors.   *The New
Testament is not the first stage of the evolution but the
last phase of the revelationary fact and deed.*   The revelation had to be interpreted for all time in order to act
on time—just as, on a lower plane, the Church of the
early centuries is put into the Athanasian Creed for all
time, and the Reformation into the Augsburg Confession.   But the plane is much lower.   For into these
documents it was the Church that put itself, whereas
into the New Testament it was Christ that put himself, in a way parallel to his self-projection in the
Church.   The creeds are not parallel to the Church,
but the Bible is.   They are products of the Church.
The Bible is not.   It is a parallel product of the
Spirit who produced the Church.   The Church was
made by faith, the Bible by inspiration.   They are two
products of one Spirit ; the one is not a product of the
other.   The Bible was not produced by the Church ; and
yet the Church was there before the Bible.   Both were
there collaterally from the Spirit.

§   §   §

I may perhaps use another illustration, suggested by
Grützmacher, which I will somewhat enlarge in the
application.   In a parliamentary discussion, if the
subject be very large, the debate may go on indefinitely,
as new aspects of the question are unfolded and new
lights cast upon it.   As the discussion is carried into the
press so much the more do new points arise, and again
fresh points out of these.   If the parliament were

enlarged to the dimensions of the press the evolution and the length of the analytic process might be interminable. And it would become quite interminable if the whole of the population were included in the debate—to say nothing of the population of the world, extended to all the population that had ever existed on the earth. Now such a process would correspond to the simple expansive evolution of the natural world in a *process*. But in practical affairs a point comes when the debate must be closed. It really does not exist for its own expansion, but for the sake of its close, in due time, in an *act*; which act is its end, and has a value and authority relatively final. It is final so far as that debate is concerned, and it is permanent amid all subsequent debates. It registers a real achievement and a point won. Even if it becomes the point of departure for future reform it is more than that. It has a real value for its present. It has added to the permanent. So the evolutionary process culminates from time to time in results which are not mere products of the process but are imposed on it by a will; and they have more value than mere points of transition or links of past and future. And if the process were on a world-scale all these ends, with their relative finality, with their permanent contribution and eternal value, would be gathered up in an end absolutely final, the end of all ends, their consummation, in which they found themselves when the mere process of their production had faded away with the ink of the cosmic Hansard. The Christian case is that this cosmic end has been anticipated with condensed finality at one point of history, for the sake of all the rest, in the absolute end, act, and personality of Jesus Christ.

But to go a step further. If parliament simply passed

its act and proceeded to a new subject what would the effect be? It would be nothing. The House would have the satisfaction of having done something, gathered up its discussion, and expressed itself, and, so far, the country behind it, in an act of public will. And it would then go to the moors, leaving behind it an academic resolution. But for public life and the public future that would be perfectly futile. The act of the House's will must by the same will go upon the House's records. It must be printed and circulated in due form. It must be accessible to the nation when the House has risen, and when that parliament has dissolved. It is not enough that an account of it should appear in the papers according to the skill of the stenographer, or the view of some publicist who studied the debates. It must be printed by order of the House. And it must carry the royal seal of finality upon it. That is to say, the form of the act is there by the same will of the Government as carried the principle of the act. The act as printed and published is an integral though formal part of the material act of will which passed it. Now, with all recognition of the difference between the strict verbiage of an act and the fluidity of much in scripture both as to word and fact, that illustration represents the relation of the New Testament to God's fact and act of Christ. The form is part of the whole act. And the illustration would be still more detailed if we included in the Act of Parliament a provision that it go to the public accompanied by certain schedules of explanation drawn up by order of the Crown. The point is that not only does the evolutionary series exist and work to a positive end, but that that material end has within itself a formal close, expres-

sion, and interpretation; which is an integral part of
it, essential to its effect, and not simply a first amateur
and tentative stage in its interpretation by the casual
press and public. The formal expression shares, in its
way, in the authority of the material act, and has behind
it the royal power. This is the authority in the Bible.
It is a factor in the finality of Christ. It is a schedule to
the act, and not a mere leader on it. We can no more
believe in the infallibility of the Bible, but we must believe
in its finality. That is the region of its inspiration. It is
a region of religion and faith. For in theology there is no
finality. What science requires is evolution, and theology
is science. But the one need of religion to-day is
finality. And for Christianity that can only be had by
an Incarnate Christ as preached in an inspired Bible.

The point, then, of this lecture is this: When the
Apostles spoke as they did upon such central matters as
the eternal sonship and due worship of Jesus Christ they
did not speak from themselves; they recorded no mere
impression, and ventured no guess to explain the
impression left by Christ; but they spoke as men in
whose experience there spoke still more the Christ who
lived in them. And, though on matters lying further
from the centre, on matters of anthropology rather than
theology (like the connection between sin and physical
death), they were less authoritative, yet when they spoke
of Christ's person or his work, they were the organs of
Christ himself, and their truth has a value for all subsequent times which partakes of the authority of that
revelation whom they interpreted.

LECTURE VI

THE TESTIMONY OF APOSTOLIC
INSPIRATION—IN PARTICULAR

LECTURE VI

THE TESTIMONY OF APOSTOLIC INSPIRATION—
IN PARTICULAR

IN positive revelation we have to do with two things.
The one fact has two constituents. We have, first, the
history or the manifestation, and we have, second, the
inspiration or the interpretation of the history. We
have, first, God entering the world, and we have,
second, this entry of God entering man. We have the
fact, and we have the word of the fact. The fact we have
in Christ; but the word of it, the meaning of it, we have
in believers and apostles moved by Christ. And especially in the apostles, whose insight becomes itself a fact,
in turn, working upon believers from faith to faith. So
that we have three things—first the incarnate fact, then,
the word or interpretation of it by apostles, and, thereby,
the fact again, but the fact enshrined in the soul of the
believing Church. To use philosophical terms, we
have the thesis, planting itself out in an antithesis, and,
then reclaiming, recovering itself in a synthesis. We
have first, the fact incarnate, then the fact interpreted,
and then the fact enthroned. But we must have the word
as well as the fact, if the fact is to do anything with men.
The word is an essential part of the fact, or, let us say, an

159

essential function of it.   It is the fact reacting on itself.
It is the vast eternal action of Christ reverberating in the
consciousness of his apostles.   It went out as power and
returns as light, doubling back luminously upon itself,
as it were, to search its old track by this inspiration.
Only in such a sense is the incarnation prolonged in the
Church.   The total revelation needs the inspiration as
well as the manifestation, the thought no less than the
thing,   "The fact without the word is dumb; and the
word without the fact is empty."

Now it is only with the interpretation of the fact that
inspiration has to do, and not with the fact itself; for we
do not speak of Christ the fact as an inspired man.   Nor
has it directly to do with the establishment of the fact as
a fact.   Inspiration has not to do with information but
with insight.   It has to do entirely with the theology of
the matter, and not with its historicity.   What a pagan
or mantic notion of inspiration they must have who use it
to discredit theology, who in the name of truth discredit interpretation by afflatus.   The facts in the
Bible were established by the usual means, as in
Luke's case (Luke i. 1).   But the meaning of the fact
—that is the field of inspiration.   The fact of the
cross, for instance, is established by the ordinary
historic evidence; but it was no ordinary means that
enabled Paul to see its interior—the atonement, the
centrality, and the finality of it for Christ's work.
The idea of propitiation, for instance, was in Judaism and its ritual.   That is something of which we
have the due historic evidence.   The inspiration of the
apostle was not in discovering the idea; it was in seeing
its real truth and consummation to be in the fact and act
of Christ.   The idea had at last become historically and

finally effective in Christ. The fact of the cross was seen
to mean that consummation. Yet the insight was the
result of that fact's own peculiar nature, working on
Paul's peculiar nature, through the Lord the Spirit. So
that the New Testament writings are really a part of that
fact ; just as the Old Testament is an essential part of
Israel's history, and not merely a description, nor only a
product of it. The apostles read God's will in the fact
of Christ; but it was from a height of faith to which
that fact had raised them. (Christ by his work made
them saints, and by the inspiration of his Spirit he
made them theologians.) The inspiration of the
Redeemer gave them that understanding. They saw
the deep things in Christ under the moral coercion
of the fact and its nature, under its creative and
illuminative action on them. It reorganised their whole
conceptual world by giving it a new vital centre, and
therefore a new reading. They saw a new world because
a new king was on its throne. And it was a vital and
creative centre. There was new vision, not simply a
new point of view, because the eyes that saw it were the
eyes of new men.

§   §   §

But why isolate the apostles and give them a unique
authority ? The apostles were not the only contemporaries of Christ nor his only followers. Yet the rest did
not see what they saw. The whole public, the whole
Church even, did not rise to Paul's height or John's.
How shall we know that the insight and judgment of the
apostles was worth more, was more true to the fact,
than that of other contemporaries of Jesus who were not
so impressed ? Why should they be right, and Judas,
Caiaphas, or Pilate wrong—as well as many better men,

like Hillel, who did not respond as the disciples did to Christ? How do we know that the apostle's view of him is the divine truth of him? How do we know that Paul's Christianity is truer than that of the Judaistic Christians who opposed him as earnestly and sincerely as the rationalists do now?

Well, in the first place they were all contemporary but they were not all intimate with Jesus. All had acquaintance but all had not knowledge. All had met Christ but all had not companied with him. Nor were they selected and taught by him in view of the future.

But even of those who companied with Jesus all did not see in Him or His cross what John, Paul, and Peter declare that they at last came to see. And Paul and the author of Hebrews did not company with Jesus; yet they go deeper than any of those that did—for John owed himself in this respect to Paul. How was it? Were the men who saw deepest more holy personally than the rest? Was it because they did the will better that they knew of the doctrine? Will that overworked principle explain inspiration? Why should we prefer the interpretation of Paul to that of the early chapters of Acts? Why prefer even the late Peter of the Epistle to the early Peter of the Acts?

Let us see what they believed and claimed as to themselves. They did claim special, exceptional knowledge, quite different from that of natural acumen or religious genius. Of this claim 1 Cor. ii. 14 is but a sample. The natural man, however brilliant or shrewd, receiveth not the things of the Spirit of God, for they are spiritually discerned. "He that is spiritual" (which for Paul did not mean he that has spirituality, but he that has the miraculous and specific gift of the Spirit, the new life of the New Creation, which makes a man a Christian) "judgeth all things and is beyond man's judgment." Or again, v. 16, "We have the mind of Christ." The context shows that this has nothing to do with the temper of Christ, or what is now known as the Christian spirit. And the "we" is admitted to mean the Apostles, as distinct from the initiates they were teaching. The meaning is that, by the supernatural gift of the Spirit, possessed only in the Church, Paul had knowledge of the intention of Christ, Christ's implicit thought, God's meaning in Christ, the theology of Christ and the cross. That is what Paul meant (whether he was right in thus thinking he had Christ's theology or not). So it was not only that the Apostles were in closer historic proximity to Jesus than other men, though that makes them historically unique. Nor was it only that they had the common faith which marked them off from the world by a new creation, as members of the Church. Nor was it only that this faith acted on a natural endowment which tended to religious exaltation, not only that some of them were religious geniuses, flushed with a new enthusiasm, and kindled to unusual insight. But, by their own account, they were uniquely instructed by the Spirit, and not merely renewed. They had what they called "the gift of knowledge" as a charisma of the Spirit. Truly it was in no ecstatic way, in no trance or such like thing. The spirit did not act merely by exalting their whole nature to a pitch of unique sensibility. Sensibility does not always mean insight. But indeed it is no more possible to describe the inner psychology of inspiration in the apostles than in the prophets. Many Christians had both the Christian facts and the Christian faith who never rose to inspiration. They had only personal religion in the Spirit. But with the Apostles it was a special gift of the Spirit, not enlarging the revelation in matter but certainly opening its interior and pointing its form. It was the action upon them of the ascended and reigning Christ—his instruction. Especially so when the call came to write, when the trying hour and the anointed spirit met. Paul was more inspired in this Corinthian chapter than in the third heaven; so close is inspiration to history. Besides the living faith and the special chrism their natural possibilities were roused also by the actual junctures in which they found themselves. The occasion of writing was some providential juncture in the affairs of the Church; and they managed and directed that juncture as men writing of final truths in which they habitually lived, truths given them to see by the indwelling Lord. They claimed to possess absolute certainty about the greatest things of God and the Soul, and the central action of Christ and His cross. They shared the self-certainty of Christ. They do not write as if any interpretation of Christ besides their own was thinkable. And they make a distinction, which was mostly clear to themselves, between what they gave as the mind or intention of Christ and what they did not so give. For some of their words they claimed a like authority with that of Christ. They claimed the obedience that the Church would give to Christ (2 Cor. ii. 9; vii. 15, Acts xv. 28). The whole of 1 Cor. ii. is of classic value for the Apostle's view of his own inspiration; and it certainly does not allow us to think that he regarded himself as groping after great truths, making great guesses, or feeling about at an inchoate stage in the understanding of Christ and his work.

§   §   §

Now was this sense of unique insight and final interpretation a delusion ? Was it inflation or inspiration ?
Was it ideal obsession or divine visitation ? Were the
apostles megalomaniacs ? And yet founded the Church ?

1. We may note here that their belief in their own
position and knowledge was accepted by the Church
then, and has been corrobated by the Church ever since.
It came home with the demonstration of the Spirit and
of power (Rom. i. 16, 1 Cor. ii. 4, 1 Th. i. 5, Ep. vi. 17).
And it is what has survived.

2. It had been provided for by Christ, who said that
in the great crises not they should speak but the Spirit
of God should speak in them.   (Mat. x. 20, xvi. 19.)

3. It was the same note of authority and finality as
sounds through all the prophets, who, over and over,
speak their words not only in God's name but in the first
person, as if, for the hour at least, not they lived but
God lived in them.

4. The apostles claimed for their words, especially on
Eternal Truth, a like permanent authority with Christ's.
They even ignore his precepts, which they seldom or
never quote to their Churches; they make their own,
and they expect for them the obedience due to Christ.
In their preaching, moreover, they drop his parable style
for one of their own.   And the homiletic of the Church
followed them in this, and did not copy either the
synoptic or the Johannine style of address, and certainly
not Christ's conversational dialectic.   In 1 Thess. iv. 15
we have, " I say unto you by the word of the Lord," as
we have it also in 1 Kings xiii. 17.   In Gal. vi. 2 we find
" Bear ye one another's burdens, and so fulfil the law of
Christ."   But there is no such precept from Christ

N

that we know of. The law is fashioned by the apostle out of the Gospel of Christ. Yet how easy it would have been to refer to some such precept of Christ as the new commandment to love one another and to minister to the brethren as he did. So, 1 Cor. vii. 10, " I give charge, yet not I, but the Lord." On this ground the apostles claimed, for their precept if not their person, the obedience really due to one whom the Church worshipped. (2 Cor. ii. 7, 9, 15, 2 Th. ii. 15, Acts xv. 28.) They were not indeed reincarnations of the Incarnate, but they were his organs. The source of their certainty was one quite different from reason and its proof (1 Cor. ii. 4, and especially verse 12 ; what they knew was " things given by God ").

The process of this certainty and authority, the psychology of it they could not explain even to themselves (1 Peter i. 10). It was not irrational, but it was alogical. Their central truth was a supernatural gift ; it was not an achievement or a discovery of theirs.

5. What they saw and said in this way was not for them the revelation but the interpretation of the revelation. It was not given them by a second revelation ; it was given by insight into the one and only revelation ; by the finished revelation filling itself out in them ; by the inspiration that distended the material fact, and thus formally completed the revelation. They saw and they said what Christ was, not what an imaginative intelligence surmised. They translated Christ, the text, who without the translation would have been a dead letter so far as history is concerned. They treated their text exegetically, not fantastically, not ingeniously. What they gave was the meaning of Christ ; and they gave it in a way that the earthly

Christ himself could not—in the light of his finished
work. The finishing of that work by the cross was
not always perfectly certain in Christ's earthly thought;
even in Gethsemane, I have said, he cherished the hope
that there might still open from the Father's will some
other way. But for Paul the cross had come and gone
—or rather had come to remain as the pivot and key of
all. The apostles' inspiration was the interpretation of
the cross as being the revelation of all the revelation in
Christ. We have in it not only the impression on
them from the historic Christ but the tremendous action
on them of Christ the glorified, of Christ in the heavenly
close and consummation of all that he was (and of all
that history was), in his cross, resurrection, and glory.
Their inspiration formed the *coda* of the crowning
movement in the total work of Christ. What they
spoke was the secret in the cross, the wisdom that
God had hidden away from thought in the mystery, or
sacrament, of the cross (1 Cor. ii. 7). They expounded
the sacrament of Godhead, God manifest in the flesh.
Their inspiration was to set forth in word and thought
the principle and power of that supreme sacrament of
the Word, namely Christ; it was to exhibit formally
the truth materially embodied in the manifestation.
Their work on it was analytic and not synthetic. Their
metier was the *knowledge* of things already *given*, 1 Cor.
ii. 12. It was to set forth the inwardness of the historic
fact and spectacle. It was the searching of the deep
things of God, the exhibition of what was hidden
(hidden, possibly, even from the earthly consciousness
of Christ himself), interpreting such spiritual things to
spiritual men (1 Cor. ii. 13).

And this they do not only through the psychological

effect of the manifestation upon their souls, but much more, through the selective, the miraculous action in them of the same Christ who was the manifestation, and is now in them his own interpreter. They did not simply echo the cross; they were anointed by Christ to decipher it. The apostolic inspiration is the posthumous exposition by Christ of His own work; and it takes as much precedence of his earthly and (partly) interim teaching as the finished work is more luminous than the work in process. If Paul felt at his vital moments that not he lived but Christ lived in him, then, surely in the great matters of insight and seasons of speech, it was not he that spoke but Christ that spoke in him. And if, as Peter says (1 Peter i. 10), the prophets had to study and clarify for themselves, by their inspiration, things that were given them to do or speak more greatly than they knew, so we may venture to say, perhaps (*mutatis mutandis*), that the spiritual Christ himself, looking back from his glory on the work of his humiliation, and still ministering it to history, opened up his manifestation then by his inspiration in the apostles, in whom he dwelt and prolonged his work through its actual to its vocal close.

§   §   §

So let us aim at some clearness when we say that Christianity is Christ. The essence of Christianity is not in the bare fact, but in the fact and its interpretation. It is not in a mere historic Jesus, evidentially irresistible, but in a Christ evangelically irresistible, a Christ who is the mediator of the grace of God. Is this not so in regard to the Old Testament? Where is our perennial interest there? Not in the chronicle but in the message, the purpose in it. The Old Testament is valuable neither as a history of Israel, nor as a history of religion, but as a history of revelation, of grace, of redemption. And the new scholarship has done us an unspeakable service in planting us at the outset at the part of the Old Testament which contains that interpretation, in planting us on the prophets. It has moved our starting point from the historic books to the prophetic, from the narrators to the preachers of the Old Testament, from the history to the inspiration. It has made the inspiration of the Apostles of the Old Testament the standpoint from which all the story is to be read and construed. They do not so much give us Israel as what God meant by Israel. And it is only carrying the same method into the New Testament when we fix on the Epistles with their dogmatic element, and make that the view-point from which the fact is to be read and the gospels themselves interpreted. It is in these interpreting books that the inspiration lies rather than in the narrative. There is more inspiration in the Epistles than in the Gospels, as Luther truly said. That is to say, in the total revelation the inspirational element predominates in the Epistles and the exhibitionary element in the gospels. It is in the Epistles that we have the essence of Christianity, what the fact means for God, and grace, and man. It is there the heart of the fact ceases to be dumb. And it is there that we have the fixed point from which to exercise the critical method upon the Gospels with truly religious historic and scientific effect. It is the whole Biblical Christ that is the truly and deeply historic Christ.

§   §   §

What we have, therefore, is results like these.

1. God *does* in Christ the one thing needful for the holy redemption of the race into the kingdom. This thing

done is the power and action of God unto salvation. It is not merely a source of power to us if we use it, but it is the act of God finished for us in Heavenly places. In Christ God redeemed once for all.

2. To make this effective in history it must be declared. What is the work for us without its word? It must be interpreted, unfolded, in thought and speech, else men would not know they were saved. The work alone would be dumb as the word alone would be empty.

There are some who recognise in Christ's death no action beyond what it had, and has increasingly, upon mankind. It did not act on God but only from Him. Those who so think may be particularly asked what provision Christ made that a work with that sole object should be secured to act on history, and should not go to waste. He wrote nothing himself. If he had it could not well have included the effect of his death—unless he had done with a posthumous pen what my plea is he did by his Apostles. He did not even give instructions for a written account which should be a constant source for the effect on us intended by his life. Nor did he take any precautions against perversions in its tradition. Yet it is hard to think that a mind capable of so great a design on posterity should neglect to secure that his deed and its significance should reach them in some authentic way. He surely could not put himself into so great an enterprise, and then leave it adrift on history, liable to the accidents of time or the idiosyncracy of his followers. He could not be indifferent whether an effective record and interpretation of his work should survive or not. He would then have shown himself unable to rear the deed he brought forth. It would have been stillborn unless the close of it in some way secured its action on the posterity which

we are told was its sole destination, on those whom alone
it was to affect or benefit.   But that completion of his
work he did secure if he inspired its transmission and
interpretation in the Bible.   If he died to make a Church
that Church should continue to be made by some permanent thing from himself, either by a continuous
Apostolate supernaturally secured in the *charisma veritatis*,
as Rome claims, or by a book which should be the real
successor of the Apostles, with a real authority on the
vital matters of truth and faith.   But, we discard the
supernatural pope for the supernatural book.   And so we
come back, enriched by all we have learned from repudi-
ating a verbal inspiration and accepting an inspiration of
men and souls, to a better way of understanding the
authority that there is in the inspiration of a book, a canon.
We move from an institutional authority to a biblical ; and
then from Biblicism we advance to Evangelism.   But it
is an Evangelism bound up with a book because bound
up with history.   The Bible is a historic book in a sense
far other than the Koran.   There is more in the matter
than personal inspiration, just as there is more in the
corporate Church than a group of sacred souls.   Were
personal inspiration all, the end might have been reached
by one great hierophant.   But we have a group of them,
with a central message in common, however complemen-
tary its various aspects are, however contradictory even
some of its minor aspects might be.   And this because,
for all the pronounced personality of each Apostle, he
was yet the representative of a whole Church, an Eternal
Saviour, and a universal salvation.   The interpretation of
the manifold work of Christ should be a corporate matter.
The salvation of the whole Church could not be duly
interpreted by one man in it ; one man could not even

make a liturgy for a Church; any such man would be too nearly its Saviour or its Intercessor. Therefore in apostles, chosen at his will, the sole Saviour became the sole interpreter, so far as the elements were concerned which made him Saviour. He was the real author of the New Testament (if the image might be pardoned), with the Apostles, as it were, but his staff, though with a very free hand. He rounded off his great work by inspiring an authoritative account of it, in records which are not mere documents, but are themselves acts within his integral and historic act of salvation. They are spiritual sources and not historic memoranda—sacraments even more than sources. And they have an authority of their own greater than is due to mere proximity—however we may be guided by the critics, as subalterns of the same spirit, in adjusting the fabric or cleansing its face.

There are two classes of historical document. There are those that simply report a transaction as a narrative of it might do, either in a book or a newspaper. And there are documents which are documents in the case, which, like treaties, focus the action, form an integral part of the deed itself, and carry not only the consent which made the act, but the signature which sends it forth, and perhaps codicils of authoritative explanation. The New Testament writings (taken of course out of the ban of verbal inspiration, or of an equal inspiration in every part), belong to the second class. They are part of the whole transaction, integral to the great deed. And we do not get the whole Christ or his work without them.

The same Christ, the same Spirit * as acted in the

---

* "Christ, who by the Eternal Spirit, offered Himself unto God." I cannot here enter on the difficult question raised by the phrase " The Lord is the Spirit."

redeeming deed acted also in the interpretation ; and
with a like novelty, a like originality, a like miraculous,
creative, and final power—with a like absolute originality, but in a different form.   The New Testament, we
have seen, is an integral part of a binary revelation,
which consists of the manifestation and the inspiration or
interpretation which the manifestation itself creates, and
creates both from its historic base and from its home
in the unseen.   The difference of this inspiration from
every other lies in the unique nature of the personal
fact, in the generic difference from every other deed
of the deed whose spirit was in both—both in the fact
and in the interpretation—the deed of the Cross.

§   §   §

3. I have said that the New Testament writings have
the originality belonging to the fact and work of Christ,
though in a form different from what it had in his
personality.   I go on to say that it is in a form different
also from our apprehension of the fact through them.   As
we have God by the miracle of Christ, so we have Christ
by the miracle of the apostolic inspiration.   (Mat. xi. 27,
xvi. 17).   If the manifested deed is miraculous, so is the
inspired.   The apostles' understanding of the cross is
miraculous, like the cross itself.   It is there by the direct
and specific action of the same Spirit as that by which
Christ offered himself to God, though the action took
another form.   So also the form of our illumination
through the apostles is different from theirs by the very
fact that they had no apostles to mediate the truth to
them.   As Christ was the direct mediator of the work
itself, having himself no Saviour, so the apostles are the
direct mediators of the central truth about it, having
therein no human revealers.   They were untaught by the

words of any man's wisdom in the great leap of finding
in Christ the reality of whatever ideas they had learned
from the age around them.

§   §   §

4. The production, then, of this original and unique
understanding of Christ in the apostles is inspiration. Of
its psychology, as I have said, we know little or nothing.
The men may have known little. At least they have
left us little. It was quite different from the trances of
which Paul had experience, but which he does not treat
as sources of inspiration. When he was beside himself
the matter was between him and God alone ; it was in his
personal religion. But when it was a matter of inspiration and of interpreting Christ to history, to men, he was
sober for their sakes. (2 Cor. v. 13.) His inspiration
was more than the originality of genius. In Galatians,
you may remember, by a wonderful flash he inverted the
values of Old Testament history, and put prophetic
gospel before statutory law even in historic order.
(Gal. iii. and esp. ver. 17). It was an intuition that
arose from no scholarship, but from his powerful grasp
of the principle of the Gospel which Christ had revealed
to him as so revolutionary for the world. It was his
theology that enabled him to divine what criticism has
only verified. It was a divination greater than that
of the line of scholarly genius which has recently set
his inversion upon a scientific base, and critically shown
the prophets to precede at least the most legal part of
the law. The apostolic inspiration was also more than
the originality of a great poet like Milton, who presents
life, but not God, under aspects so fresh, new, and deep.
It answers the question, What is He going to do with us ?
It is concerned with God's whole and final purpose

for man and history, and with the inversion of man's
thought and action about it by the cross. Through
Christ, then, this redemption took place; through the
apostles' interpretation it entered history. *He* did the
thing, *they* saw its meaning and proclaimed it; and they
knew they were doing so in a final way, though not in a
final system. If Christ had not done the thing, but only
proclaimed God's doing of it, the apostles would have
been but his pupils and successors in the work, instead of
his subjects and organs. But *He* revolutionised man's
relation to God, and thus revolutionised human nature;
they made the change current and set it afloat in history.
But as the act of Christ was one which no genius
could do, so the apostles, as integral agents of that
act by way of its interpretation, were in a different
category from religious genius; however their native
religious sensibility may have been the point of attachment for the Spirit's use of them.

§   §   §

5. It may be asked whether the synoptic Christ, when
read without the medium of the epistles, could have
floated Christianity out into the world. The first answer
to that is that the three gospels were written for people
living in the theological atmosphere of the epistles. The
second answer is No, by themselves they could not have
launched the faith, so far as we can see. If we ask
farther, could the Synoptics keep Christianity a world
power now, with the certain reversion of the world's
mastery soon or late? Again, No. It was the interpretation in John or in Paul that made Christianity historical
for men—though it was Christ's act that made it vital
for God and God's treatment of men. The one gathered
and impelled the race which the other had redeemed by

a new creation. The act made the soul, the gospel of it made the Church. Or again, if it is asked whether, with Loisy at one end or Dale at the other, we could dissolve the Gospels and leave their Christianity, the answer must be a very clear, No. You cannot sever the life from the word and keep the Church as a vitality detached from the message of the cross.

§   §   §

Apostolic inspiration, therefore, is a certain action stirred by the heavenly Christ in the soul, by which his first elect were enabled to see the moral, spiritual, and theological nature of the manifestation with a unique clearness, a clearness and explicitness perhaps not always present to Christ's own mind in doing the act. Inspiration is thus much more than the impression made by Christ's character or personality. It was a special charisma, the charisma distinguished from others by Paul himself as that of wisdom and knowledge, 1 Cor. xii. 8 ; where it is put first, as if it were the apostolic prerogative.

§   §   §

Of course, any modern theory of inspiration distinguishes between miraculous insight and miraculous dictation, between finality and infallibility of interpretation. The notion of the writers as being mere penmen is quite incompatible with the great description of inspiration in 1 Peter i. 10, which at least indicates the psychological and even critical atmosphere in which the supernatural gift worked. We must connect inspiration with the personal and moral experience of the inspired (little as that fact entitles us to bemean the great word inspiration as we do to-day in using it of the personal experience of faith's rank and file, and even of happy suggestions in common affairs). It was not hierophantic. It was not the communication of occult truths quite unapprehended. It was not psychological magic. True, it is of the nature of genius, which is always inexplicable—only it is more so. But genius is an innate predisposition, while this is a positive gift at a later stage, and on the top even of genius. Genius is an election, this is more, it is a special call. Genius is impelled from within, this is moved from without. Genius has its inspiration in the nature of the man's personality, this has its inspiration from the positive nature and action of a manifestation which visits it. Genius works itself out, this works out the fact and the person with whom it is in such causal and organic connexion. It is true that for Paul the Gospel of Christ did not mean the personal religion of Jesus; it was a faith of which Jesus was the object, and not the subject. And yet he was its subject, in that it came from him—not, however, from his earthly teaching, but from his heavenly glory in his task for ever done. For Paul the Gospel of Christ was not only a Gospel which treated of Christ, but one which proceeded from Christ. It did not come from the teaching and partial Christ (whose teachings, if they were to be more relevant than a dreamer's to an incomplete historic situation, must have been also incomplete), but from the whole Christ in his complete person and act. To divide up the personality, and detach the heavenly Christ from the earthly Jesus is not a feat of criticism so much as a failure of religion, or an intellectual freak and a confession of unfaith.

Apostolic authority, therefore, is not official but personal, not statutory but experimental, not external but internal, in the sense that it is a thing of the soul and not of a mere society or its heads. The apostles are authoritative, not because they were in the Gospel group, not because they formed a college to which Christ had given a charter. For I have said that not all the group of disciples became apostles; and the greatest apostle was not in the group. But the apostolic authority is that of those who by a spiritual election had a gift of supernatural insight—and insight is always more or less miraculous, whether naturally in a genius or supernaturally in an apostle. Why should we resent it ? We do not resent the authority of the real illuminates elsewhere. For in its nature it is inward and congenial to the soul, however outward it may be in spatial position or historic sequence, or in its spiritual invasion of our consciousness.

§   §   §

As to the authority of the Bible, especially on a matter like the Godhead of Christ, we may note this. The mere historical aspect of the Bible is a matter of learned inquiry. Its evidence for a mere historical fact must stand at what it is historically worth. The difficulty only begins with facts which are more than merely historical, whose value lies not in their occurrence, but in their nature, meaning, and effect. It is not the crucifixion that matters but the cross. So it is not reanimation but resurrection. And here the authority of the Bible speaks not to the critical faculty that handles evidence but to the soul that makes response. The Bible witness of salvation in Christ is felt immediately to have authority by every soul pining for redemption. It is not so much food for the rationally healthy, but it is medicine for the sick, and life for the dead. All the highest interpretation of the Bible comes from that principle of grace. Even historical criticism, which is a real part of theology, should be pursued on that basis. It should be a work of the Church much more than of the schools. And from the Church must come the final correction and appraisement of the criticism of the schools. It is only knowledge with a soul of faith that grasps the full scope of revelationary history. For it is the history of a revelation we have to do with in Christianity, it is not a revelation of history. Mere history does not need to be revealed; it can look after itself by its own scientific methods.

The authority in the Bible is more than the authority of the Bible; and it is the historic and present Christ as Saviour. The Gospel and not the book is the true region of inspiration or infallibility—the discovery of the one Gospel in Christ and His cross. That is the sphere of inspiration. That is where inspiration is infallible. Inspired men have been wrong on points and in modes of argument—just as, even with Christ living in them, they sinned in life. They have not always been right by the event. But they were right in the interpretation of the Gospel in Christ as the final work of a holy God for the race. They were not infallible, but they were penetrating and they were final, final as to the nature of the Gospel, of Christ, and of the Church. The true region of Bible authority is therefore saving certainty in man's central and final part—his conscience before God. And all its parts are authoritative in the degree and perspective of their relation to that final salvation. What distinguishes the Bible from other books is not appreciable by those that seek no revelation, no spiritual footing, no other world amid this, and no security in the other world. It is only intelligible in its core to those who are being saved in some positive way.

It is to what the Reformers called justifying faith that the Bible appears most unique and authoritative—to faith in a justifying God. And it has been said that the canon is authoritative so far as this, at least, that we have no writings outside it that could eject one of those within.

It is by the Bible that Christ chiefly works on history. All the Church's preaching and work is based on it, on what we only know through it. As no man could succeed the apostles in their unique position and work, but their book became their true successor, so no book can replace this. The apostles are gone but the book remains, to prolong their supernatural vision, and exercise their authority in the Church. In so far as the Church prolongs the manifestation and is Christ's body, the Bible prolongs the inspiration and is Christ's word. The writers were and are the only authentic interpreters of Christ. They said so, under the immediate shadow of Christ's action on them, whether his historic or his heavenly action. They never contemplate being superseded on the great witness till Christ came. If they are wrong in that, where are they right? And where are we to turn? To a critical construction of what they said— they including the evangelists? But does that not make the critics, the constructors, to be the true Apostolate? And if it come to construction (as I have already said) I prefer the Apostolic to the critical, if we must be forced on a choice. If the Bible is not inspired but only documentary we are at the critic's mercy. For what does it give us apart from its inspiration? Nothing of Christ's, but only of the Apostles. In so far as it is a record it is not so much a record or document of Christ but of the apostolic view and message of Christ in his salvation. But it is really a document for apostolic inspiration, for the apostolic reading of history, rather than for history as such. It documents not so much the history of the revelation as the revelation in the history, a certain construction of the purpose and meaning of the divine coming and the divine action. If this apostolic view of things be without inspiration, then about Christ and his meaning we must simply guess according to our needs and sympathies. But if it be authoritative anywhere it is on the place, person, and work of Christ, and not merely on the facts, sequences, or pragmatisms of his biography. In its substance it is a part of the revelation; its penumbra; and it is as authoritative *in its way* as the manifestation whose vibration it is. It is of eternal moment to the soul whether it take or leave the Christ that this book as a whole preaches to the world. For it does not give us the data for a Christ but Christ's own interpretation of himself.

§   §   §

From all this what follows? It follows that the view of Christ's place and person which pervades the New Testament is authoritative for us. The Christ it preaches is the Christ God sent. The depth, directness, sureness, and uniqueness of the inspiration guarantee the reality and deity of the manifestation. If God produces a special understanding of the fact he must have produced the fact. If apostles so moved saw in the resurrection of Christ such significance, then the fact itself is not at the mercy of mere historical evidence. The act of faith when it rises to inspiration gives us the reality of its object in giving us its power. If God made men so to read and trust the resurrection power, He could not be misleading them as to the creative fact it streamed from. The same spirit

o

effected both. If inspired knowledge grow out of a certain fact that fact is a part of God's revelation. We cannot take the resurrection gospel and leave the resurrection fact. So also with the cross; and so with the person of Christ. If the apostles were right in believing that their interpretation of the central things, the creative things—details and peripherals do not concern us—were given them from the Lord :—if it was Christ who taught them to believe in himself as the Eternal Son, then the fact was so. He was the Eternal Son. If they were right about the source of their knowledge they were right about the object of it; these were one and the same. It is a great "if," I admit. If they were wrong about their authority and their centre, the outlying pieties of such fanatics have little moral worth, however beautiful. If they were wrong there they were of little value anywhere else, except among the pieties and beauties of faith, which, however, do not need apostles to their warrant, but appeal directly enough to our spiritual æsthetic. Only they do not lift us above an æsthetic religion. Divine love, were it certain, is easily believed to be all that it sounds in the love-song of the Christian Church, in 1 Cor. xiii. The question is, is it certain? Was and is Jesus Christ that love for good and all? And is there anything that can separate us from that love of Christ's? Could angels or powers or things to come from new heights or depths? Could a later revelation come, and a more complete, to detach us from it, and to release us from its obsession for some revelation still more divine and more nearly final?

§   §   §

A certain nobleman possessed a house in a fine park; and he owned also a great picture of his late countess, painted by a classic artist in the days when her beauty was the talk of the town.   He was so proud of it that he had it placed on an easel near a large oriel window on the ground floor, so that not only his guests within but the public who were allowed to stroll round the house in the absence of the family might see it.   Now a certain stranger was staying at the hotel in the village by the park gate while the family was at home and the domain was closed; who spent much of his time in rambling about the neighbourhood, and sketching many of its fine points.   Of course he turned his glass often upon the mansion with a curious eye; and one day he fixed it upon the window with the picture.   He was much arrested and impressed with the lady he saw there, and could not banish her from his mind.   Day after day he stalked the window with his lens; and, though the time of the day and the falling of the lights did not always enable him to see her, yet he did see her so often that, being a highly romantic young artist, he fell deeply in love with her, and neglected his sketching to haunt the most commanding point at the hour when he mostly saw her sit and meditate there.   At last the family went to town and he had access to the grounds—only to discover that he had been fooling himself; that his love was silly, and it could never be answered even were all the obstacles he had thought of removed.   For she was a work of genius but she had no life.   Her beauty was great but she had no heart.   She could neither love, nor scorn, nor help, nor speak.

If the supernatural figure of Christ that we see set out in the New Testament is not real it is but a picture at the great window to fool poor men.   With all its beauty and spell it is no more to keen and hungry souls than the magic canvas to the dreaming youth.   A far plainer reality would better have met his heart.   A real prophet would mean far more to us than any Christ if the Christ were but an apostolic phantasy.   The apostolic family might surround their picture with all pious care, admiration, and observance.   They might set it full in the window, rhapsodise about its beauty, and about the way they felt it. But it is not the mistress of the house.   And it cannot do or be for any the thing they need most of all.   It can mock them by its very unearthly beauty but it cannot love their love back.   It is a world's wonder of a picture, but it is only painted on the window; and it cannot open the door of its own house to any either to come or to go.

LECTURE VII

THE TESTIMONY OF EXPERIENCE IN THE SOUL AND IN THE CHURCH

LECTURE VII

THE TESTIMONY OF EXPERIENCE IN THE SOUL
AND IN THE CHURCH

I

Our present Protestantism is historically composed
from the union of two streams, which take their rise in
two different sources. They still flow alongside with a
fusion so far very incomplete; and they react on each
other with an amount of irritation somewhat inexplicable
till we perceive that the streams *are* two, distinct in their
origin and direction. They are the Reformation and
the Illumination: the Reformation from the sixteenth
century, and the diversified movement which marked the
eighteenth century, and which is compendiously known
as the Illumination or the Aufklärung.* They are the
old Protestantism and the new—the one resting on the
objectivity of a given revelation, the other on the subjectivity of human nature or thought; the one finding
its standard in a divine intervention, the other in im-

---

* For a full account of the situation we should really have to recognise
three streams. We should have to distinguish within Protestantism the
old objective tendency, resting on history as the authoritative source
(in the Bible), and the newer subjective tendency, resting on Christian
experience, originating in Anabaptism, revised in Pietism, and rewritten
in Schleiermacher. The one represents classic Protestantism, the other
romantic. But for the present purpose it will be better to confine our
attention mainly to the two currents named in the text. Of course, the
subjectivity of human nature, which I mention immediately, becomes in
Pietism the subjectivity of Christianised human nature.

manent human reason more or less generously construed ; the one emphasising a divine redemption, the
other human goodness and its substantial sufficiency.
The face of the one movement is towards the Church
and the Bible, the face of the other is towards civilisation and culture. The one falls back upon historic
humanity, upon the history and the revelation there ;
the other on intrinsic humanity and the revelation there.
It is a distinction much more penetrating than the
somewhat vulgar antithesis of Orthodoxy and Heterodoxy. It is not so much two theologies as two methods
—if not two religions. And neither is pure. The one,
the Reformation stream, carries down with it much of
the débris of mediæval doctrine ; because at its source,
in the monk Luther, it was mainly a religious and
ethical change rather than a theological. The other, the
Illumination, carries with it much of the pagan débris
of the older Renaissance and of classic antiquity ; since
its element was not so much religion as thought, and its
achievement is not faith but culture, and especially
science. It was really directed at first not against
religion, but against what it thought a false basis of
religion. It sought to replace imagination by induction as the foundation of our conception of the world.
It asserted the intrinsic divinity of nature, and it would
make the spiritual life but the highest of natural
phenomena. While, therefore, the direct legacy of the
Reformation laid fundamental stress upon the sense of
guilt, and the action of grace, the legacy of the Illumination laid stress on native goodness, the sense of rational
sympathy, and the sufficiency of human love spiritualised.
For the one, man was the lost thing in the universe, and
the greatness of his ruin was the index of the dignity of

his nature; for the other, man was the one saving thing in the universe; and the greatness of his success in subduing the world to his thought and will was the badge of his heroic divinity, soiled, perhaps, but indelible. The one lived by redemption and regeneration, the other by evolution and education. For the one forgiveness was essential, and it was identical with the new eternal life; it put life on a quite new track, it was a redemption, a revolution. For the other forgiveness was incidental, and simply removed obstacles or redressed lapses in man's developing career; it put the train on the old track, after some derailment by accident, or some loopline by error. It was a restoration. The one cultivated theology and sanctity, the other science and sentiment, criticism and romance. The one saw the new Jerusalem descending out of heaven from God, the other saw it rise "like an exhalation" from earth. The heaven of the one was in the blue sky, for the other it was in the growing grass. For the one the great matter was God's transcendence over the world, for the other it was His immanence in it. So the one degenerated to Deism, the other to Pantheism. For the one the Incarnation is nothing but miracle, inexplicable but sure; for the other it is nothing but universal immanence. For the one redemption is an interference, for the other it is an evolution. For the one Christ is absolute, for the other He is but relative to the history from which He arose. For the one He closes the old series totally in the new creation of another, for the other He but mightily prolongs it. In the one case we believe *in* Christ, in the other we believe *like* Christ. For the one Christ is the object of our faith, for the other he is the captain of our faith, its greatest instance. In the one we trust our whole selves to Christ for ever, in the other we imitate him. In the one he is our God, in the other our brother. It is well that the issue should be clear, if our choice is to be as intelligent and effectual as a faith should be.

These are the two streams whose junction forms current Protestantism, and can you wonder that the situation is complicated and even confused? We should trivialise the whole subject if we saw in the serious religious differences of the day no more than orthodoxy and heterodoxy—the propriety of certain individuals on the one hand, faced by the perversity of certain others on the other. The conflicting views of Messrs. X and Y are but the points where old opposing forces for the moment emerge and meet.

And we must own each movement has its relative justification. The old Protestantism had come to have great need of the Illumination. It was growing cumbrous, hard, and shallow. It needed especially to be trimmed down and cleared up from the critical side of the Illumination, and to be deepened and humanised from its romantic side. In just the same way mediævalism had called for the Renaissance. But all the same it was not the Renaissance that really took Europe in hand at that crisis. It was no Paganism that could save Europe for the true Church, or the Church for Christianity. That was done by the self-recuperative power of Christianity itself. It was done by the self-reformation of the Church, by the restoration of faith, and not the renascence of culture. Remember, the Reformation was not something done *to* the Church, but *by* it, and therefore by its faith. It was the vital Element in the Church disengaging and asserting itself. And so to-day it is not to the

Illumination, it is not to any culture, theological, æsthetic, or scientific, that we are to look for our salvation from the Protestant scholasticism which choked faith by orthodoxy in the seventeenth century, and still survives in the popular levels. That deliverance can only come by a movement from the interior of faith itself. I know it would be untrue to say that all the liberalising influence in the Protestantism of to-day is due to the direct action of the Reformation spirit of faith or religion. In so far as that liberality is a correction of our views about God in the cosmos, it is due quite as much, if not more, to the Illumination, which was quite independent of the reformers and rose rather from the philosophers. But the real matter is not the correction of views but the correction of real religion, of practical relations between God and the soul. And that is due, not to the action of either reason or romance, but to the renovation of faith by the piety and genius of men like Spener, Francke, Schleiermacher, and Wesley. *

§   §   §

It is not here a question whether each tendency must ban the other, for we need both; but it is a question which of them must be dominant for Christianity, and especially for original, essential Christianity. I mean for Christianity as first preached, the Christianity of the Bible and the apostle. In proportion as it ceases to be a κήρυγμα, Christianity ceases to be Christianity, whether it die in the direction of a sacramentalism or a humanism. It seems to me that this is constantly overlooked by the spokesmen of a Christianity which is liberal or nothing. They become as much the doctrinaire victims of a specu-

---

* I do not forget the influence of the romantic movement on Schleiermacher, but it was perhaps upon his weaker and less permanent side.

lative theology as our forefathers were the victims of an orthodox theology. The experimental Gospel in each case ceases to be life, and evaporates to a *caput mortuum* of certain views broad or narrow. I read a criticism of a positive theologian by a liberal of the academic stamp in which occurred this naïve saying: "It looks as if the problems of theology were here confused with the practical declaration of the Gospel by preacher or pastor." There is not one of the apostles that would not be hit by the remark. And it applies with even more force to our Lord Himself. Where are we to go for our Christian theology except to their practical declaration of the Gospel? The New Testament is no collection of theological *loci*. And how are we to test a theology at last but by its service for the purposes of the Gospel? Of course, if it is not a theology we are after but a theosophy, if our interest is in the philosophy or psychology of religion as a product of the human spirit, the case is altered. But with that the Gospel and the preacher have little directly to do. It is very interesting, but it is not vital. It belongs to the Schools, to the interpretive efforts of man upon the world; it has little to do with the Church and its interpretive message of man's destiny, and its Gospel of God's reality in His redemptive work.

When the question is forced, therefore, whether the positive or the liberal movement must rule in a historic Gospel, we have no hesitation about our choice. We take the Reformation side of our Protestantism for a stand, and not the Illuminationist. We may even go so far, when the issue is forced, as to say that Illuminationism or Rationalism is not Protestantism. We find our charter in history, and not in human nature; in the

Word, and not the world. The seat of revelation is in
the cross, and not in the heart. The precious thing is
something given, and not evolved. Our best goodness is
presented to us rather than achieved by us. The Kingdom of God is not a final goal, but an initial boon. You
will say, perhaps, the one does not exclude the other.
But for the practical issue on which all turns (except to a
doctrinaire intellectualism), for the last reality, it is more
true at this juncture to press the antithesis than to slur
it. The Gospel stands with the predominance of intervention, and it falls with the predominance of evolution.
Grace is essentially miraculous. Christ is more precious
to us by what distinguishes Him from us than by what
identifies Him with us. The Gospel turns entirely upon
redemptive forgiveness; and if evolution explain all, there
is no sin, and therefore no forgiveness. The Gospel turns
on the finality of Christ ; but on an evolutionary idea
there is no finality except at the close; it is therefore
inaccessible, for the end is not yet. There can be no
finality on that basis, in anyone who appeared in a middle
point of the chain.   So far, therefore, Christ is provisional and tentative till a greater arise. The positive
Gospel, we say, is the dominant thing by which modern
thought must be gauged and its permanence tested. We
may take from the modern mind and its results so much
only as is compatible with a real, historic, redeeming,
final Gospel. That Gospel is the preamble, and the
subsequent clauses that contradict it must go out.

We shall not be foolish enough, sectarian enough, to
make a sweeping condemnation of modern thought in
advance. For one thing, it is very hard to know what is
meant by it. Does it mean the mental world of Kant, and
Goethe, and Browning, or of Spencer, Fiske, and James,

or of Nietzsche, Tolstoi and Ibsen? Because they are in many respects as incompatible with each other, and hated by each other, as they are opposed to evangelical Christianity. And, for another thing, we have already accepted many of the results of modern civilisation. It has thrust back the frontier of the Church, and given a mandate to the State to take up province after province which the Church used to control, in art, science, philanthropy, education, and the like. Well, we largely agree. We accept the emancipation of these from religious dictation. Church discipline gives way to civic rights and police protection. The number of public subjects on which the preacher is entitled to a respectable opinion grows fewer, while at the same time there are more aspects than ever of his own subject open to his study and demanding his official attention. We accept the modern repudiation of an external authority in the forms of belief and uniformity of confession. We accept the essential inwardness of faith even when we press its objective. We accept the modern freedom of the individual. We accept the modern passion for reality, which owes so much to science. We accept the methods of the Higher Criticism, and only differ as to its results. We accept the modern primacy of the moral, and the modern view of a positive moral destiny for the world. And we repudiate imagination, whether æsthetic or speculative, as the ruling factor in the religious life. We have assigned another place and function to the miraculous in connection with faith. We accept the modern place claimed for experience in connection with truth; we recognise that the real certainty of Christian truth can only come with the experience of personal salvation. In these and other respects we have already accepted

much which would have scared even the stout reformers.

II

I would single out for particular stress the place now
given to experience in religion in consequence of the
Reformation view of faith, co-operating with the inductive
method of science—our experience of Christ especially.
What Nature is to science, that is Christ to positive
faith. I would direct notice to the form of the great
issue presented in the question : Are we to believe *in*
Christ or *like* Christ ? Are we to trust ourselves to Him,
or to the type of religion He represents ?

I am struck with the absence of any sign of an experience distinctively Christian in many of those who discuss
the sanctuaries of the Christian faith—such as the nature
of the Cross, or of the self-consciousness of Christ. To
them Christ's first relation is to human power, or love,
and not to sin. They cultivate not trust in Christ, but the
"religion of Jesus." We are driven from pillar to post,
and left with no rest for the sole of our foot. Can we
rest on the Gospels ? No. Criticism will not allow that.
Can we on the Epistles ? No. Protestantism will not
allow that. It would be taking the external authority of
an apostle for our base, and that ends in Rome. But is
there no such thing any more as the *testimonium Sancti
Spiritus* ? No. Some of these scholars, to judge from their
writings alone, do not seem even so much as to have
heard of a Holy Ghost. And they have a fatal dread of
pietism, and methodism, and most forms of intensely personal evangelical faith. They are, like Haeckel, in their
own way, the victims of an intellectualism which means
spiritual atrophy to Christianity at last. No, they say,

if you fall back on your experience, you may land anywhere.

But am I really forbidden to make any use of my
personal experience of Christ for the purposes even of
scientific theology ?   Should it make no difference to the
evidence for Christ's resurrection that I have had personal
dealings with the risen Christ as my Saviour, nearer and
dearer than my own flesh and blood ? (Is His personal
gift of forgiveness to me, in the central experience of my
life, of no value in settling the objective value of His
cross and person ?) My personal contact with Christ, our
commerce together, may I found nothing on these ?
" No," it is said, " nothing of scientific objective value.
These experiences may be of great personal value to you,
but they give you no warrant for stepping outside your
own feelings.   They may be useful illusions in their
place, but you must outgrow them.   You can never be
quite sure that the Saviour you meet is a personal reality.
You can never make it certain to any that He is a continuous personality with the historic Jesus.   And it is even
laid upon us to make it doubtful for yourself."   " In your
so-called communion with Christ you have no more real
right," we are told, " to build on the objective personal
reality of your *vis-à-vis* than the Roman Catholic girl had
to believe in the real presence and speech of the Virgin
at Lourdes.   If it is Christ who visits you, it was the
Virgin that visited her.   Of so little worth is the fact of
the experience in vouching for the content of experience.
If you commune with Christ, do not gird at those who
traffic with the saints."

§   §   §

Now, might I have leave to say that I had to meet that
problem for myself several years ago ?   And the answer

I thought satisfactory was twofold. First, it was personal ;
second, it was historical in two ways.

I take the first first.   There is, and can be, nothing so
certain to me as that which is involved in the most
crucial and classic experience of my moral self, my conscience, my real, surest me.   A vision might be a phantom,
and a colloquy an hallucination.   But if I am not to be
an absolute Pyrrhonist, doubt everything, and renounce
my own reality, I must find my practical certainty in that
which founds my moral life, and especially my new moral
life.   The test of all philosophy is ethical conviction.
That is where we touch reality—in moral action (God as
Spirit is God *in actu*), and especially in that action of the
moral nature which renews it in Christ.   Now, my contention is that my contact with Christ is not merely
visionary, it is moral, personal and mutual.)   Nor is it
merely personal, in the same sense in which I might have
personal intercourse from time to time with a man in
whom I am little concerned between whiles.   Because
what I have in Christ is not an impression, but a life
change ; not an impression of personal influence, which
might evaporate, but a faith of central personal change.
I do not merely feel changes ; (I am changed.)   Another
becomes my moral life.   He has done more than deeply
influence me.   He has possessed me.   I am not his loyal
subject, but his absolute property.   I have rights against
King Edward, however loyal I am, but against Christ I
have none.   He has not merely passed into my life as
even a wife might do, but he has given me a new life,
a new moral self, a new consciousness of moral reality.
In him alone I have forgiveness, reconciliation, the grace
of God, and therefore the very God, (since neither love
nor grace is a mere attribute of God).   There has been

P

what I can only call a new creation, using the strongest word in my reach. I owe him my total self. He has not merely healed me, in passing, of an old trouble, but He has given me eternal life. He has not only impressed me as a vision might—even one projected from my own interior—but he has done a permanent work on me at my moral centre. He has made a moral change in me which, for years and years, has worked outwards from the very core of my moral self, and subdued everything else to its obedience. In my inmost experience, tested by years of life, he has brought me God. It is not merely that he spoke to me of God or God's doings, but in Him God directly spoke to me; and more, he did in me, and for me, the thing that only God's real presence could do. Who can forgive sin but God only, against whom it was done?

Thus the real Catholic analogy to his action on me and in me is not visions of the Virgin, or the ecstacies of saints, but it is the Sacraments. In the Catholic view these are objective and effective upon the inmost substantial self; so is Christ objective, effective, creative, upon my moral, my real self, upon me as a conscience, on sinful me. He is the author not of my piety merely but of my regeneration. My experience of him is that of one who does a vital, revolutionary work in that moral region where the last certainty lies. And in that region it is an experience of a change so total that I could not bring it to pass by any resource of my own. Nor could any man effect it in me. And any faith I have at all is faith in Christ not merely as its content nor merely as its point of origin, but as its *creator*. The Christ I believe in I believe in as the creator of the belief, and not merely its object. I know him as the *author* as well as object of my faith in God. I know him, therefore, as God. The great change was not a somersault I succeeded in turning, with some divine help; it was a revolution effected in me and by him, comparable only to my entry on the world. The very fact that in its nature it was forgiveness and regeneration makes it a moral certainty, the kind of certainty that rises from contact with my Judge, with the last moral and personal reality, who has power even to break me, and with my Redeemer, who has power to remake me as his own.

§   §   §

If certainty do not lie there, where can it be found in life? If he is not real, moral reality has no meaning. There are hallucinations in religious experience, but not here. They might be connected with the affections but not with the conscience at its one life crisis. They might be as impressive as a *revenant*, but no more morally creative and redemptive. If you claim the right to challenge the validity of my experience, you must do it on the ground of some experience surer, deeper, getting nearer moral reality than mine. What is it? Does the last criterion lie in sense, or even in thought? Is it not in conscience? If life at its centre is moral, then the supreme certainty lies there. It must be associated, not with a feeling nor with a philosophic process, but with the last moral experience of life, which we find to be a life morally changed from the centre and for ever. To challenge that means rationalism, intellectualism, and the merest theosophy. Do not forget that philosophy is but a method, while faith, which is at the root of theology, presents us with a new datum, a new reality.

You refuse the mere dictum of an apostle. But if we may not rest upon the mere dictum of an apostle, may we not upon our own repetition of the apostolic experience, of the experience which made them apostles? I say repetition, but might I not say prolongation? We rest on our own participation in the ageless action of the same redemption in the Cross as changed them, after many waverings, for good and all. Is it not the same act, the same spirit, the same real personality acting on us both, in the same moral world? And, expanding my own experience by the aid of theirs, may I not say this: I am not saved by the apostle or his experience, nor by the Church and its experience, but by what saved the apostle and the Church. When Christ did for me what I have described, was it not the standing crisis of the moral macrocosm acting in its triumphant way at the centre of my microcosm? Was not the moral crisis of the race's destiny on Christ's cross more than echoed, was it not in some sense re-enacted at my moral centre, and the great conquest reachieved on the outpost scale of my single crisis? The experience has not only a moral nature, as a phase of conscience, but an objective moral content; as is shown by the absolute rest and decisive finality of its moral effect in my life and conduct. If it be not so, then we are asked to believe that men can produce in themselves these changes which permanently break the self in two, or can lift themselves to eternal moral heights by their own waistband. But, if so, what need is there for a God at all? Do not even the positivists likewise?

There is no *rational* certainty by which this *moral* certainty of a creator Christ *could* be challenged; for there is no rational certainty more sure, or so sure, and none that goes where this goes, to the self-disposing centres of life. This moral certainty is the truly rational certainty.

[margin note: Rational certainty can't enter same realm as moral certainty.]

Christ approves Himself as a divine reality by His revolutionary, causal, creative action on that inmost reality whereby man is man.   That centre from which I *act* (and therefore am real), meets, in a way decisive for all life, with Christ in His act on the Cross.   If this contact represent no real formative activity on me, if it be but impressionist influence, then the whole and central activity of my life, whereby I confront it in kind, is unreal.   If the Saviour be unreal and my communion an unreality, a mere mystic or moody mingling of being, then there is no reality, and everything is dissolved into cloud and darkness and vapour of smoke.

§　§　§

I do not wish to say anything disrespectful of these academic critics to whom we owe so very much in the way of laboratory theology, but they are the second, not the first.   A higher hand must make them mild.   A deeper insight must enlarge their truth.   And I much wish they had more of that ethical realism of Carlyle or Ibsen, only turning it upon the conscience at the Cross.   But so often (just as a vast memory may impair the power of judgment) you find the finest critical faculty, and the most powerful scholarly apparatus, conjoined with a moral nature singularly naïve, and beautifully simple and unequal to the actual world.   Their experience of life and conscience has no record of lapse or shame.   Their world is a study of still-life; it has not the drama, the fury, the pang, the tragedy, the crisis of the actual world at large, with its horrible guilt and its terror of judgment.   It opens to them none of the crevasses where glow the nether fires.   They inhabit, morally, the West End. They are in no touch with damned souls.   They have lived in an unworldly purity, and have never been drawn from the jaws of hell, or taken from the fearful pit and its miry clay. They have been reared, many of them, in the sacred and pious atmosphere of the German manse, and cradled in the godliness of the most Christian of homes. The paradox is this, that if purity be the test of truth, and obedience the organ of theological know-ledge, if that be the meaning of "will do, shall know" (as it is not), if they are as right in their views as they are of heart, then evangelical Christianity would be dying of its own moral success.

III

The second part of my answer to the suggested analogy between communion with a saint and communion with Christ our Lord is this. It would enlarge what I have been saying to the scale of history. Christ has entered actual history, with piercing, crucial, moral effect, in a way the Virgin never has, nor any saint. He has entered it not only profoundly, but centrally and creatively; she is adjutorial at most. By his effect upon human experience he created that Church within which the worship and contact of the Saints arose. The Church arose as a product of something which Christ produced— namely, saving faith. And it is not only the effect of Christ on the Church that I speak of, but, through the Church, his effect on history at large. Christ affects the moral springs of history as no saint has done. They but colour or turn the stream; he struck from the rock. I make all allowance for the fact that, by the Church's fault, he has affected history less than he might have done. But it remains true that all we have and hope in the new humanity owes to Christ what it owes to no other. And it owes it to a Christ felt and believed to be generically different from every rival or every believer. What we owe to Christendom, or to great Christians, they owe to a Christ who owed himself to no man. He has entered the history of the Church at least as He has entered my history—not as the mere postulate, nor even as the spring, but as the Creator of the new life, the new self, while he himself needed no new self or new life. I make all allowance for the reasonable results of historic criticism, yet he stands in history as a defined consciousness and a creative person, who is powerful not in the degree in which he is appreciated by our experience, but in a way which creates experience, and which can only be appreciated by something greater than our experience —by our faith. We know him by faith to be much more than he has ever been to our experience. I know him, and the Church knows Him, as a person of infinite power to create fresh experience of himself, which is experience of God. My contact with him by faith is continually deepening my experience of him. And as my experience deepens it brings home a Christ objective in history, and creative of the experience, and the life, and the deeds of a whole vast Church, meant, and moving, to subdue mankind not to itself, but to the faith of the Gospel.

§   §   §

But how can an individual experience give an absolute truth ? How can an experience (which is a thing personal to me in, say, my own forgiveness) assure me of the world ? How can my experience, my forgiveness, assure me of the world's redemption ? How can it assure me of the final and absolute establishment of the Kingdom of God ? I may experience my salvation, but how can I experience the salvation of the world—which is for all (and is so felt by some) a greater concern than their own ?

The answer is this.   My experienced salvation is not a
passing impression but a life faith.   It is not a subjective
frame but an objective relation, and even transaction.
The peace of God is not glassy calm but mighty confidence.   My experience here is the consciousness not of
an impression on me, but of an act in me, on me, and by
me.   It is not an afferent but an efferent consciousness,
as the psychologists would say, like the muscular sense,
the sense not of rheumatism but of energy.   And, to go
on, it is the sense not only of myself as acting in the
experience called faith, but it is the sense that that act is
not perfectly spontaneous but evoked, nay, created by its
content and object.   And, still to go on, it is the sense
that it is created by another and parent act—which is the
one eternal decisive act of an eternal Person saving a
world.   I am forgiven and saved by an act which saves
the world.   For it not only gives me moral power to
confront the whole world and surmount it, but it unites
me in a new sympathy with all mankind, and it em-
powers me not only to face but to hail eternity.   And
this it does not for me, but for whosoever will.   Surely
the Christ who re-creates me in that faith in God must
be God.   This is the report of my faith, and of the
Church's faith, upon the act to which it owes its own
existence as an act.   Is it to be amenable to unfaith?
Actor sequitur forum rei, said Roman law.   The venue of
criticism is in the court of the challenged faith.   That is,
the true and fruitful criticism is that within the believing
Church under the final standard of grace.   It is a part of
that self-criticism of the Church whose classic case is the
Reformation.

What Christ has done for me has become possible only
by what He did even more powerfully for others whose

faith and experience have been deeper and richer than
mine, but who reflect my experience all the same, even
while they diversify and enlarge it mightily. Standing
over my experience is the experience of the whole
evangelical succession. And standing over that is the
historic fact of Christ's own person, and His consciousness of Himself ("All things are delivered to me of the
Father") as Lord of the world, Lord of nature in
miracle, of the soul in redemption, and of the future in
judgment. When I meet Him in my inmost soul I meet
one whose own inmost soul felt itself to be all that, and
who has convinced the moral flower of the race, in the
whole historic Church, that He *is* what He *knew* Himself
to be. And in that conviction the Church has become
the finest product of Humanity, and the mightiest power
that ever entered and changed the course of history from
its moral centre.

Our experience of Christ is therefore an absolutely
different thing from our experience of saint or Virgin.
In their case, granting it were actual, the visitation
might be but my experience; in His case it is my faith,
which concerns not a phase of me whereof I am conscious, but the whole of my moral self and racial destiny
whereof I am but poorly conscious. (Faith is the grand
venture in which we commit our whole soul and future
to the confidence that Christ is not an illusion but the
reality of God. We may respond to a saint, but to
Christ we belong.

IV

The third part of my answer would expand what I
have touched on, a few words back, in regard to the
consciousness of Christ.

I have referred to the individual experience, and to its expansion in the experience of the Church. But is this enough to give us the reality of a supernatural (or rather a superhistoric) Christ? If it were, then we should be in this difficulty, that the experience of believers would be the seat of God's revelation to us. And fresh difficulties arise out of that. If it be so, then do we not give the Church (as the collective experience) a prerogative which, even if it does not rise to the claim of Rome, yet puts the individual conscience too much at its mercy, and obtrudes the Church between it and Christ? And, again, if it be so, what was the seat of God's revelation to the very first Church of all, to the first believers with no Church behind them? And what place is left for the Bible, the record, at all, except a mere subsidiary one in support of the supreme experience of a Church? Whereas the Bible, no less than the Church, was a parallel result of the Gospel, and part of the revelationary purpose of God. The gift of the Spirit * to the Apostles was not simply to confirm personal faith but to equip them efficiently for their apostolic, preaching, witnessing work.

We must pass within the circle of the first Church's experience and testimony, and find a means of stepping off the last verge of its direct documentation on to sure moral ground where the documents cease. We must pass by faith from the field of the first faith certificated in the documents to the historic reality behind the wall of documents, and within the ring fence of the testifying Church.

---

* The difficult question as to the relation between Christ and the Spirit (especially for St. Paul) is too large for side treatment. I only note that our communion is not with the Spirit, but in the Spirit, with Father and Son.

And we are compelled to do so by the very nature of that faith and those documents themselves. If we are not to stultify the first Church and all its history, we must recognise a point on which critics so antagonistic to each other as Schaeder and Lobstein agree,* that the Gospel about Jesus in the first Church truly reflected Jesus' Gospel of Himself, and grew inevitably out of it. We could not speak of Jesus with any respect if his influence not only could not protect His first followers from idolatry in placing Him where they did—beside God in their worship—but actually promoted that idolatry. If *they* included Christ in his own Gospel, then *he* did. It was not in the teeth of him that they made him an object of faith and worship along with the Father. They could never have treated him, those disciples who had been with him, in a way which would have horrified him as much as some apostles were horrified at the attempt to worship them at Lystra. If they found him Saviour through death from sin, found him the Son of God and the Eternal Christ, then he offered himself as such in some form or other.

Accordingly the question becomes one of the interpretation of his self-consciousness as the Gospels offer it upon the whole. We are borne onward by the experience of the Church upon the experience of Christ in so far as he revealed it. The Church's first thought of him was substantially one with his own thought of himself. What was that? Was it a thought which placed him with men, facing God and moving towards God, or with God facing men and moving to them? Was he not always with men, but from beside God?

* See *Die christliche Welt*, 1907, No. 19, Sp. 529.

Can our relation to him, if we take his construction of it, be parallel to our relation to any apostle, saint, virgin, or hero? Into the self-consciousness of Christ I have already gone. I can only refer again to all the passages of the Gospels which have their focus in Mat. xi. 25 ff.,* and which reveal the sense of his complete mastery of the world of nature, of the soul, and of the future. He forgave the soul and claimed to judge it. He determined our eternal relation to God. And he used nature at will for the supreme purposes of grace and eternity.

§ § §

But we must here take another step which replaces us where we set out, though on a higher plane. This power of which Jesus was so sure was not there simply to make a vast and placid self-consciousness. He was not there simply as a reservoir of moral power instead of its agent. If he had the power it was not as a miser of power, to enjoy the satisfaction of possessing it in self-poised and self-sufficient reserve, not to be a quiescent character reposing in God. He was there to exercise the power in historic action. And as it was moral power, it could only go out in moral achievement. He was there for a task in which the whole of his power should be expended. He was there to do something which only his power could do. If he had power more than all the world's, it was to overcome the world in another than the individualist and ascetic sense. It was to subdue it to himself. The Son was not only to affect it, but to regain it for the Father. He was not simply to rule, but to redeem. He was there for action; and

---

* Surely the criticism which dissolves this passage leaves us with little but dissolving views of anything.

it was action commensurate both with his person, and with the world, and with the world's moral extremity. He was there to do that which all the accounts declare was done in the Cross—to conquer for mankind their eternal life. It was not simply to fill men's souls at His as from a fountain, but to achieve for them and in them a victory whose prolonged action (and not mere echo) should be their eternal life. With all his power he was there for one vast eternal deed, which can only be described as the Redemption, the new Creation, of the race. Nothing less could afford scope for the exercise of such power as his, if it was a power that must work to an active head, and could not be held in mere benignant self-possession, in quiescent, massive, brimming Goethean calm. The moral personality must all be put into a corresponding deed. What is the deed which gives effect to the whole tremendous moral resource of Jesus? There is not one except his death. If we reduce that simply to his life's violent and premature close, then we are without any adequate expression in action of so vast a moral personality. That personality becomes a truncated and ineffectual torso; or it becomes but an æsthetic quantity, an object of moral and spiritual admiration, and the source of profound religious influences and impressions, but not of living faith and of eternal life. It is a grand piece of still-life, spectacular but not dramatic, with spell but not power. It can refine but not regenerate, cultivate but not recreate. And had Jesus not found in his death the regenerative outlet for the infinite moral power in his person, He would have been rent with the unrest and distraction of prisoned genius. He would have been no expression of the peace that goes with the saving power of God, peace which he then could neither have nor give.   But the finality of what he did as God on the cross is the source of that unearthly rest which is the peculium of the true Church.   And it is lost from all the Churches that are more earnest in bringing a Kingdom than in working out a Kingdom already brought.   These Churches and their efforts may have much power, but they lack the divinest power which is also spell; and they fail to attract those that crave from power not only results but peace.

LECTURE VIII

*THE MORALISING OF DOGMA, ILLUSTRATED
BY THE OMNIPOTENCE OF GOD*

LECTURE VIII

THE MORALISING OF DOGMA, ILLUSTRATED BY THE OMNIPOTENCE OF GOD

In all the Churches but those of sheer external authority dogma has succumbed to the solvent of criticism. By which word dogma is not necessarily meant positive truth, but dogma as such, the specific theological constructions from the past which have been sealed with ecclesiastical authority as formally final. A Church must always have a dogma, implicit or explicit. A cohesive Church must have a coherent creed. But it must be a dogma the Church holds, not one that holds the Church. The life is in the body, not in the system. It must be a dogma, revisable from time to time to keep pace with the Church's growth as a living body in a living world. The study of theology must go on and go forward. Solution after solution of the great problems must be both attempted and encouraged by vital faith. First the pursuit and formulation of *doctrine* by individual thinkers or groups must be pursued and honoured as an energy inferior to none in the varied lifework of the Church. And then, at certain stages of the process, certain Churches may feel that a point of agreement has been reached, which enables them, if other reasons make it desirable, to state their common view in a new form, as a breathing place for their mental energy, a salute to other Churches, or a guide for their own catechumens. The idea of a dogma, as the organised declaration or confession by any Church of its collective doctrine, is only the intellectual counterpart of the idea of the organised Church itself. No Church can live without more or less organisation, which must include not its machinery only but its thought. A mere brotherhood needs no theology; but then it has no stay and no influence in history. It is only a sympathetic group. But a Church must have a creed, either tacit or express, else it is no church. Christianity certainly is more than its truth, but there is no Christianity apart from its truth. A religion of mere affinities is no more a religion than one of mere freedom. There must be a belief, and an entrusted entail of belief. The difficulty begins with the question how far the collective belief is to be pressed upon individual members or ministers—the question of subscription. The two questions are constantly confused by thoughtless people. A creed which is but declaratory, and corporate, and binding on honour is confused with particular and individual subscription to it, binding in right and giving legal status. And the confusion is increased when people jump to the conclusion that dogma, or the collective expression of a Church's belief, must be final in a given form. It is now widely recognised that every form of belief must be changeable in proportion to its detailed length, and permanent in proportion to its condensed brevity. And the influences that now recast the great old fabrics of faith, once so new and adequate, are part of the action of the same divine spirit which put them there on a time to serve

their hour and age.   It is now preparing a new synthesis
from the old and positive faith.

To-day the great fabrics of historic dogma not only
succumb to the calm decay of time, but they crumble
faster than ever under the acid that now fills the air—
under modern criticism.   This is a source of grief and
fear to many at one extreme, while to some at the other
it is a source of almost unholy joy.   For the great
Churches which have publicly and expressly pinned
their existence to specific dogma, patristic or mediæval, it
is of course a most serious thing.   The Roman Church
appears to be honeycombed with a modernism that may
lead either to its disintegration or to a new reformation.
On the other hand, for those free lances of the genial
heart and sterile mind, who face theology as a bull greets
scarlet, and regard positive views as a tramp does four
walls, the collapse of the old structure seems as the
opening of the prison-house to them that are bound.

§   §   §

Dogma is the science of faith.   Every department of
science has its dogma; and in the hierarchy of the
sciences these dogmas qualify and supplement each other.
In one region we have the dogma of gravitation; in
another that of evolution; in another that of affinity;
in another (if it be another) the molecular dogma; and
so on.   Thus in the region of spiritual life we have also
a science.   We have a science of faith.   And the truth
of it is accepted for fundamental by the Churches, the
living bodies concerned, just as gravitation and the
like are accepted by the universities, which do not, for
instance, enter discussion with the man who challenges
the rotundity of the earth and starts an apostolate of
its flatness.

Dogma is the science which underlies the mentality of those living and moving societies. And it exists upon experienced faith in the holy love of a changeless and saving God in Christ, just as physical science exists upon a faith in the uniformity of His action in Nature.

But there is an ambiguity which we must realise and avoid in the phrase, a science of faith. There are things it seems to mean and does not. It does not mean a science of thought attached to faith, like Greek metaphysics. It does not mean a metaphysic of Being, or a philosophy of jurisprudence, imported into the Christian faith by the circumstances of its history and growth. Nor on the other hand does it mean a science of the subjective religious acts, a psychology of religion. Far less does it mean that the psychology of religion shall provide the dogmas or " broad general truths of religion," to whose test every belief of faith must submit, as the modern way is. But it means the science of religion when religion rises to the positive faith we have in Christianity, the science of religion as a moral relation, a living and historic relation between two personalities, two consciences; which in Christianity is a redeeming relation. It is the science of realised redemption. It is a science wherein faith is not so much the observed object as the observing subject. It is faith thinking and not only faith thought of. It is the view of things created by the new man and not discovered by the modern man. And it is upon the lines of such an ethical religion alone that we reach that moralising of dogma which is the demand of many who are not prepared to dismiss it.

§   §   §

No dogma has been affected by the influences of the age so much as that of the person of Christ. It was *the*

doctrine of the Church in the first age, when a united
Church laid the lines of its dogma down; and none has
felt like it the dissolving effect of a divided Church.
And the Chalcedonian or Athanasian form of the belief,
which is embalmed in the current formula of two natures
in one person in Christ, may be said to have been
seriously shaken wherever modern conditions have been
realised. This has occurred the more readily as the
creeds in which it was embodied served for their day the
purpose rather of repelling errors than of adjusting truths.
The truths were not really and inwardly adjusted, but
only placed together; and they are thus the more easily
shaken apart. They were married but not wedded, or if
wedded not welded; and though they lived in the same
house, it was not without friction. The human
mind, the moral experience, were not yet ripe enough.
Psychology, and especially religious psychology, had not
then come into existence; and, while the strongest
assertions were made about the coexistence of the two
natures as a postulate of faith, it was beyond the power
of the metaphysic which then prevailed to show how
they could cohere in a personal unity. The attempts
failed even at a later date, when a doctrine of mutual
permeation (or περιχώρησις) took the place of a doctrine
of conjunction and mutual action (or συνάφεια and
ἀντίδοσις). With the modern growth of psychology,
and the modern revolution of metaphysic, such formulæ
were bound to dissolve. They were based on an early
metaphysic of natures and a crude science of personality. But the metaphysic of history, the modern
primacy of personality, and the new stress on experience,
coupled with a critical historicism equally modern, have
opened a better way; and they keep Christ and his

problem from retiring into the outskirts of thought.
No dissolution of the old dogma prevents the Christological question from still being the question of the
hour and of the future for religious thought, when we
are not monopolised by the modern social problem.
The discredit of the dogma has also been increased by
the modern return to the Bible and its Gospel.   We
find the scripture doctrine of the subject, inchoate as
it is in form, to be more satisfactory than the
ecclesiastical development of it for a starting point.   And
it is satisfactory for this reason.   It remoralises the
whole issue by restoring it to personal religion.   Yet let
it not be thought that the moralising of dogma makes it
less urgent, less incumbent, less dogmatic.   For what is so
insistent, inevitable, and dogmatic as the categorical
imperative which is at the moral centre ?

At the Reformation, with its concentration of religion
on the conscience, and on the guilty conscience, Christianity became once more personal and evangelical; that
is, it became predominantly ethical.   The key to the
religion was found in personal faith.   It was not in the
institutes of theology or the institutions of the Church.
It was in moral and religious experience, in the contact
of a historic Redeemer with our living and personal
experience of redemption.   That was what had really
made Christianity in the first century.   And it was
what was lost in a Church dominated by Chalcedonian
metaphysic with an Aristotelian editing; till the personal
faith of the New Testament was rescued from a religion
chiefly institutional and creedal at the Reformation.
Three centuries later another powerful effort was made
by Hegelianism to scholasticise Christianity anew, and to
rationalise Christology on the largest lines.   The older

and narrower Rationalism had simply abolished Christology by reducing Christ to a mere man, and any science
of him to the psychology of genius.   And Hegel seemed
to restore all by discovering a Christology in the very
nature of thought and being.   But the capture of Hegel
by his extreme left has brought his system to much the
same effect as the old rationalism.   While the reformed
and evangelical spirit has, by its revival, notably in
Schleiermacher, Ritschl, and others, discredited all the
Hegelian constructions.   The Incarnation, being for a
moral and not a metaphysical purpose, must be in its
nature moral.   Its metaphysic should therefore be a
metaphysic of ethics, and not of thought as pure being.
And we are shut up to the method of experience to
explain the act of grace in Christ's coming, and to
release it from rational permissions in order to be an
autonomous power.   Religion is an ultimate in consciousness—according to its most recent psychology.
And the higher it is, so much the more ultimate, and
the less vassal to rational permissions.   It is living
faith that has the promise of understanding the object
of faith.   Certainly nothing but faith can decide
whether Christ is properly an object of faith or only its
chief subject.   No historic inquiry can decide that, as we
shall see. A religion of moral redemption can only be
understood by a Church of the morally redeemed, as
rational science, in its area, can only be pursued by
rational minds schooled to its method.   The theology of
such a gospel opens only to a Church of broken and
converted men. Only the saved have the real secret of
the Saviour. That is the religion of the matter, which
carries its theology. The Godhead that became incarnate
in Jesus Christ did so not to convince, but to save. God-

head became incarnate so far and in such fashion as the purpose of redemption prescribed. It became incarnate in the manner the work required. (Man's need determined God's deed.) Christ was almighty—to save. In a word, the work of Christ, realised in the Church's experience through faith, becomes the avenue and the key to the person of Christ. Soteriology is the way of access to Christology. But where we come down to a bland version of salvation, to the ebbs and flats of religion, to a lay, light, and level sense of holiness, sin, judgment, and grace— when we arrive there (either through lack of " fundamental brain work," as Rossetti called it, or of radical soul work) then the person of Christ becomes unintelligible; impressive, in a sense, but unintelligible. And the effort of the Church's thought to pierce its mystery is dismissed as mere metaphysic, in favour of an æsthetic or a sentimental regard for his character and message. Most elusive of all is the effort to retain the old passwords, while reducing them to no more than disguises in luminous paint for the subjective processes of a self-saving Humanity.

§   §   §

In speaking of the moralisation of Christology by the Reformation and the modern movements in its train I do not think I can do better than offer here a free translation of a passage in Melanchthon, one sentence of which has recently been much used as the motto for this whole tendency. It is taken from the preface to the Loci of 1521.

" If a man know nothing of the power of sin, of law, or of grace, I do not see how I can call him a Christian. It is there that Christ is truly known. The knowledge of Christ is to know his benefits, taste his salvation, and experience his grace; it is not, as the academic people say, to reflect on his natures and the modes of his incarnation. If you do not know the practical purpose for which he took flesh and went to the cross what is the good of knowing his story? Is a doctor but a botanist? Is he content to know the forms and colours of his herbs? It is their virtue that counts. So with Christ. He is given us as our remedy, or, in Bible phrase, our salvation. And we must know him in another way than the scholars. To know him to purpose is to know the demand of the conscience for holiness, the source of power to meet it, where to seek grace for our sin's failure, how to set up the sinking soul in the face of the world, the flesh, and the devil, how to console the conscience broken. Is that what any of the schools teach, metaphysical, critical, or literary? Paul in Romans, when he wants to condense Christian doctrine into a compendium, does he philosophise about the mysteries of the Trinity, or the method of incarnation, or an active and a passive creation? He does nothing of the kind. He speaks of law, sin and grace; of conscience, guilt and salvation. These are the topics on which a knowledge of Christ turns. You do not know Christ until you know these. How often Paul declares to his believers that he prays for them a rich knowledge of Christ. He foresaw that we should one day leave the saving themes and turn our minds to discussions cold and foreign to Christ. What we propose to do, therefore, is to sketch the inwardness of those passages that commend Christ to you, that settle the conscience, and establish the soul against Satan. Most people look in the Bible only for classic instruction about goodness and evil.   But it is a philosophic more than a Christian quest."

§   §   §

The modern moralisation of religion thus prescribes a new manner of inquiry on such a central subject as the person of Christ.   It plants us anew on the standpoint of the Bible, where all human ethic is pointed, transfigured and reissued in Christ's new creation of the moral soul.   This rebirth of the race is not a thing yet to be done, but a thing already done and given into our hands ; " God hath regenerated us in the resurrection of Christ from the dead " (1 Peter i. 3); and it is prolonged in the Christian experience of many centuries.   What, then, does such a tremendous and revolutionary fact involve ?   How must we think of him who brought it to pass ?   As the incarnation of natural and arbitrary omnipotence ?   No, but as one who was potent for everything morally required by the one need of sinful Humanity, and the one demand of Holy Eternal Love.

Was it by a moral way, by moral conquest, that Christ came to his final glory ?   Then it must have been by a moral way that he left it.   Is the end of our salvation a moral glory ?   Then the origin of it must have issued from moral glory.   Is it an eternal salvation ?   Then its moral glory rose in a moral Eternity.   Did the Eternal come by a transcendent moral act ?   Then that act began in Eternity.   A final salvation means a saving act eternal and absolute. Some metaphysic is here involved, certainly, but it is a metaphysic of the conscience.   It starts from the conviction that for life and history the moral is the real, and that the movements of the Great Reality must be morally

construed as they are morally revealed. The spiritual
world is not the world of noetic process or cosmic force,
but of holy, *i.e.* moral, order, act, and power. Now concerning the union of the two natures in Christ the old
dogma thought in a far too natural and non-moral way.
Its categories were too elemental and physical. It conceived it as an act of might, of immediate divine power,
an act which united the two natures *into* a person rather
than *through* that person. It united them miraculously
rather than morally, into the existence of the incarnate
personality rather than by his action. The person was
the resultant of the two natures rather than the agent of
their union. They were united into a person whose
action only began after the union, and did not affect it.
It began (according to the dogma) in the miraculous conception, which was not an ethical act, rather than in the
grace of the eternal son, who, for our sakes, from rich
became poor. There can be no unity of spirits like
God and man except in a moral way, by personal action
which is moral in its method as well as in its aim. As
Christians we are united with Christ by a moral,
i.e. a personal, process; and can we think otherwise of
the manner of his union with God which is its base?
It is only in the way of moral modulation that the
divine Logos could become true man. That is where the
Christian differs from all pagan notions of incarnation.
And the Christian idea is so different, so ethical, because
its origin and its seat is in the cross, which is the axis of
the racial conscience, and the historic focus of moral
mediation. It is the cross and not the cradle that has
the secret of the Lord.

But, indeed, it is ethically misleading to speak of union
in such a case. Union is a term too physical, too natural.

Even terms like permeation or interpenetration are so. And this is the cardinal error of the old dogma. It works upon a spiritual subject with physical instead of moral categories. Its incarnation takes place not by spiritual power but by natural power, however vastly magnified and deified, by a fiat rather than a moral act. The error is very persistent. I admit that some Bible phrases give the wrong lead, as when we read of the Spirit being poured out, and without measure. You find it in some of the recent liberal interpretations of Christ as a human personality completely filled by the Spirit. But that is really docetic, however imposing. It dehumanises, it depersonalises, and therefore it degrades, the human nature to a vessel for the divine. It reduces the human below the personal level by treating it as a mere receptacle or tenement of the Godhead. This is a poor and passive idea of humanity instead of a moral, which must be active even in its receptivity. And we are but repeating a form of the old error which construed the human nature as no more than a coat which was put on, while the divine became but a palladium dropped from Heaven in human form, with an action more mechanical than moral. Whatever may be said against the Kenosis doctrine, at least it made the whole Christ on earth the result of a grand moral act in the Heavens.

§   §   §

We might, perhaps, put the matter in this way. Let us examine a dogma which underlies so much popular religion and creates so much popular scepticism—the dogma of God's natural omnipotence. Jesus, we say, was the incarnation to the world of the power of Almighty God. But, it is at once objected, we see in Jesus neither omnipotence nor omniscience. He claimed neither. Do you claim for him, say, divine omnipotence ? The answer to that question must be Yes and No.

Surely we must distinguish two ideas as to the relation of power and goodness. Must we not distinguish between the power which, though it has another and lower nature, may be put wholly at the service of justice, and the power which in its nature *is* justice ; between the might that serves right and the might which is right ? Can we not distinguish between a visible thing, like the might of armies employed in a just cause, in the cause, it may be, of universal justice, between that and a spiritual power which is the intrinsic might of justice, the might of holiness, when Truth unarmed uplifts its head, and shows how awful goodness is ? Is there not the power that works for righteousness and the power that is righteousness at work?

All our natural life, of course, starts from the former, from the idea of physical power, which may or may not be brought into the service of justice ; and we have that conception of power fixed upon us by the start. When we begin to examine our notions we find that established in possession. So that justice at best is understood but socially—as natural happiness made general. Socialism is simply the Christianity of the natural man, the Church of the not yet born again. What is the idea, the expectation, by which natural men seek to judge if the course of the world is worthy of God, and the experience of life compatible with His goodness ? Is it not the idea of omnipotence for happiness—the unlimited power to possess and spread happiness. That is the standard of their theodicy. If my life, if multitudes of lives, are lamed or crushed by calamity how can I believe in a just, kind and omnipotent God ? This is the question of the natural man. The *métier* of a God is to use His omnipotence for human happiness of a high and wide sort. When this happiness seems to fail the result is scepticism and pessimism, more or less bitter. Think how the Lisbon earthquake of 1755 shattered the rational optimism of that thin time to start the deliberate pessimisms of to-day. It is the inevitable result of the attempt to measure the whole of anything so spiritual as life or God by its power to satisfy natural expectations. That is not God's prime object; it is not His regimen of the world in the final account he gives of Himself, His purpose, and His creature's destiny in the cross of Christ. His is not the omnipotence that natural happiness requires, far less that the natural imagination pictures; but it is the omnipotence that His own *holiness* requires, His own purpose not of love simply but of holy love, the omnipotence required by His own perfection, the omnipotence required to establish in the world as we find it, in a sinful world, a kingdom of complete communion with His Holy Self and His Eternal blessedness. All power in heaven and earth is delivered to the victorious *Holy* One, and to Him alone.

We thus begin with such notions of power as we imbibe from our first contact with it in natural force, elemental instincts, or imperious wills. And we carry that order into our thinking. We construe omnipotence accordingly. We form ideas of omnipotence which are suggested to us by nature, and then we demand that a revelation from God shall begin by accrediting itself to those natural notions—especially by some miracle. But we demand an impossible thing when we look for such a revelation in Christ—a human being omnipotent in that sense. A human being with natural omnipotence would

[Handwritten margin note at top: Two kinds of omnipotence, one in natural world, other in realm of moral]

be a monster. Christ did not come with natural omnipotence either for his weapon or for his credentials. He
did not come with a power of unlimited miracle, with a
blank cheque on the universal energy. His omnipotence was not of the kingdom of nature but of grace.
His power was both held and used under moral
conditions, as we see in the cases where it was arrested
by unbelief. He came much rather to convert that
natural method, nay to invert it. He revealed that
holiness *was* the divine power, and did not wait on
power; that the forces of creation had their end,
charter, and scope in a moral redemption, and they
could not exceed their terms of reference; that holiness,
that moral Godhead, could only establish itself in the
world by its own nature, and not by natural force; that
his Church could only be established by its Gospel, and
not by anything at the disposal of States, or at the
command of Empire. His kingdom was not of the world.
This principle gave rise to a struggle within Himself,
in the temptation He mastered; as it has done also
within His Church, in the temptation to which she
succumbed. The power He incarnated was the intrinsic,
supreme, and final power of divine conscience, that is, of
holy love, for the destiny of the world. This is the
true power of God which was incarnated in Christ—
this morally irresistible power of holy love.

In the natural, arbitrary, and unregenerate sense in
which we understand the word, God is not omnipotent.
All things do not work together for an omnipotent God,
but for love's good on God's scale, for an absolutely holy
purpose, to them that love God for His holy purpose
(Rom. viii. 28). At least the God of Christ is not omnipotent in any other sense than that. The God incarnate in

[Handwritten margin notes: Christ came not with natural omnipotence, was in realm of grace. Holiness is to be established by own nature, not by natural force]

Christ is not. He can do only the things that are congruous with His moral, His holy nature and purpose. But in this moral sense is he omnipotent over the world? Is he in final command of history? Is he secure of the reversion of time? Well, what omnipotence is required for that? Is it not the power of holiness, not to do anything and everything suggested by human egoism or fantasy, but to do everything required for its own effectual establishment on the world? The purpose of a world created by a holy God must be holiness, the reflection and communion of His own holiness. Can God secure it? What the world actually is we know, if we let our conscience speak its verdict on history. Is it in the power of the Holy God, through the very holiness smitten by our sin, to secure such a world's holy destiny still? That is the ultimate question in life. That is what, in one form or another, occupies the first-class minds. And to that question Christ and His cross are the answer, or they have no meaning at all. They reveal in their foregone victory the omnipotence of holiness to subdue all natural powers and forces, all natural omnipotence, to the moral sanctity of the Kingdom of God. And if they do not reveal that we are left without any ground of certainty about a holy ending for the world at all. And our guesses will be hopeful according to our sanguine temperament, our happy circumstances, our small insight, or our low demand. It is a tremendous revelation and achievement in the cross of Christ. "How awful goodness is." The more we know about cosmic forces, antres vast, deserts horrible, Alps of thick ribbed ice, seas, continents, vastitudes of every kind; of geological ages, stellar spaces, solar storms; of creature agonies, of social

miseries, devilish wickedness, civilised triumphs, historic
heroisms, the grandeur of genius and unquenchable love;
of all the passion, for evil on the one hand, or, on the
other, for the Eternal, Immortal, and Invisible good—
so much the more we must feel how awful is the holy
love of God, that has secured the grand issue for ever,
that surmounts all principalities and powers, things past,
present, and to come, every other omnipotence; surmounts, nay exploits, them all, in the Holy One of God,
who by His cross is the same world-conqueror yesterday,
to-day, and for ever. It is a tremendous claim. And
the improbability of it is either a pious absurdity; or it
is the quiet irony of a God who has it already done in
the hollow of His hand. Like every ultimate interpretation of life it is a matter of insight—insight into the
world, the Christ, and the Cross. What is lacking
to the seers and geniuses of our time, like Swinburne,
Meredith, or Hardy, is still lack of insight. They
see into "Love in the valley"—and how lovely—what
they do not see into is love *in excelsis*.

§   §   §

The formula of the union of two natures in one
person is essentially a metaphysical formula, and the
formula of a Hellenic metaphysic, and it is more or less
archaic for the modern mind. The term "nature" is a
purely metaphysical term, and one which characterises a
scholastic metaphysic of being rather than a modern metaphysic of ethic. The metaphysic of being, if not banished
from modern science, tends to be retained only in so far
as the moral is regarded as the real, and the key to being
is found in personality. Even if we do speak at all now of
two natures in one person the accent has moved from the
term nature to the term person. We start with the

R

historic reality and unity of Christ's person. We work with such ethical categories—with ideas like personality, history, and society. These are what command thought, rather than ideas like being, substance, or nature, wherever thought works out its new creation in Kant and comes to close quarters with life. Now the ideas of personality and society, which mean so much for history and religion, are condensed in such an idea as marriage, which is at once the keystone of society and the great symbol of Christ's relation to man. And in marriage the ideal is (however far we may be yet from its general realization) that of two personalities not only united but completely interpenetrating in love, and growing into one dual person. " The two shall be one flesh " —one spiritual personality. This interpenetration is something of which personality alone is capable. Any notion like " a nature " is too physical in its origin and action to rise really above the impenetrability of matter, and the mutual externality of each such nature. This is one reason why a union of natures complete enough for personal unity has been so hard to compass with the old metaphysic, which did not rise beyond a finer physic, or pass εἰς ἀλλὸ γένος. The marriage relation is the brief epitome of the social principle of the kingdom of God, of the unity of Christ, and the kind of unity in a Triune God. It is impossible to keep Trinity from Tritheism if we interpret personality by the categories of being or substance, instead of interpreting being by the categories of personality. A personality is much more than intelligent or conscious substance, however refined. In this sense personality has not a nature. We speak at times of Christ as being Himself the Kingdom of God ; and it is not the extravagant phrase that some minds declare it to be. At least it points to a social plurality in Him in whom His whole Church lives. Which is an idea of the same class as a divine dualism, the complete interpenetration, in that "public person," of human and divine personality. It suggests their interpenetration in a way of which wedlock gives the symbol or ideal, however far short it might fall as yet of being the actual analogy which it will one day become in the Christian evolution of society, and of thought to correspond. As the supreme human interests grow more ethical, as the ethical categories more and more come to dominate thought in a life whose first concern is personal action, by so much the more must the great problems that surround the historic Christ be handled on such congenial and fertile lines. The ethical notion of the true unity as the interpenetration of persons by moral action must take the place of the old metaphysic of the union of natures by a *tour de force*. Unity of being need not be denied, but it will be approached and construed on those ethical lines which alone consist with personal relation and explain it. The Church has worked long on the old lines which were laid down by pagan thought rather than by a final revelation in a person : perhaps, when we have worked in this new and living way as long, then we may expect results for which we are not yet prepared but which we can already forefeel along the line of the true method. The moral and experimental method in theology will give us, from its congeniality with the source of our revelation in a personal Saviour, results as great and commanding in their sphere as did the application of the other experimental method of induction so appropriate to natural science.

§　　§　　§

Taking this moral method we seem shut up to one of
two theories. If the incarnation was the result rather
than the cause of Christ's moral action then it was the
result either of a great and creative moral decision of his
before he entered the world—which preserves his pre-
existence, and seems to require some form of kenosis. Or
else it was the result of the continuous and ascending
moral action in his historic life, wherein his moral growth,
always in unbroken union with God, gave but growing
effect to God's indwelling; while the final and absolute
union took place when his perfect self-sacrifice in death
completed his personal development, and finally identified
him with God. So that we then have a progressive
incarnation of God and a progressive deification of man
in a rising scale of mutual involution; which requires
some form of adoptionism.

In either of these cases everything turns on moral
action (either in the world or before it), whose historic
consummation was in the cross and its redemption.
Either the cross was the nadir of that self-limitation
which flowed from the supramundane self-emptying of
the Son, or it was the zenith of that moral exaltation
which had been mounting throughout the long sacrifice
of his earthly life, it was the consummation of the progressive union of his soul and God. I do not see why
we may not combine the two movements, as I shall hope
to show. But in either case the supreme moral act of
the cross is the key to the nature of the process. There
the new moral value was really introduced into Humanity,
and if the incarnation did not take place for that purpose
it has no sense or end. The new element was introduced, it was not evolved. An evolutionary incarnation
is none; it is but blossom. The element of miracle

must be there.   And it was introduced by a moral
miracle and not a magical, a miracle corresponding to
the nature of moral freedom.   A moral end can only be
reached by moral means; and if the nature and end of
redemption be moral it means that the incarnation which
made it possible must be moral in its nature too.   No
moral redemption would be possible if the God who came
to do it did not assume his manhood by a moral miracle,
a miracle of grace, as real as that which finished it.   If
Christ began from a magical act, a prodigious act, a
mere exercise of power, as I have said the dogma* makes
him do, and if emphasis is removed from the atonement to
such an incarnation, as Catholicism tends to do, then it is
very hard to give real moral effect to his closing work.
And history has shown how hard it is.   Popular thought
at least is diverted from the cross to the cradle.   Evangelical belief, and especially Catholic belief, has had
many unsatisfactory ethical results.   Ecclesiastical ethic
is not always Christian ethic (to say the least).   And the
reason lies to a great extent in the incongruity between
the moral nature of the Church's Redemption and the
non-moral nature of the Incarnation which was offered
to explain it.   Since the incarnation lay interior and
fontal to the redemption, its metaphysical nature over-
bore the moral action of redemption, and much was
pardoned to the conscience of a man who assented to
the dogma.   It is often urged among ourselves that the
evangelical construction of Christ's death as atonement
is not as prolific as it should be of moral results—nay
that a certain moral obtuseness has too often gone with

---

* I might here beg that the difference be not overlooked between the
dynamic union of the two natures (of which I have spoken and which I
have chiefly here in view) and the miraculous birth.

evangelical orthodoxy and zeal.   That is not to be roundly denied.   In many quarters it is throwing men of the better (but hastier) sort upon a non-evangelical Christianity.   And the reason is that the atonement at the Church's centre is not conceived in truly ethical terms.   It is not grasped as the focus and spring of all the divinest ethic of the conscience, and therefore of the world. And the reason why it is not so grasped is that its truly moral and evangelical interpretation, as adjusting the conscience directly with a perfectly holy God, has been alloyed with mediæval, Catholic, and dynamic notions of incarnation.   These being more metaphysical than moral, arrest its ethical effect, and divide the unity of the divine action in Christ.   The Reformers, with all their new departure in the *religion* of Redemption and Justification, took over the substance of the old *theology* about the divine nature that gave Christ His redeeming power. With all their moralising of the close of Christ's life they did not duly moralise its beginning, or the heavenly act which preceded and prescribed its beginning.   And so we have a paralysing division down the middle of the divine action in Christ.   We have the ethical effect of Christ on man crossed by an initiative on God's side, when Christ left heaven, which was more metaphysical or miraculous than it was moral.   And the two disparate things much confuse that general Christian mind, or ethos, from which, more than from individual conviction, so much of our Christian ethic proceeds.   Christ could only redeem into God's holiness if it were from the act of that holiness that he came : he could only create a holy ethic if it was in the holiest of acts that his creative life and work arose.   The moral problem set in our need of salvation can only be solved by a moral movement in

the God who undertook it.   A redemptive work is moral
or nothing.   But if its first ·condition is an incarnation
made possible only by such an act of power as underlies
the union of natures into a composite person, then the
redemption is unreal.   It is a phantasmagory.   If it was
the mere possession of a divine nature and a rank worthy
to atone that gave Christ His saving power, if it was not
the moral quality of his action in the doing of it (either
on earth, or in heaven before coming to earth), then his
work has a moral discount which is bound to reduce the
value of its practical effect, if not to turn it to an
unreality.   If his conquest of our moral weakness was
not a victory of his own moral strength, but merely the
power or strategy of a Miltonic omnipotence getting the
better of the prince of this world, can we wonder that
the moral effect on us of such a trial of strength between
two giants is qualified ?   Theories of incarnation which
make all turn on the natural omnipotence or omniscience
of the Redeemer are beside the mark.   It was not the
rank or power of the Redeemer that made his death
precious for redemption, but his worth.   It was his
moral value as the Holy that gave him power, both with
God and man, to prevail.   It was his holiness, with
which the Holy Father was perfectly pleased and
satisfied.   That is the only Christian doctrine of satisfaction.   If the incarnation was not above all things a
moral achievement by God the redemption cannot be a
moral conquest of man.   The divine coming and action is
then magic, however exalted or massive.   And revelation
becomes not the self-donation of God in sacrifice, but a
phantasmagory, a transparency, a placard (Gal.iii.1),which
leaves the conscience untouched, though it may move the
imagination to the most magnificent ritual in the world,
and the intellect to the most architectonic orthodoxy.

THE MORALISING OF DOGMA, ILLUSTRATED
BY THE ABSOLUTENESS OF CHRIST

LECTURE IX

THE MORALISING OF DOGMA, ILLUSTRATED BY THE ABSOLUTENESS OF CHRIST

I HAVE been speaking of the moralising of dogma. I applied that method by saying that the cross of our redemption was the historic origin of the theology of the incarnation ; that by the cross also it passes back from a theological conviction to a life experience; and that the practical value of the incarnation lies in its being the necessary foundation of the cross. It is when we are remade at the cross that our eyes are opened to see at its base the door and the stair that lead down to the incarnation at the foundation of our moral world. Christ's self-consciousness of His own divine nature must (I have said) be very powerful for our theological conviction. The value of the apostolic inspiration, (I have added), cannot be much less for the same purpose. But it is the new creation in the cross that translates the belief into spiritual life, and indeed makes that life, by making Christ the element of our own final spiritual consciousness. I would now farther illustrate the moralising of dogma, first in regard to theological dogma, by continuing to dwell on the cross as the avenue to the

incarnation and the incarnation as the foundation of
the cross; and second, in regard to philosophic dogma,
by translating the doctrine of the absolute into the
terms of religious experience.

§   §   §

It does not matter what happens to any creeds or
orthodoxies on this subject, if we but get at the truth.
Let us not resolve beforehand that it is impossible to
modify the old confessions, or to resume, after a slack
interval, the long movement of the Church's thought
to pierce and clarify the mystery of godliness in Christ.
Let the doctrine be reconstructed, reinterpreted, re-
stated—what you will.   Provided two things.   First that
the task be publicly essayed by competent and reverent
people and not by amateurs, with but a natural religion
and a poor education or none on the subject; for the
worst heresy is quackery.   Indeed, the work can really
be done only by the collective Church in earnest faith,
working on the contributions of individuals intellectually
equipped and morally serious.   And, second, provided
that what is aimed at is religious truth, which is so
much more than the results of severe historical criticism; truth as it is in Jesus and not about Jesus; truth
which is the Church's supernatural faith giving a
rational account of itself; the truth of a faith which is
not natural religion, but an invasion of the natural
man, and an enclave in the course of history; the order
of truth which has made Christ what he has been to
the Church and the soul.   That is not necessarily the
truth exactly as the Church has formulated it, the
truth as stated in the Church's conception, or dogma;
but it is the substantial, distinctive, and evangelical truth
of the Church's experience; the truth, operative however

conceived, which has made Christ for his Church something totally different from what Buddha is for his Church;
the truth of the dogmas in distinction from the dogmas
as true.

§   §   §

The Church has always held fast to the formula about
"the Eternal Godhead in Jesus Christ." What is
under that phrase? Surely it means more than that Jesus
himself was but a unique human personality, and that
the divine element in him was the presence or Spirit
of the Father, dwelling in him as in us, only more so;
to whom he was completely sensitive; with whom he
was filled, in the affectional sense in which one personality may be said to fill another, through love's
saturation and obsession?

Does the Godhead in Christ mean only that the
Father was in the closest communion of affection with
Christ's human personality? Or does it not mean that
the personality that met the Father so completely was
itself of the nature of Godhead, and always had been
a divine *vis-a-vis* to the personality of the Father? Only
in the latter case should we really speak of the deity of
Christ; only if he was the Ego in some form of the
Eternal Son; only if he was increate, and had a share
which God could delegate to no creature in the creation
of the world, a share in the world's origin as real as
his part in its Redemption, Reconciliation, and Consummation.

To compare great things with small, that powerful
genius Emily Brontë makes the heroine in Wuthering
Heights to say, "I *am* Heathcliffe. He is always, always
in my mind; not as a pleasure, any more than I am
always a pleasure to myself; but as my own being." Borne

on the current of her passion, she goes on to say, " I
love him because he is more myself than I am.   Whatever our souls are made of, his and mine are the same."
And did not the insight of the Church go on to say the
like *sub specie eternitatis* of the Son's relation to the
Father? Is unity of being not the postulate of a love so
engrossing and complete as the genius of the Church's
faith realised that of Father and Son to be ? It is
not only in theology that passion gravitates to metaphysic.   We need but remember also Shakespeare's
sonnets and minor poems to feel that.

It would be better method (and better ethic as well)
if we confined the expression " Christ's Godhead, deity,
or even divinity," to the more thorough-going idea.
There is nothing so necessary to belief and its moral
purposes as more clearness, courage, and conscience in
deciding what we mean by terms.   The chief plague
and heresy of the hour in this region is that with the
popularising of religion God tends to become the most
fluid of all words.   The prime certainty becomes the
great haze.   The living God becomes but as the ether
of life.   He pervades, but he does not purpose.   He
saturates all, but all does not centre in him.   Discussion
thus becomes impossible, from the fact that the intellectual conscience grows damp and limp in the mist.
Terms become so liquid that they run into any mould,
and are sometimes no more tractable than a cloud that
you cannot even mould.   The intellectual ethic of
some to-day would ruin them if it took a commercial
instead of a mental form.   Clear, strong and honest
heresy is a negative contribution to clear and strong
belief.   But heresy in rolling cloud is only stifling,
depressing, and demoralising.

§   §   §

The Godhead of Christ can only be proved religiously.
Indeed, the only true confession of the Incarnation is
living faith.   It can only be based on what is involved in
the idea, the experience, of God that proceeds from Jesus
himself.   Is He necessary to the being of the God He
revealed?   If we do not regard Jesus and his full gospel
as God's supreme revelation, as God's ultimate word,
there can be no talk of his Godhead.   If we do not
bring all other religious truth to this test; if we place
above Christ's word those ideas of God which we
draw from the world of nature or reason, those conceptions of Absoluteness, Omnipotence, and the rest
which would be called common-sense notions; if we
take from these, and not from Jesus, our notion of
what God is—then we shall very likely fail in proving
his Godhead.   If we seek in Jesus absolute power, in
the natural sense of the word, we shall not find
it.   If we decree beforehand that God is not present
where omniscience is not in evidence we shall drop
the question about Godhead in Jesus.   But absolute
Omnipotence or Omniscience is no direct part of a
saving revelation.   Absolute power and authority indeed
belongs to Godhead, but it is not the whole of it, it is
not the outgoing element in it, which is love.   And an
incarnation may be possible of that element in Godhead
which rather represents absolute obedience, and absolute
holiness of response.   That element of subordination
and sacrifice must be there surely.   For if there be in
Godhead absolute authority it is hard to conceive of it
without thinking of absolute obedience as there also;
unless the obedience cease to be correlative with the
authority, unless authority once existed without obedi-

ence, unless there could be an Eternal Father with but a temporary son, unless obedience be an undivine thing, and the only divine thing is to lord it, and to wrap one's self in conscious power with no outgoing love. And then where is our Christian ethic, or the real divineness of humility? And then why should Nietzsche not be the true prophet, and a *deus humilis* a mere figment fostered by the weak majority to strengthen their case and better their lot?

The self-consciousness of Jesus I have indicated as being of immense value here; but how do we know that his God was not a figure in the window and his Father his dream? His self-consciousness taken alone is only a historic datum. We must have something that turns that past to our perpetual present. We must have the Lord, the Spirit. To the evangelical experience, that Jesus becomes our present Saviour; and such a Christ, who has become our experienced Salvation, is certainly involved in his own God. Christ can only save if we have God saving in him. A theology of incarnation must be a theology of the saved. The fulcrum of any vital doctrine about the person of Christ must be an experimental faith in him as Redeemer. Christ is very God to me because, and only because, he has been God's saving grace to me a sinner; He has not simply preached it, or brought it. We cannot convince the man in the street that Jesus is God, nor the man that feeds his soul on modern culture. We do not go to the world of the hearty, alert, interesting, rational man, even when he has developed some religious attention and some theological curiosity; we do not go to the ordinary able man and propose to convince him by argument, consecutive, cumulative, or convergent, that

We do not try to convince men by argument that Jesus was God, but by experiential faith resulting from redemption.

Jesus was God. That would be to attempt the impossible. It would mean that we could have no real
faith in a moral atonement till we were first convinced
of a rational incarnation. And it would mean, as I
have said, that we set about proving that Jesus
possessed the qualities which the natural man of
common-sense, or of common-sense organised into a
philosophy, associates with the idea of God—a supreme
Being, all-knowing, all-present, all-blessing, capable of
all prodigies. No such attempt could succeed. Indeed
it can easily seem absurd. And apart from the incongruity of attaching these qualities to a historic
personality, no such claim is made in the New Testament.
It does not offer an omnipotent Christ or an intellectual
paragon. Its appeal is not to the average rational man.
That would be a legalist and not a gospel appeal. To
reject the New Testament appeal is not stupid, not
irrational, as the cheap apologists are prone to say.
The appeal is not made to the shrewd and logical; it is
made to the heart and conscience in a real experience;
and to neither of these acting normally, but to an
abnormal and concerned condition of both. It is made
to men created for love who yet do not or cannot love,
to men created for goodness who are in sin, and who are
either uneasy or miserable in it, or too lost to be either.
The need to which Christianity appeals is the need of
the conscience, its supreme need of grace from the God
whose holiness troubles its days or oppresses its nights.
And the first condition to be satisfied by any doctrine
about Christ's person is that it shall be necessary to the
central principle of Christianity that 'in Christ we have
a gracious God.' Not that we have such a God through
Christ, but that in having Christ we have Him. That

s

is the marrow of Christianity, running through Paul, Athanasius, Anselm, Luther, Schleiermacher, Wesley, and indeed all the great evangelic and apostolic succession.   The sum of a religion of commandment, of a legal religion, may be the mere love of God and love of man.   But Christianity is not a legal religion, and such love, though not far from the Kingdom, was yet outside it (Mk. xii. 34). There is no real faith in the Godhead of Christ apart from the evangelical experience of God's gracious love of us.   And that experience has always required behind it, for its full force, a real incarnation.   The pre-existence of the Son of God who became incarnate in Jesus has always been considered requisite for the evangelical faith of the Church, the faith that God in the cross really forgave and saved, and that he was not merely believed and declared to have done so, even by the greatest of all prophets and the holiest of all saints, Jesus.   We should be clear about the issue.   Even a Roman Church that worships Christ, has a social and a spiritual future denied to a rational creed that but admires and honours Him.   (Christianity is either Evangelical or Socinian at last.   And if it is not the latter it must stand on the fact that the God we sinned against was in Christ, really forgiving the sinner at first hand, that Godhead was actually living in Christ and reconciling—not sending, visiting, moving, or inspiring Christ, but living in Him and constituting Him. Certainly more than inspiring Him, for it is a poor response to the history to think of Christ simply as inspired, or visited by a Spirit which came and went. And I have tried to show that we cannot think of Him adequately as tenanted by the Spirit, even in an abiding way—as a created personality quite filled, and always filled, with the influence of the Spirit, always and perfectly answering the Spirit. We may of course reject the apostolic interpretation and follow a different line from the New Testament. And we may justify ourselves in doing so by various considerations—when we do consider. But if we follow the New Testament as a whole and as a Gospel, we must think of the divine element as constituting the historic personality; and we must think of Christ's earthly life itself, with all its passion and choice, as due to a great and critical volition of the same will in a heavenly state. That is a view essential to apostolic Christianity, and one of the facts which it believes to be of first necessity for the redeeming work which is Christianity, and which created the Church. In the Bible men are preoccupied with the reality of an incarnation whereof all the pagan ideas and legends about gods descending and walking the earth were but presentiments, adumbrations, prophecies, and even prayers for it. Those Judaistic notions of Messiah, Redemption, Expiation, and all the train of ideas which the religious historical school use to dissolve Christianity into a very effective syncretism, were really a part of that providential *preparatio evangelica* which fell into place and found itself in Christ.

So, when we base our belief in the Incarnation on the Evangelical experience that is a case of the moralising of dogma in the theological plane.

§   §   §

I wish now to illustrate the process of moralising dogma by applying it in the Christological interest to another dogma than omnipotence, the philosophic dogma of the Absolute.*

* For the moralising of such a doctrine as Atonement may I refer to my little book *The Cruciality of the Cross* (Hodder & Stoughton, 1909), and especially its last part.

What is most keenly discussed in many cultured circles at present is the *Absoluteness of Christianity*. What does that really mean? Has it any meaning for the Church and its preachers? It does not, cannot, mean that a philosophical Absolute can be proved by the Christian revelation in a systematic way which compels theoretic conviction. It does not mean that Christian theologians profess to have solved the problem in which Hegel failed. They have indeed a solution to the world; but not to the same version of its question as the philosophers put. The idea of the Absolute has for us not a philosophic but a religious, practical, experimental value. It really means, in more familiar language, *the finality of Christ* for the experience of life and reality—the soul's last reality. That is the form which the truth of the incarnation assumes in face of the challenge that marks the present day. The insight this luminous age lacks is insight into the greatest moral fact of history—into Christ. What we need, what preachers of all men need, is not so much affection to Christ but insight into Christ. That is the Church's need, however it may be with individuals. It is not impression but inspiration. Christianity must stand or fall by an insight which discerns the finality of Christ as to life and its destiny. And, from what I have already said as to the place and function of the cross, you will not be surprised if I say now that this finality of Christ is the same thing as used to be described as his " finished work," his transfer of Humanity, for good and all, from death to life in relation to God. It is always the cross that is the offence to the world. It may be the philosophic world of Hegel with its Absolute; or the "gothic" world of Nietzsche, Henley, Shaw, Kipling, Davidson or Wells with its superman, its assertion of the

individual and his instincts, its cult of the violent life,
and its protest against humility, sacrifice, poverty,
chastity, or obedience.   Or it may arrest the natural
healthy world of comfort and success.   The only authoritative ethic in the face of these egoisms and subjectiv-
isms is one that is based on the finality of the
historic Christ and his redemption.   We are in a world
which has been redeemed; and not in one which is being
redeemed at a pace varying with the world's thought and
progress, or the Churches' thought and work.   To believe
that the kingdom has come is another religion from the
belief that it is but coming and that we have to bring it.
It produces a totally different type of faith and life.   And
it is the only type that can save Christianity from being
politicised, socialised, and secularised out of existence.
And I would say three things about this belief, of which
that matter of experience is the first.*

§   §   §

(1) For Christianity the Absolute is not in an idea but
in an experience.   It is a layman's matter.   It is the very
soul of our universal faith.   It is the affair of every man,
if his eternal soul is worth more than all the relative
world.   It has little directly to do with the results of
speculation or of comparative religion.   Our absolute is
not the last common summit of all thought; for we do
not rally about a minimal point of light that shines dear in
the sky for all quarters, like the pole-star for the sea, or the
shining Fusiyama for Japan.   Not is it the least common
denominator of all faiths; for we are not united most by
the thin thread of belief which divides us least.   Of
course, a philosophic Absolute cannot be out of relation

---

* See Hunziger *Probleme*, p. 79, for much that follows.

to the Christian God; and there is a metaphysic of faith;
but it is not the Gospel that Christianity brings, nor the
claim it makes.   The Gospel does not say that all religions are right with their claim to be absolute, right in
the sense that they all bring us to contact with the
Absolute in differing degrees, though none finally—not
even Christianity.   That relativism rests on a conception
of the Absolute somewhat abstract and formal—too much
so for the faith of a living and eternal soul, or for its
trust of itself to a living and eternal God.   The Christian claim to absoluteness is a thing of more depth,
breadth, and volume than that—more simple, vital, and
passionate.   It has more flesh, blood, content and conscience.   For, among faiths, there is in Christianity a
difference which is qualitative and not merely gradual, a
difference in kind and not in degree only.   Christianity
does bring us into contact with the Absolute God—like
other religions; but (if the phrase were allowed) it does
so absolutely and finally.   The other religions had a real
message; Christianity has something beyond a message
more real still.   They all told us truth with whatever
error; Christianity goes beyond a gift of more truth and
less error.   Christianity takes us out of the formal region
of truths more or less true; it takes us out of the region
even of absolute truth, truth absolutely true, out of
mere theology.   Its revelation is the gift of a true
God, not of truth about God.   So long as truth is
propositional or formal, so long as it is any kind of
statement, however exalted and kindled, about God,
it is below the kind of absolute that the soul requires, that life requires, that the world requires.
Christianity gives us a new and absolute *life*, an absolute,
not in form or truth, but in content and experience.   It

does not give us anything about God, but it gives God Himself—the living God to living men.   Its revelation is not doctrinal but sacramental.   And in its light—in its psychology if you will—we can interpret all other faiths. We then see that the vital thing in every religion is not an innate evolutionary movement towards an absolute God, but the absolute God breaking in upon the spiritual consciousness, breaking up through it in essential miracle. The foundation of the whole world emerges in the moral and religious life of the soul, takes command, and anchors us upon something which Eternity cannot shake.   For this *is* Eternity.

§   §   §

(2) For the absoluteness of Christianity lies in an experience of the historic and most human Christ as a superhuman visitant, and as the one moral mediator of personal communion with the living, and holy, and eternal God.   It is an experience of Christ as the absolute conscience, *i.e.*, as the judge of all, and as the Redeemer, *i.e.*, the saving health of all—in a word, as the God of all.   It means that the person and work of Christ alone gives the moral soul to itself.   He does for us the ultimate thing of the soul, its one thing needful.   He gives it its own eternal place and communion with an absolutely holy God.   God is the only world in which the soul can find itself.   Christ gives us our God and our soul at once. God finds us and we find God.   In Christ the end of all makes himself in his love the means to that end.   What is there to be done beyond that, when that is done on the scale of the race?   To be in living, loving, holy communion with the living, loving, holy God for ever is the soul's perfect consummation and final bliss. And that is Christ's gift.   What do we want, what

can we conceive, in any farther revelation? We are here at a finality and its rest. Endless discovery, of course, remains, endless explication within the gift unspeakable; but in the way of revelation what more is possible than that God should in his love give Himself to man completely, though not at any point exhaustively? What more can we pray than that He should give us his whole and holy self, and so bring us to our true and whole self? And this in Christ, to the classic religious experience of the race, He has done. The point, you perceive, is not that this is what a final revelation *would* do if we had reached it, but that this is what God in Christ has done and does. That is the real issue of the hour. Not, Is Christ *a* revelation of God? but, Is he *the* revelation, the final and complete revelation, of which all that we may call revelation besides is but a factor? Most whom we need here consider admit that Christ is a revelation of God; but all do not admit that he is the final revelation, that we have in him God Himself, and the whole Eternal God, with His last word, with man's last judgment, his last justification, his last destiny. This is a matter which cannot be settled by proofs or evidences of Christ's deity, but only by experience—the soul's experience of eternal Redemption in a Church of souls. There is no basis for a belief in the Incarnation but this basis of faith. Nor is there any other basis for certainty of the world's final good. The poet trusts that somehow good will be the final goal of ill; the believer knows that this is how it must be so, for so it is.

§　　§　　§

(3) The final thing, the Absolute, in Christianity is the experience not simply of contact with Christ, not simply of a revelation given, nor even of a deliverance wrought,

[handwritten marginalia: Creator of new life]

but of a new creation effected in Christ. The Son is as creative as the Father. What he brings is not a revelation which can be tested by the formal tests of truth, and called final by its coincidence with a final philosophy— a philosophy of the Absolute. That was the dangerous method of the early Apologists. It was a dream which misled many a century ago to think that Hegel's philosophy, as the last word of thought, had countersigned for the moderns Christ's revelation as the word of God; with such a reference the Gospel was good for any amount for which we might draw on it. But the final thing in Christianity is an experience in which Christ is not simply the ideal nor the channel, but the creator of the new man. He is the real principal, and not a mere intermediary. In his person we have the permanent divine ground of our communion with God, and not merely its divine agent once. The work of Christ is the work of a Christ eternally working for us. If we are brought to God by the historic Christ we go on to find that we remain in God only as we abide in the same Christ as the Eternal Son. It has been so found in the history of the Church. It is on the ground of Christ that we are forgiven, daily forgiven, it is not simply by means of Christ. He is not the ground of our trust simply but of our salvation—not an *Erkentnissgrund* but a *Realgrund*. The means is in him identical with the end. He is God dealing with men directly, though mediatorily. Now I beg you here not to say such words are meaningless. That they are not; for the thing has been often said, and by the greatest. And no one is entitled to deny it till he has grasped the meaning, and is sure on good ground it is wrong. God in Christ deals with men directly but mediatorily. He is the Mediator and

not the medium, not the agent.   Buddha was a divine
agent.   Can we refuse to say he had a commission from
God?   But Christ is the offended Holiness itself exer-
cising forgiveness and salvation; and doing so in such a
way as to set up, not recognition, not belief, not welcome
even, but communion—on the scale of the race and of
Eternity.   To be in Christ is to be in God.   He is not
the herald of God's will but God's will in action, God's
final will in universal action on me; and so acting on
me as not simply to impress me but so as to remake
me, and thus build every soul into an everlasting kingdom.   It is not a new mood, or a new conviction he
gives me, but a new life, an Eternal Life, a new world, my
Eternity, my own Eternity, destined, forfeit, and restored.
There is nothing more left for God to give man, but the
appropriation, in experience and in detail, of this one and
final gift of Himself in Christ and his Eternal Life.   For
if there be a Mediator in this sense there can only be one.
He can have no successor.

§   §   §

It is a mighty matter to have to do with, a vast venture
and committal to make, when we put our soul in
Christ's hands for God and for Eternity, and when we
take in him the Almighty and Eternal into our soul.   It
is a step for good and all.   We risk all we have on that
pearl.   We sell all we have to buy it.   It is a tremendous
assertion we make when we go to the world with Christ.
How true it is that society to day needs nothing so
much as the lost sense of God in its midst—holy,
judging, amazing, terrifying, comforting, healing us.
There are those who while they feel that feel it so poorly
and unworthily that they think it can be recovered by
literature, or the stage, or some such mop for the Atlantic.

But is there any way to set God in the midst but His own way of setting Christ there ? It is a tremendous thing to go to the world with our Christ, and to many a pretty wit a thing ridiculous and despicable. I do not wonder people do not believe us. Christ Himself was disbelieved, and he grows credible but slowly. I cannot myself claim to have been free born in this faith ; with a great price have I procured its freedom. I have envied those who took naturally and sweetly to Christ—though they have helped me little. And I should count a life well spent, and the world well lost, if, after tasting all its experiences, and facing all its problems, I had no more to show at its close, or carry with me to another life, than the acquisition of a real, sure, humble, and grateful faith in the Eternal and Incarnate Son of God. All is still well if the decay of everything else but fertilise the knowledge of him (Phil. iii. 8). Only, let us not increase the difficulty by misunderstanding. It is indeed a tremendous thing to say that the historic Christ outweighs all the world, the race, its possibilities and its development. Think of the range of history, the dimensions of the Cosmos. Tell over in your imagination the whole population of earth, past, present, and to come. Conceive what it is when we learn that it would take an express train 114 millions of years to the nearest star. And Christ outweighs all that cosmic greatness ! It is beyond flesh and blood to believe it. But do not let us misconceive the terms of the demand. Do not let us succumb to mere bigness. There is no religion in an infinite merely extended, but only in an absolutely holy love. We do not weigh Christ against a numerical race, but a fallen. And we do not mean that Christ was as the end of all development ; for the development *in* Christ is far greater than the

development *to* Him.   He is God's seventh and last day,
in which we men for ever live and grow. No stage, no form
is final. As mere history Christianity is not imperfectible.
What is final is intra-historic, super-historic. That is the
real *continuum*. It is Eternal Life. But that means much
more than an indestructible spiritual energy with endless
power to vary. All the variations are on a fixed theme.
It is more than the mere spiritual vitality upon which
the Catholic Modernists seem to stand as the essence of
the Church. It is a positive work, word, and message.
It is not the vitality of the Church but the holy will of God
in Christ. The Lord is the Spirit. God is Spirit. Yes,
but a cognisable spirit with inalienable features—a Holy
Spirit. Christ is not a will that might decree anything,
but God's holy will in action for our Salvation, His will
as His saving self, His will as Himself and not a function
of Himself.

§   §   §

What is meant then is that as (in Butler's great
saying) "morality is the soul of things," with Christ we
have all things in principle, that the gift is for ever
compendious and insuperable. It means that the gift,
Christ, has a supernatural history not only after it,
but before it and in it, that it is an eternal act and deed
in a historic soul ; that it has in it the final power not
only to enter history mightily but, being there, to
subdue all things to itself, to compel, monopolise,
and consummate history, and so to grow to the goal
latent in its own increate beginning. It is meant that,
as in creation this world is given in its own plane of
Time once for all, so, on the second and eternal plane,
the spiritual and heavenly world is given once for all in
the New Creation in Christ. Christ works upon man

with the same absolute creative power as the Father
does; that is the meaning of the Godhead of Christ.
We do not indeed attain once for all, but we are
apprehended once for all. We do not mean that our
religion is final, but that God's revelation is. The
religion must grow; but its growth is in the power of
appropriating its own finality—as Christ himself did,
in becoming what he always was. We have an absolute
revelation but not an absolute religion. We have in
Christ an absolute grace, crucial for God, which we meet
with an appropriate faith, crucial for the soul. God's gift
is the Eternal Act; our taking or refusing it is our
eternal doom. It is the issue of Eternal Life or Death.
Yet we only gradually become conscious how final, how
crucial for Eternity, the faith is that meets a grace so
free. But that slowness matters less; because it is our
revelation we have to preach and not our religion, it is
our Christ and not our faith, our word and not our
sermons. We have to preach God and not advertise
Him. The gospel still means far more for God than the
martyrs do; and the redeeming Christ is more than the
confessing Church. In Christ we have the whole of God,
but not everything about God, the whole heart of God but
not the whole range of God. We have the final kind of
God but not the final compass of God, the kind and will of
God that history cannot supersede; the whole counsel of
God but not all his counsels; all God but not yet all good.

But with even that qualification it is a mighty matter
to believe. *Magna ars est conversari cum Deo.* It is the
greatest thing in the world. And in two ways it is this
vital thing. It is vital in the sense of being a matter of
life and experience. And it is vital in the sense of being
essential to the life of Christianity in the world, and
decisive for the destiny of the soul.

LECTURE X

THE PRE-EXISTENCE OF CHRIST

LECTURE X

THE PRE-EXISTENCE OF CHRIST

To explain Christ and his final work there were two
ideas current in the early Church—his Virgin Birth and
his Pre-existence.

It is possible, of course, to hold both of these. But
the temper and tendency of our time is against the old
emphasis on the former, especially on critical grounds;
and more particularly because of its absence in cases
where, as in St. Paul, all turns on the uniqueness of
Christ's nature and origin. It is to be noted also that
were the Virgin birth beyond historic criticism it might
not by itself give us a pre-existent Christ, and it need
not give us more than an Arian. It might indicate no
more than a supreme son of God *created* then or before
through the Holy Ghost for the special purpose of a
sinless redemption.

If, however, we relax the emphasis on the Virgin Birth
we must increase it upon the pre-existence, as St. Paul
did.

And we are the more moved to this since, while Jesus
makes no sort of reference to his human birth, sat very
loose to family ties, and rebuked, and even renounced,

T

his mother in a way (Mk. iii. 21, 31) hard to adjust to the current hypothesis, yet it is difficult to remove from him entirely all reference to his pre-existence. Were these ample and explicit, of course, were his own consciousness of an antenatal life put beyond doubt, any difficulties of ours would be quite minor as to how such a life became possible in human conditions. Questions as to the psychology of the kenotic act could well wait, if we were perfectly sure from such a source as Christ's own words about its reality.

But the pre-existence of Jesus is one of those points where, in the present state of opinion about the fourth gospel, modern thought is apt to feel insecure from lack of express data and from distrust of theological venture. Faith is too timid to-day to stray far from the shore lights of explicit statement, to launch out into the deep things of God, and sail by observation of the heavens. It asks, where are we told this or that? Such non-theological religion can do but a coasting trade. You have the same textual habit of mind both in the hard believers and the hard critics. A verbal Scripturalism has gone, but it has given way to another kind, which has not ceased to be narrow by becoming critical, and has not become really liberal just by ceasing to be literal. There is a mental cramp, and certainly an imaginative, which too easily besets the meticulous scholar. And it is a poor exchange to fall out of the hands of the theologian, narrow as his imagination could be, into those of the critic, narrow as he can be for lack of any imagination at all. There is an amplitude and an atmosphere about the great dogmatists of theology which is absent from the dogmatists of research. These have the great way with them. The great theologies are epics, with a fascination for

Miltonic minds. In their sphere they have the scientific
imagination so praised by Tyndall, and the cosmic
emotion which W. K. Clifford pursued. And in matters
of the soul it is better to have the dogma of the tele-
scope than that of the microscope. It is better to
have the dogma of Melanchthon, or even Calvin, than of
Wellhausen or Schmiedel (whom I name with due respect
for the great work they represent). The one has the
positivity of infinite revelation, the other the positivism
of the present age. The one descends from the great
sky like a bride adorned, the other struggles from the dust,
with clipped wings and short strokes, to meet a Lord
too much in the air. Each is a dogmatism; but the one
dogmatism represents, in forms now partly obsolete, the
spacious consciousness of a whole living and believing
Church, gathering up the best thought of its age; the
other betrays the straitened and esurient air of a
scientific school whose thought does not feed its soul.
There is much in the old dogmatism that needs correction, and there is much in the new mind to correct it.
But how much needs chastening in the new may be
exemplified in the warped and rash acumen of those
critics who venture to assure us, for instance, that it is
now proved that Jesus never claimed to be the judge of
mankind. And this is done in face of the patent fact
that among critics quite as competent there is an equally
decided conviction the other way. In several such cases
we feel how much truth there is in the observation made
by a liberal theologian. " It is remarkable how often
men who can set out admirably the thought of the past
show themselves quite incapable of understanding the
features of their present." The scholar, the historian,
submerges the thinker. Harnack, for instance, is much

Hanrock
great histo-
rian but
not so great
a historian
(theologian

more happy in dealing with the history of Christianity than with its essence. He is a great historian, and a valuable apologist; but as a theologian he is—not so great. And yet the half-taught mind concludes that eminence in the one direction makes a man an authority in the other. It really takes a great deal of theology to revolutionise theology.

§　§　§

I may illustrate what I mean by the treatment of a passage which is of great moment for the question that engages us. The allusion by St. Paul to the pre-existence and kenosis of the Son in Phil. 2, is almost a ἅπαξ λεγόμενον, (except 2 Cor. viii. 9.) Now what is the interpretation put on that fact, that singularity, by the extreme critics?

There are two possible. We may think that such an allusion is but a brilliant flash that looked in upon the writer's mind only to be mentioned and then to vanish without settling in his thought. It is a mere happy thought, an injected parenthesis, a jewel dropped on the way by a rich and lavish mind, too urgent in his spiritual flight to stop and recover it up for further use. The rarity of reference is then interpreted as a sign of the comparative eccentricity of the idea in the writer's mind. Or, on the other hand, we may be more impressed by the weight of the reference than by its rarity. We may think that the isolation and length of the passage in a practical book is due to its greatness. We may recall that the whole New Testament (and especially the Epistles) is occasional in its nature, much of it pastoral, edificatory, intending Church business and not theological system. St. Paul was not what orthodoxy made Luther—a professor of Dogmatics. The theology comes in by the way, as the ground of the religious or moral appeal. However fundamental, it is allusive and incidental; it is not dwelt upon in that proportion to its intrinsic value which it would have if the writer kept chiefly in view the majesty and proportion of Christian truth.

Now of these two possible views about rarity of reference, the tendency of mere criticism is to prefer the former. The latter requires a finer, ampler, literary instinct, a more imaginative psychology, a judgment more sympathetic and flexible, with more spiritual *savoir faire*. The critical tendency is to say that the idea in question counts for little in St. Paul because it is a passing allusion. This is an inference the more strange from men who otherwise depreciate the Apostle as a systematiser, and find his greatness in the suggestive wealth, the vistas, of his experiential thought.

There are other instances. It is held to be a mere theologoumenon, for instance, to say that in his death Christ really judged and executed the sinful principle, paralysed it at the core of human nature and history, and broke the heart of its objective power; on the ground that St. Paul, the great expositor of his death, seems only to allude to it in a parenthetic reference to the action of his sacrifice as "condemning sin in the flesh." The development of the idea in the fourth Gospel seems overlooked—the destroying of the prince of this world.

And the tendency I am speaking of, this quantitative criticism, this concordance criticism, reaches a climax when it is applied to Christ's own references to his pre-existence or his atoning death in the Synoptics. Because they are few, therefore they are comparatively insignificant. They are few, it is said, because the matter did not bulk in Christ's own consciousness. But a criticism with some psychological imagination may suggest another interpretation. They may be few just because they bulked *unspeakably* in Christ's mind. His thoughts about his death were unutterable, except in an act; just as in the Last Supper, when all his teaching had failed, he resorts to what Keim so finely calls "his last parable," the object lesson, the enacted revelation, finished in the supreme ἅπαξ λεγόμενον of the cross, (which is also ignored by much criticism). These thoughts were too great and engrossing to be spoken of, especially to his dull entourage. "How am I straitened." Too straitened in doing the thing, when it came to a head, to be other than silent about it. The captain is not loquacious in the rapids. He does not talk about seamanship in the storm. The pilot does not teach navigation in shooting a savage bar. Remember, moreover, that the first bearing of Christ's great and crowning action was upon God and not man. He was adjusting the relation between God and man, and not impressing individuals, or doing a thing calculated to impress posterity with a religious message in a religious way. He was dealing with God for the race. Hence, as the crisis deepened, his words and thoughts were oblivious of men and their reception of Him, and engrossed with what he was doing with God. If his supreme object was to act on men, the ἅπαξ λεγόμενα on the inmost matters are not intelligible. They are inadequate for the purpose.

The more rare the reference the more seminal it may be, and often has been. Isaiah 53 is quite unique in the Old Testament. Yet one might venture to say it is *the* passage in the Old Testament which is the link with the

New, yea, the germ of it, and the passage, which has most affected the conception of the most unique thing in the New Testament—the cross—both with the Saviour, the Church, and the world. And so also the kenotic passage in Philippians ii. has had an effect upon Christian thought, faith, and adoration out of all proportion to the space the New Testament gives to the idea ; as it must have had a power in a mind like Paul's far larger than the space it covers in his letters.

§   §   §

Criticism, in its vigorous and rigorous reaction from the Teutonic extreme of Idealism, has sometimes about it, if not a narrowness, yet an exility, not to say a stridency, a want of atmosphere and of space, which is unfortunate in dealing with a reality like Christian faith, or a book like the New Testament. There is what might be called a Synoptic positivism ; which corresponds, in its sphere, to the Comtist empiricism in philosophy ; and it makes criticism, in its present phase, too much the victim of its own age to be the final interpreter of History. It applies religious psychology ; but the critical science of religions cannot give us the psychology of religion. A mere objective psychology of religion, we are told by an authority so great as Troeltsch, does not avail without a field of observation in the living faith of the inquirer. So that in religion a scientific impartiality and personal disinterestedness is impossible ; and at the root of all we have a venture of faith and the dogmatic method. No mere Historicism has the key to history, especially religious history ; it only cleans the wards of the lock. The weighing of evidence seems at times even to impair the power to weigh ideas, to divine personality, or to assess faith. Great lawyers are often poor theologians. There is a realism which bars the way to reality; and to-day we are much straitened by it. The religion of the chair may not lack scenery, but it does often lack horizon, and even sky. It has hues but not atmosphere. It has detail, but not distance. The place is strait and the light is poor. It is of Ruysdael and not of Turner. Or it has *genre*, but not style.

§   §   §

In nothing are these features more apparent than in our attitude to such a question as the pre-existence of Christ. Except in the 4th Gospel he says nothing directly about it, therefore, we are told, it cannot be real. It seems to be forgotten that the consciousness is inseparable from the great ἅπαξ λεγόμενον of Matthew xi., 27, which is treated in the way I have just described. It seems even to be forgotten that the kenotic explanation of his limited knowledge in certain other respects should apply here, and should suggest an oblivion in Christ of his eternal past indispensable both to the reality of his human life and to the efficiency of his divine work for us. Such oblivion may have been necessary to Christ himself in the doing of that work, however impossible it was to those to whom he spoke when the work was done, and made them think out the explanation of it, and of his glory who did it. The apostles could not evade the idea of a pre-existence which may have come home to Christ himself only in the uplifted hours and the great crises. For his Godhead cannot mean that at every hour he was fully conscious of all he was. Probably St. Paul's belief in the pre-existence of Christ was mainly reached by the way of inspired, and I would say guided, inference. It did not rest on Christ's words. It was an inevitable rebound of spiritual logic under his faith's obsession by the Christ in glory. Such glory, such Godhead, could not be acquired by any moral victory of a created being within the limits of a life so brief as that of Jesus. In a similar application he worked back from the faith that all things were made *for* Christ to the conviction that, as the end was in the beginning, all things were made *by* Christ; and by a Christ as personal as the Christ who was their goal. And so, from the exalted glory of Christ, Paul's thought was cast back, by the very working of that Christ in him and in the whole consciousness of the Church's faith, to the same Christ from all Eternity by the Father's side.

§   §   §

I do not think that to-day we can evade this same retrospective pressure of our faith, when its tide is full, any more than the apostles could.

First we consider this. Such a relation as we believe our Saviour now bears to the Father could not have arisen at a point of time. It could not have been created by his earthly life. The power to exercise God's prerogative of forgiveness, judgment, and redemption could never have been acquired by the moral excellence or religious achievement of any created being, however endowed by the spirit of God. I confess (if I may descend so far) I had long this difficulty, which lowered the roof of my faith, and arrested the flight of devotion. And I am afraid from the state of our public worship, I was not alone in that difficulty. I could not get the plentitude of New Testament worship or Catholic faith out of the mere self-sacrifice of the human Christ even unto death. Nor could I rise to it from that level. I was too little moved by his earthly renunciations to rise to the dimensions of the Church's faith, for I am not speaking of its creed, which was my own. The cross of such a Christ, who was the mere martyr of his revelation, or the paragon of self-sacrifice, was not adequate to produce the absolute devotion which made a proud Pharisee, yea a proud apostle, glory in being Christ's entire slave, and which drove the whole Church to call Christ Lord and God, in a devotion the most magnificent the soul has ever known. Such worship seemed too large a response to anything which Jesus, with all his unique greatness, did or determined in the course of His earthly life alone. The Synoptic record alone would not account for the Christian religion, nor produce the plerophory of Christian faith. Christ's earthly humiliation had to have its foundation laid in Heaven, and to be viewed but as the working out of a renunciation before the world was. The awful volume and power of the will-warfare in which He here redeemed the world, and turned for Eternity the history of the race, was but the exercise in historic conditions of an eternal resolve taken in heavenly places. He could never be king of the eternal future if he was not also king from the eternal past. No human being was capable of such will. It was Godhead that willed and won that victory in Him. If it was God loving when he loved it was God willing as He overcame. The cross was the reflection (or say rather the historic pole) of an act within Godhead. The historic victory was the index and the correlate of a choice and a conquest in Godhead itself. Nothing less will carry the fulness of faith, the swelling soul, and the Church's organ voice of liturgy in every land and age. If our thought do not allow that

[margin notes] Human sacrifice of life not enough to appeal to, + produce absolute devotion.

[margin note] The cross the historic act within Godhead.

belief we must reduce the pitch of faith to something
plain, laic, and songless, and, in making it more homely,
make it less holy, less absolute, less adoring. The adoration of Christ can only go with this view of Him in the
long run. Nothing lower takes with due seriousness the
superhuman value of the soul, the unearthliness of our
salvation, and its last conquest of the whole world. It
would reduce the unworldly value of the soul if it
could be saved by anything less than a Christ before
the worlds. It came upon me, as upon many at the
first it must have mightily done, that His whole life
was not simply occupied with a series of decisions
crucial for our race, or filled with a great deed then
first done; but that that life of His was itself the
obverse of a heavenly eternal deed, and the result of
a timeless decision before it here began. His emergence on earth was as it were the swelling in of heaven.
His sacrifice began before He came into the world, and
his cross was that of a lamb slain before the world's
foundation. There was a Calvary above which was the
mother of it all. His obedience, however impressive,
does not take divine magnitude if it first rose upon earth,
nor has it the due compelling power upon ours. His
obedience as man was but the detail of the supreme
obedience which made him man. His love transcends all
human measure only if, out of love, he renounced the
glory of heavenly being for all he here became. Only
then could one grasp the full stay and comfort of words
like these "Who shall separate us from the love of
Christ?" Unlike us, he *chose* the oblivion of birth and
the humiliation of life. He consented not only to die but
to be born. His life here, like His death which pointed
it, was the result of his free will. It was all one death for

him. It was all one obedience. And it was free. He was rich and for our sakes became poor. (What he gave up was the fulness, power, and immunity of a heavenly life.) He became "a man from heaven." When Paul spoke so he was not thrusting upon his Churches the rabbinical notion of an Adam Kadmon, or ideal man, in heaven, in the same sense as Judaism spoke of an ideal existence of the Temple itself, or the Law, or the Mother Jerusalem from above, or the heavenly city which came down out of heaven from God. Probably enough he knew the notion, but only to transcend it, to use it freely as a suggestion and not succumb to it merely as a dogma. God sent his Son, he did not emit him, he did not think him. The heavenly side of salvation was not ideal simply but historic, though it was premundane history. It was an eternal and immutable transaction. Things were done there. God sent; the Son came. And he came consenting to earn a glory he was entitled to claim. In all most precious things must we not *erwerben* what we *ererben*, and appropriate our greatest rights? Godhead came in Him, only not in force but in virtue, not gross and palpable but in moral power. He could have had his legions of angels. He could have come and taken possession of the world as a ἀρπαγμόν, as an Alexander seized a country. He could have come as an Apollo King, and taken the world as a prize of war, by moral storm, manly beauty, and heroic action. But, though he came as God, he came to win the world as his Father's gift, and by the Father's way of the cross as part of the gift. The self-determination to be man went the whole divine length to the self-humiliation of the cross. The Son expressed his true nature as a servant; but it was glorious

as the service of the Eternal Son.   He was son before he
became man; even as in his earthly life it was his sense
of Sonship that gave him his sense of Messiahship.
It is what he did in becoming man, more even than what
he did as man, that makes the glory of his achievement
so divine that nothing short of absolute worship from a
whole redeemed humanity can meet it.   Nothing short
of that heavenly deed can stir the absolute worship which
is the genius and the glory of his kingdom.   Nothing else
can enable us to measure the love of God, the thorough-
ness, the finality, the eternity of it.   When God spared
not his own Son, and yielded not even to the prayer of
Gethsemane, it was a piece of Himself that he forswore;
and in the grief of Christ he cut off His own right hand
for the sake of the Kingdom of His Holiness.   What
God felt and did then was not through some relation
to us that came into being with Christ's earthly life, but
it was through something that underlay it.   For had it
came into being then, to see and judge the world in Christ
would have been a step so new as to affect the unchange-
ableness of God.   Grace would have begun, and so been
finite.   But it was a step which lay in the nature of
Godhead for ever, in the eternal, personal, holy, and
obedient relation of the Son to the Father, and in the
act of renunciation outside the walls of the world.

Of course, when we come to discuss the precise mode
of the son's pre-existence with the father, or the psychological process of the kenosis, we are entirely beyond
knowledge.   The act is a postulate of saving faith, but
the mode of action is insoluble.   Logical difficulties may
be raised against any view.   But a kenotic theory so far
has less than some, as I hope we shall see.

§   §   §

It is a fact well recognised that Christ's references to his pre-existence are much more explicit in the fourth Gospel than in the Synoptics. And when we consider, it is not so strange as it seems. If we take those Johannine references, and couple them with the indubitable prevalence of the belief both in Paul, in Hebrews, and the Apocalypse; if we notice, farther, that the writers treat the belief not as a new idea which they have to insert but as a current faith which they would enhance; we are driven to conclude that it was a view early common in almost all sections of the young Church. Is it possible to think that that could have been the case if the belief had no point of attachment in the words of Christ himself? It was a belief whose challenge went to the heart of Jewish Monotheism. So much so, that, when Paul had broken with Judaism, the result is expressed most pointedly in the fact that he went about preaching Jesus as Lord—as the κύριος by whom, for an Israelite, Jehovah alone was meant, Is it possible, then, that the fourth Gospel especially should have placed such a belief in the mouth of Jesus himself if there had been nothing in any of his sayings to justify it? There is much loose talk about what his first believers put in the mouth of Jesus; and too much of it among amateurs who have never framed any scientific canon to regulate the principles or limits of such ascriptions, but who simply remove what does not fit their views.

§   §   §

Of course that does not solve the problem created by the comparative absence from the Synoptics of the express statements we find in John. But I find as little difficulty in believing that Jesus had an esoteric teaching on some subjects as that there were large areas of his

consciousness on which he was entirely reserved—such as
his most intimate communion with his Father. I say
nothing here of regions where he was for the most part
kenotically ignorant. And it may well have been that it
was these esoteric hints that were expanded in the fourth
Gospel. Traces of them appear in the Synoptics—especially in the well known Mat. xi. 27, that embryonic fourth
Gospel to which I so often allude. But we can hardly
be surprised if, in documents for general use in Churches
that were but working their way to a public largely
Jewish, there should be little use made at first of an idea
so startling to a Jew and so blasphemous in effect. For
its effect was to set another personality than the Father
alongside of Him on his throne. It is quite true, as I
said, that the Jews were not all unfamiliar with the
notion of the pre-existence of their Great Sanctities. But
it was quite another thing to assign a pre-existence to a
personal Messiah; and both Bousset and Dalman, who
are among our chief authorities on the theology of
Judaism, are at one against the view that it cherished
the idea of a pre-existent Messiah. Judaism certainly
could not tolerate the pre-existence of a Messiah invested
with those functions and titles of Jehovah which the New
Testament ascribes to Jesus. Recall the method of Jesus
with his public in the less serious matter of his Messiahship. For most of his life he was reserved about it; and
he bore it home, even to his disciples, only in an indirect
way that made them seem to discover rather than accept
it. It dawned but slowly, and it shone so briefly that
they lost it at the end. How much more need for reserve
on a matter so much more grave? If he had been explicit and categorical about his pre-existent life it would
have been to invite from a Jewish crowd a death as

certain as Rome's suppression of him would have been
had he raised the Messiah's flag.   When his end did come
it was on the charge of making himself equal with God.
But if the thought was in his mind it would be sure to
look out at some side window even if it did not call into
the street.   And there are such glimpses.   Return to the
passage I quote Mat. xi. 27, "No man knoweth the
Father but the Son."   I deal with that at more length
elsewhere.   I only ask here whether, if question about
the pre-existence did not arise from other sources,
that idea would not be the first to occur in explanation
of these words.   If they appeared in John we should all
say at once that it was by the notion of the pre-existence
they were to be explained, whether the writer was foisting
it on Jesus or not.   The Eternal Father would demand
for correlative the Eternal Son, to explain, by solidarity
of being, the Son's exclusive and adequate knowledge of
such a Father.

But the truth which Christ could not hope to impress
by his words he impressed by his crowning act of death
and resurrection.   There at last he came into his own.
To these add his expository work in the Church by his
Spirit.   It was such things that forced on the Church its
belief in his pre-existence.   It was slowly forced, more
slowly than his Messiahship.   It could not be otherwise.
But it was inevitable, as the scope and depth of that final
revelation made its way into the mind of faith.

§   §   §

It is important at a time like the present that we
should keep clearly in view the interest which is served
by our belief in the pre-existence of Christ.   Why should
we press it?   Why was it pressed in the New Testament?   Was it in the interest of some scheme, either of

philosophy or theology, which aimed at making more definite God's relation to the created world ? Was it to provide some explanation for Christ's miraculous power, and especially for his resurrection ? Was it to provide a large system of dogma with a celestial warrant ? Was it to equip a religion with a central figure calculated to impress and command the imagination ? Was it because the impression made by the historic Christ was so weak that it succumbed to the current notions of pre-existence which floated in from the surrounding air and settled down to germinate in the warm soil of faith ? It was for none of these reasons that the idea took the place it did, and has kept it. It was not in the dogmatic interest that it arose or survived, but in the religious. It was to give full and infinite effect to the condescending love of God, and to give range to the soul's greatness by displaying the vast postulates of its redemption. *Tantae molis erat divinam condere gentem.* If we feed on Christ it is on bread which came down from Heaven. The soul's saviour could be no less a power than the soul's creator. It all arose from a sense of soul-greatness, from a direct, intimate, and intense relation between the soul and the Saviour, to which we grow daily more strange. It arose out of that experience ; and not from the necessities of a system, or the infection from systems around. These would have been easily ignored had they given no means of expressing the experience that worked so mightily. It points in the same way when we note that Paul, in Philippians ii., uses the idea, as it was forced on living faith, for the purposes of that faith's moral culture To promote a self-renouncing love he dwells on the act of self-renunciation which gave them for a Saviour God himself in a life of humiliation, and no middle

U

being who was a mere emanation from God in a world process.

§   §   §

What, we may ask, has experience to say on our question? Can it have anything to say on the pre-existence of Christ when it cannot even speak of our own? Let us see. Is our experience of Christ parallel with our experience of ourselves? To experience ourselves is a piece of psychology; is that all we have in the Church's experience of Christ.

It seems plausible enough to say that the pre-existence of Christ is not verifiable by our Christian experience. But everything depends on the experience to which you appeal. Is it that of the critic? Or of his age? Is it simply the experience of a mystic mood, a pious frame, a sympathetic religiosity? Or is it the classic experience of the regenerate, of the Church within the Church, the really significant elite of faith? Is it the experience of the average Christian who "loves Jesus," or that of the elect who show what the average Christian means and must rise to be by his New Creation? Is the experience of the ordinary Christian normative for faith? It is certain that the spiritual riches of Christ, as understood and realised by the Apostolic succession of the fit and few, especially in relation to sin, means what lay Christianity is too ready to pooh-pooh as theology, and to ban as metaphysic.

It is indeed one of the most great and fertile of modern principles that our faith has much more directly to do with the benefits of Christ than with the nature of Christ. 'It is by what the Saviour has done for me that I know what he is for me; it is through the work of redemption that I know the person of the Redeemer; it is the work

which reveals to me the worker.' But it would be an
abuse of this principle if it were made to mean that
Christ is no more, either to me or to the Church, than
he is felt at any point of time to be. If I am deeply
moved by the example or the ideal he has stamped on
me, I am not therefore justified in saying that he is no
more than ideal or example. If I am touched, humbled,
and cheered by the way in which he reconciles me to
God, I am not therefore warranted in declaring that his
one work for me and for mankind was in this reconciling
way alone, and that it was a work with no action upon
God, and no relation to judgment. I am not entitled to
say that the reconciling effect upon men exhausts the
whole personality of Christ. The work does not reveal
the whole of the workman—directly, at least. And there
is always the question how far our sense of the work is
entitled to prescribe the compass of it ; that is, whether
experience is to be the measure as well as the organ of
faith. The apostles at least were driven by their experience into a cosmic interpretation of his work who
produced it, far transcending individual experience ; and
they have carried the greatest with them. If the effect
of Christ on us be but our reconciliation, if the benefits
be construed but in that subjective sense, if they do not
extend to redemption from some thing more objective
than our own frowardness with God, that is an effect
that might have been produced by a prophet and martyr
of unparalleled sanctity and unquenchable love. Such a
subjective construction of the benefits of Christ would
not call for the life, death, and resurrection of the very
Son of God. And we need feel no surprise that to-day,
when Christ's work is thought to be exhausted with the
reconciliation of men, the men affected by it should be

very unsteady, not to say light, in their views of his divine person and its range of being. There would be no necessity, in such a subjective construction of Christ's work, for the belief to which the early Church was driven by the apostolic sense of what they had in Christ—the belief in his pre-existence.

§   §   §

The reconciling and redeeming work of Christ is, indeed, our grand avenue to his person in its fulness; but it does not exhaust it, unless that work be interpreted as the new creation *in nuce*. And certainly if (like so many good but *bornées* souls to-day) we reduce the reconciling work of Christ to his earthly life, character, and teaching, apart from their consummation in a death which was more than worth them all, if we cherish a 'simple' sermon-on-the-mount Christianity, it is quite impossible to erect on that basis a personality so great as its advocates really revere. The greater the personality the more impossible it is to give it full expresssion in life. We have already seen how large a part of the activity of his person Christ reserved in the secrecy of his private and personal contact with the Father. And we may also observe that, as the crisis of his death drew on, it was this hidden life that overspread his soul. He became less and less engrossed with his prophetic effect on man, and more and more with such priestly gift to God as God alone could offer, and no man.

By all the deepest experience of the Church the benefit from Christ is not exhausted in the satisfying of the heart or in the pacifying of the conscience. Christ does more than fill or fortify us; he sanctifies. His work, consummated on the Cross, is yet larger than a deliverance at a historic point. It is the energy of the whole

eternal person who culminated in that act. He does
more than release us; he has to uplift and transform us.
He does more than inspire the race, he completes it. He
brings it to the glory for which it was destined by God.
And for this no saintliest man could be enough. Nothing
lower than the Holy God could re-hallow the guilty
human soul. Only the creator of our destiny could
achieve it. Of course, the *extent* at any one time of the
Church's response to Christ, or the soul's, may be
limited. The horizon of its experience may be partial
and confined. But what is of more moment is the *nature*
of that experience. It is not psychological, but theological. It is not an experience of the soul's old past, nor
even so much of its new self, but of its new creator and
king, its Lord and its God. That changes the nature
of the experience from a subjective to an objective, from
me to one who makes me. It is not simply the experience of an immense impulse, a vast promotion in goodness, a change of sentiment towards God, the clearing
up of misunderstandings, and the wiping of the slate.
What is cured is not merely distance, nor merely estrange-
ment from a loving God, but the obsession by hostility to
a holy God, and the guilt of it all. The forgiveness is
an absolute gift, but it is not an amnesty; nor is it a
revival; but in its nature it is a new creation. Christ
does not bring us mere absolution, he is the giver of a
new Eternal life. His charge is the second creation, and
the divine consummation of humanity.

Now for this creative work no mere man is sufficient.
The creators of the greatest works of genius are quite
unable to create the new heart within us, the new communion, and to put us beyond all cavil as to our final
destiny in God. They cannot make themselves the

guarantee and surety of that destiny. But Christ does do this. And he has never ceased to do it. Throughout the ages there is a ceaseless succession of confessors of such a theological salvation and not only a psychological only, of a new act of creation and not a quickened process.

If, then, such be the benefit begun and assured, the agent of that blessing no more began his work when he appeared on the earth, than he ceased it when he left the earth, as man's way is. A man might reconcile me to God; but could any greatest man so keep me as to ensure that we did not fall out again; or that if we did the due reconciler would again appear? A man might reconcile us to God but he could not unite us for ever with God in the way that an eternal holiness requires. He could do no finished work. The greatest thought and passion of the Church, its experience, and not its philosophy or its theology alone, has been driven to postulate behind all the acts of Christ's will on the earth, behind all his pity and power, an act of *his* (not merely of his God and ours), eternal in the heavens, an act which held all these earthly acts within it. His person has been felt to be greater than these earthly acts could express. They had all a volitional foundation in the heavens, which, because it was action and not mere substance, did not impair their reality but enhanced it. They had a moral substratum in the act of his premundane personality, whose power was not exhausted in our rescue alone—unless that rescue be viewed as the first stage of a New Creation which had all the consummation of humanity in its scope.

§   §   §

We are thus driven, by the real existence of an Eternal Father and our experience of his grace, to demand the

existence of an equally real eternal Son—both being
equally personal and divine.   The question, then, is what
is the relation between the Godhead of the Eternal Son
and the man Jesus Christ, and how did it come to pass.
Such questions at once arose among believers; and they
engrossed the Church's thought during the early centuries
in the many Christological systems that succeeded the
Trinitarian strife.   There was a teeming variety of
opinions on the subject in the redeemed community—
as indeed there must always be; and room must be
made for them.   Christian faith insists on the reality
of the incarnation as a fact if we take in all its
seriousness the experience that we have in Christ a
gracious and holy God truly with us; but the mode of
its process is an open question, on which it cannot be
hoped, and hardly wished, that all the Church should
think alike.   And we may have occasion to note that
many who reject the incarnation do so not only because
they wrongly require from it the satisfaction of a
philosophic rather than a religious demand, but, even
more, because they cannot see *how* such a process could
take place.   Which is much as if we refused to act on a
cable from America because we do not understand the
modes of electric action and transformation.

§   §   §

It is impossible with due reverence to speak in any but
the most careful and tentative way of the relations within
the Godhead.   It has not pleased God to make these
matter of revelation.   As we know of Christ only what
he chose to reveal in his vocation and work, so we really
know of God only what He chose to reveal in His Christ.
We practice ourselves a reserve about our inmost experiences and relations which may make intelligible, at least

in some measure, God's own reserve with the sons of Time. On the other hand He wills to be inquired of. It is not the questions that are intrusive. We are not called on to sacrifice our intellect, if only we do not idolise it. And we are not debarred in advance from all inquiry as to the conditions of Christ's supramundane existence. St. Paul did not feel so hampered. We are surely free at least to say some things which it could not be—could not be consistently with such an idea of God as Christ himself revealed. There was that in the earthly personality of Christ which in the heavenly could not be. For instance, in the earthly personality there was growth; in the heavenly there could be none—unless perhaps he were an Arian Son, a being created prior to the world's creation. What is of Godhead does not grow: it is from Eternity to Eternity. The indubitable movement and change in the living personality of God does not take the form of growth. Growth belongs only to corporeal personality; and in his incarnation the Son of God did not become for the first time personal but only corporeally personal, personal under the limited condition which involve growth. He did not enter personal conditions but historic. If growth be essential to personality in every form there can be no personal God; and our question then becomes of a quite different kind. There may therefore be in Eternity a personal Being that does not come to Himself and His perfection by growth. Whether two or more such can cohere in the one God is again another question, with its own methods of discussion. But the growth of a divine personality in Eternity is a much more impossible thing than the co-existence of three.

§   §   §

In Jesus Christ we have one who was conscious of standing in an entirely unique relation to the living God. It is the prophet's prophecy that reveals God, but it is Christ's person; and as *the* Son it reveals Him as *the* Father. If His Father be *the* Father, his Sonship is *the* Sonship. He held a relation to God as Father that never existed in any man before. Nay more, it was one that no man can ever reach again. Geniuses are repeated, but Christ never, the Son never. *For this relation constituted his personality.* He was not a person who became a son, or was destined to be a son, but his whole personality was absolute sonship. This is not true of us. We are not sons and nothing else. The relation made the personality in Christ's case. I do not mean that the relation *made* Jesus grow into a personality, but it made up *his* personality, made the essential thing in it. That is not so with us. His personalty had another foundation in God than ours. His person is born of God, ours is created. We are indeed related to a personal God, as his offspring, in a way that necessitates our being persons too. But not such persons. We can reach and develop personality without reference to God; he could not. Destroy his sonship and you destroy his personality. His personality shaped his work, our work shapes our personality. Indeed his work was identical with his personality. Not so with us, whose work is always less than our personality. Our work is a means for our personality, his personality was the means of his work. Of no man can it be said that his relation to God constitutes the whole personality. But in the case of Jesus the whole relation to the Father, namely, sonship. did constitute that personality. Think it away and nothing is left. His whole relation to the Father would be an abstract phrase were it not embodied in an actual personal Sonship, corelate with the living Father, knowing the Eternal Father as the Father knows him, and at every point in Eternity, therefore, so knowing because so known.

§　　§　　§

There are various views among those who try to justify in thought their belief, or their effort to believe, that a great gulf divides Christ from all other men.

There are those for instance who view him as the realisation of the divine *idea*, whether of Humanity or of the Church. The only pre-existence Jesus had was of that nature. It was not personal but ideal. I shall have occasion to refer to this view more than once ; and I will only say here that it seems to me quite inadequate either to the New Testament or to Christian experience. Such a faith could have produced neither. It is too remote and pale to be the source of such a passion as evangelical faith has been in the history of the Church. If you reduce the Eternal Sonship to an idea you will reduce the Eternal Fatherhood to the same tenuity. And all history follows.

There are others who come nearer reality by conceiving Christ as the realisation of the divine *purpose*. This is so far an improvement that it brings Christ into immediate relation with God's will and action rather than with his thought. He is due to the act of God. He is the supreme object of the divine election, " the captain of the elect," the object, though not the eternal object, of an eternal election—just as human souls are, though in a pre-eminent and even collective way. He has no personal pre-existence. His election is thus paralleled to that of the Church ; and we are not taught the actual pre-existence of the Church.   It is not denied that an element in Godhead passes from ideality into personal reality; what is said is that its passage is due to no movement or process of thought, but to a personal act and purpose of the Father.

That is the advantage of the view. It has a more ethical note. But its defect is three-fold. First, it does not recognise the difference between a Church chosen *like* him and a Church chosen *in* Him. Second, if he owed his personal existence to God's choice, he was but one of many choice men, and so we do not rise above the Socinian idea; it reduces Christ from the assessor of God's throne to the organ of God's purpose. And, third, it leaves no room for the consenting act on the part of the Son. But it is not enough for Christian purposes that the Father should send; it is equally necessary that the Son should come, and that the one will should be as original and spontaneous as the other. A fourth defect is that sufficient room is not left for the mystical element so essential to Christian faith.

Besides, there is a criticism which applies to both these views. They come too near the notion that, when the idea, or the purpose, was at last realised in Christ's moral achievement of his full personality, there was a real addition to the riches of Godhead; that Godhead at last fully found itself in Christ; and had attained by development that which it had not the full consciousness of being before. What I said a little ago about divine growth in Godhead may be applied here.

§   §   §

Instead of speaking of the realisation of a divine idea or purpose it meets the case better if we speak of the

redintegration of a divine person.   This will be more
clear I hope when we come to discuss kenotic theories
in the next lecture.   The whole moral history of Jesus
on earth was the ethical resumption of such personality
as he laid down by an act equally ethical in its nature.
The advantage here is a very great one.   We have the
act of the Son correlative with that of the Father.
We have the Son acting from love as truly and creatively
as the Father.   Otherwise it need not be that Jesus,
as the agent of God's purpose and his great gift to
man, should really himself love them, if only he so
loved the Father as to carry out loyally and effectually
His great behest.   It need not follow that we are
inseparable from the love of Christ; who might conceivably retire from active and direct concern with us
when he had done his task, handed us over to the
Father, and restored us to a love *like* his own, the
Father's will.   But the Christian love of God is not
a love like Christ's, but a love for ever to Christ and in
Christ.   The love of one so creative as Jesus could not
have been without spontaneous initiative at the heavenly
outset of his work.   If he came as love it was love that
moved him to come, and not a suggestion or a precept,
far less an emanation, from the Father's love.   If he
love to the endless end, he loved from the timeless
beginning, and in no mere passive obedience.   His
dependence on the Father was no mere passivity.
Christ's receptivity of God is the mightiest act in human
history; and a personality so mighty and creative
could never have come there as a mere created product,
or passive precipitate, of the divine purpose.   He could
be no mere intelligent means or organ of that purpose.
The whole New Testament conception of him as a

worshipped being is that of an end and not a means, for
whom God's judgment is his judgment, God's kingdom
his own, and on personal relation to whom turns our
eternal relation to God. His was a sovereign spontaneity;
which is not affected by the fact that he prayed the
Father for power; unless we deny all analogy in the
region of the increate to the real causality in created will,
or to the true initiative of inspired prayer.

§   §   §

I am afraid that the effort to compress into one dis-
course each of the great themes to which the last three
lectures are devoted involves considerable cost in the way
of clearness. May I point out, as I close this lecture and
prepare for the next, that I have in the rear of my mind
throughout one question which I yet try to keep more or
less in view. It is this. If we hold to the personal pre-
existence of Christ do we not render His life as the
historical Jesus unreal? We shall see how pointed the
question grows when we come to sharpen it to the issue
involved in the principle *non potuit peccare*. And in that
form an answer will be suggested to it shortly. But what
I have been trying to do in the present lecture is to
answer it in the more general form shaped by the pre-
existence alone. Could a pre-existent Christ be a real
man? Could he have the effect upon history of a real
personality if he was believed to have existed before
entering history?

And by way of answer let us close this lecture by
clearing our minds of *à priori* notions of what a real
personality might be presumed to require, a character
that would strike us as æsthetically true if we found it
in a work of imagination. If the whole Christ that fills
the faith, worship, and conquest of the long Church

could have been imagined and presented in a work of literary art beforehand, every Aristotle, Longinus or Quintilian would have joined to declare it an unreal and impossible conception. Such a miracle and inversion of values was effected by Christ, such an extension of the ideal and resource of personality. Let us here observe that the reality of a historic influence is not to be measured simply by what may appear to be the psychological postulates of a character æsthetically complete, but by the magnitude, reality, and permanence of his effects in history. These must be our first standard of personal reality. A personal unreality could never become the first personal influence in history that the Christ from heaven has become. The Christ that has become such is not the humane and residual Christ of much current religion, but the whole New Testament Christ. It is a Christ who had not to be stripped by early criticism of his heavenly life in order to become a real power; but on the contrary one whom the faith he created had to place in partnership with the Creator's Eternity in order to account for itself. The more the Church felt the reality of his influence on it, the more it acted with him upon present history, the more it found through him an even greater reality in the future than the present, so much the more has it been driven to construe his total reality as including his personal action in the infinite past. His pre-existence, that is to say, has not robbed him of the reality that is shown in vast historic effect. And it may be observed in conclusion that if the influence of the Church upon the world is less to-day than it once was, that loss of effect is at least concurrent with an unprecedented weakening of belief within the Church itself in his life before life and his ante-natal will.

LECTURE XI

THE KENOSIS OR SELF-EMPTYING
OF CHRIST

LECTURE XI

THE KENOSIS OR SELF-EMPTYING OF CHRIST

It is all but impossible to discuss a question like the Kenosis without entering a region which seems forbidding to the lay mind, and is certainly more or less technical. And yet some appeal may perhaps be made to the ministry, among those Churches where the education of the ministry has been taken seriously and theologically. It is only when the ministry despises theology and sacrifices it to a slight and individualist idea of religion, that the Church immolates intelligence and finally commits suicide. It parts with staying power in order to capture a hearing, and surrenders faith to gain sympathy. The minds that are trained enough to ask relevant questions on such a subject are also trained enough to know that they cannot be answered without considerable effort on both sides—effort both to present and to grasp. And such earnest minds are in possession of some at least of the postulates here involved, the ideas handled, or the methods used. The real difficulty is with those who will neither qualify to understand such questions nor let them alone.

If there was a personal pre-existence in the case of

Christ it does not seem possible to adjust it to the historic Jesus without some doctrine of Kenosis. We face in Christ a Godhead self-reduced but real, whose infinite power took effect in self-humiliation, whose strength was perfected in weakness, who consented not to know with an ignorance divinely wise, and who emptied himself in virtue of his divine fulness. The alternative to a Kenosis used to be a Krypsis, or conscious concealment of the active divine glory for practical or strategic purposes. But that is now an impossible idea. While on the other hand an acquired Godhead would really be none. It would be but deification. And at bottom it is a contradiction. No creature could become God.

I am aware of the kind of objection raised to the kenotic theory. Many difficulties arise readily in one's own mind. It is a choice of difficulties. On the one hand living faith finds it difficult to believe that the Christ who created it was not God. And on the other thought finds it hard to realise *how* God should become Christ. But it is something gained to note that the chief difficulties arise on the latter head, in connexion with the *way* in which the fact came to pass rather than with the *fact* itself. That is, they are scientific and not religious. When we are not so much questioning the fact as discussing the manner of it—not the *what* but the *how*—it is a matter of theological science not of religious faith. And the science of it can wait, but the religion of it cannot.

§   §   §

We cannot form any scientific conception of the precise process by which a complete and eternal being could enter on a process of becoming, how Godhead could accept growth, how a divine consciousness could reduce its own consciousness by volition. If we knew and could follow that secret we should be God and not man. It is a difficulty partly ethical, partly psychological. Even if we admit psychologically that certain attributes could be laid aside—the less ethical attributes like omniscience, omnipotence, or ubiquity—could self-consciousness be thus impaired and a love still remain which was fully divine? And how can an infinite consciousness be thought of as reducing itself to a finite? God's infinite consciousness might indeed determine itself so as to pervade, sustain, and bind a variety of finite detail without losing consciousness. An immanent God, we believe, does so in creation. But if He parted with His self-consciousness as infinite would it not come as near to suicide as infinite could?

That, indeed, is what Ed. von Hartmann says is the very thing the transcendent God must do. His task is self-redemption from the blunder and *impasse* of a world. He must retract himself, retrace his excursion into a cosmos, and restore himself by a universal negation of will from a condition of wretched actuality to the set, grey, apathetic state of mere potentiality. By that self-renunciation he recovers the true deity out of which he stumbled and fell into a conscious and actual world. The divine Sinner becomes the divine Redeemer—and first of himself. In redeeming the world from its immanent misery he redeems himself from his transcendent misery of egoistic consciousness and desire. (*Relig. d. Geistes* p. 266). This seems a resurrection of the Gnosticism of the second century, as so much of our modern speculation is. And it is only a philosophic parody of the kenotic process; which does not think of the divine self-consciousness as going out of existence, but only of its retraction, concentration, or occultation, in one constituent of the Godhead. The suicide of God is no part of the kenotic idea, which turns but on self-divestment as a moral power of the eternal Son; who retains his consciousness but renounces the conditions of infinity and its precreate form.

§   §   §

But leaving the metaphysical psychology of the matter for a moment, have we any analogy in our experience that would make this intelligible or even credible?

I am not sure that we have not.

(1.) I will first allude to the familiar experience of reducing or obscuring the self-consciousness by a drug voluntarily taken. Here the really effective cause is not the drug but the will to use it. Let us put a case. Suppose an Oriental court, a foolish young Sultan, and a venerable vizier, wise, vigilant and devoted, amidst a ring of plotting pachas. As the vizier sits next to his master at a feast he observes a pinch of poison stealthily dropped into the imperial cup. He has heard some rumour of a conspiracy; and he knows that poison. It means slow paralysis and lingering death. In a moment he must decide; and he takes the resolve. There is no other way. He challenges the king to a pledge in exchanged cups. And in due course he feels the consequence in the impaired powers with which he drags through a year or two of life. He lives thus till the ruler at last learns of his devotion, is stung to his feet by the sacrifice, and show his gratitude by such a change of life and a growth in royal worth as rewards his saviour's love for all it had borne. Now what was it that really eclipsed the good statesman's powers? It was not the drug, but the love, the will, the decision to take it with

open eyes, and to part with all that made his high place
and peace, when no other course could save the youth
he loved.

(2.) Again, are there no cases where, by an early act
of choice and duty, a man commits himself to a line of
life which entails an almost complete extinction of his
native genius, tastes and delights. Could no story be
made of a great musical genius, say in Russia, who,
being as full of pity as of genius, was also a passionate
sympathiser with the people; who deliberately committed
himself, while young and in the flood of artistic success
to certain democratic associations and enterprises, well
knowing what would happen upon discovery; who *was*
discovered, and deported to Siberia, to an exile both
rigorous and remote, where the violin and all it stood for
was denied to him and all his comrades for the rest of
their life. He must spend his whole heart in loving
fellowship with the commonest toils and needs, and in
patient ministrations to a society which prison debased.
After a lifetime of this the first brief years of artistic joy
and fame might well seem to him at moments almost to
belong to another life, and the æsthetic glory and power
be felt to have turned entirely to social love and service.
And all as the consequence neither of a spiritual process,
nor of a mere indiscretion, nor of a martyrdom only
forced on him, but of a resolve taken clearly and gravely
at a point in his spiritual life.

(3.) Or again. A student at the University develops
an unusual faculty and delight in philosophic study, and
even shows clear metaphysical genius. He is not only at
home in those great matters which live next door to the
very greatest, but he offers promise of real, not to say
striking, contribution to the historic development of that

high discipline. Or his gift may be in poetic or plastic art, to the like high degree. But he is the only son in a large family ; and, at a critical period in the family affairs, the father's death makes it his duty to leave study, learn an unpleasant business, pull things round, and devote himself to them for the rest of his life with the absorption demanded by modern industrial conditions. He has to resign his intellectual delights, call in his speculative powers, unlearn his native tastes and associations, and give himself up to active conflict with a vexatious world doubly galling to him. And in due course he comes to forget most of what it was once his joy to know. He becomes subdued (in no ignoble way, in a way of duty) to the element in which he has to work, and he is acclimatised to a world both alien and contemptuous towards his congenial treatment of the greatest realities. His contact with reality must now be by the way of faith and action, and not by the way of thought. He becomes at his best a practical mystic and amateur, who might have been a leading genius. Economic, social and ethical interests, even to drudgery and heart sickness, come to take the place of the more solemn and unearthly concerns at the divine call. And the old high joy of thinking, or art's old calm, must be postponed until another life ; with many an hour of longing, and many a homesick retrospect to what is, after all, the native land of his suppressed powers. He loses a life but he finds his soul. Is this not a case where a moral and sympathetic volition leads to a certain contraction of the consciousness ; not indeed by a single violent and direct act of will, but by a decision whose effect is the same when it is spread over a life ? He has put himself (*sich gesetzt*) in a position where he is put upon (*gesetzt sein*). And, in applying the illustration to the theology of a kenosis in Eternity, where a thousand years are but as one day, the element of time between choice and result in the earthly case is negligible.

(4.) Speaking more generally, is there not often in our experience a connection between the resolutions and the limitations of our personality? By certain deliberate and early acts of freedom, love, and duty we so mortgage and limit ourselves that in due course, as we follow them up, the moral consciousness ripens. We come to a spirituality which is really ethical and not merely instinctive, a thing of moral discipline and not naïve nature, something which comes to itself by way of challenge and conflict, and is not mere legacy. We become men of faith and not mere religion, men of moral sagacity and not mere honest impulse. By voluntary discipline we may come to love truth for truth's sake and not for our own; we learn to hold by habit and not mere heredity to the "ought" of conscience; we lose self in the love and worship of God, or in the service of man. But for the most part these conscious heights are touched but in rare hours—though they may be the hours of decision and committal that fashion life. We may soon grow weary in the course we have taken up. The very physical, or psychical, nature which was the organ of our first free resolve, asserts itself, and makes us feel its clouding power as we pursue the path to which only our freedom, our supernatural self, committed us. By our will we have come where our will is itself often obscured and hampered; and our first estate, where the choice was made, is recalled but in a dream. So also Godhead, by the same free and creative will which gave His creation freedom, may pass into a state where He is not only acted on by that creation but even submerged in the human part of it; and where He is victimised, indeed, for a time by the perverse freedom He created, and is imprisoned in its death; by consenting to which death, however, He gives the supreme and saving expression to his divine will and life. He lives out a moral plerosis by the very completeness of his kenosis; and he achieves the plerosis in resurrection and ascension. And thus He freely subdues to Himself the freedom which in His creative freedom He made.

§   §   §

The more moral the original power is, so much the more strength there is to sacrifice glory to service, and enjoyment to benediction. So that were the moral power that of deity itself, the power of self-disglorification would be enhanced accordingly. Just because He was holy God, the Son would be morally capable of a self-dispowering more complete than anything that could be described by human analogy. As God, the Son in his freedom would have a kenotic power over Himself corresponding to the infinite power of self-determination which belongs to deity. His divine energy and mobility would have a power even to pass into a successive and developing state of being, wherein the consciousness of perfect fulness and changelessness should retire, and become but subliminal or rare. The world of souls was made by Him; and its power to grow must reflect some kindred mobile power in him whose image it is. The infinite mobility of the changeless God in becoming human growth only assumes a special phase of itself. Had the myriad-minded creator of souls no power to live perfectly in the personal and growing form of the souls he made?

But sin ?   There, indeed, we do reach a limit.   *Non potuit peccare.*

But, then, it is at once said, his personality and manhood were not real.

But what if it were thus ?   What if his kenosis went so far that though the impossibility was there he did not know of it ? The limitation of his knowledge is indubitable—even about himself.   He was not perfectly sure that the cross was his Father's will till the very last.   " If it be possible let it pass."   Did that nescience not extend to the area of his own moral nature, and so provide for him the temptable conditions which put him in line with our dark conflict, and which truly moralise and humanise his victory when *potuit non peccare ?*   He knew he came sinless out of each crisis ; did he know he never could be anything else ?   How could he ?   Would it have been moral conflict if he had known this ?   I am, however, well aware how relevant and how effective is the question whether even then, whether if that foregone immunity were there, known or unknown, the battle could have been moral conflict like our own ;   whether he could have been tempted in every respect like us ; whether the victory could be real.   And in reply one might go into the well-known distinction between physical and moral omnipotence, between formal and moral peccability.   I could remind you how possible it is for you to steal some article from a shop on your way home, and yet how impossible.   You could, but you simply could not.   Leaving that, however, I would rather answer by an analogy from the Saviour's own work in his Church.   It is the business of the believing Church to urge on its members the most real and mortal moral conflict for the world—for a world, that is, whose redemption our faith

yet knows to be already achieved and secured by all the
power of God. " Work for the Kingdom ; for it is the
God, who has already secured the Kingdom, that
worketh in you." He cannot fail, but it would be our
worst sin to fold our hands upon that foregone impossibility. We have sometimes even to act as if it were not
so, as if we never knew it was so, and as if all turned on
our moral effort and success alone. And from work we
pass to prayer and remind ourselves how essential to
the soul it is to lay our needs before the Heavenly Father
who knoweth what we need before we ask Him.

§   §   §

But there are also farther answers to be made. The
question, remember, is, whether a complete kenosis
would not involve such a renunciation of divine immunity,
such a self-identification with man, as involved a personal
experience of man's sin ? And the farther answer is twofold. First, every touch of personal guilt would have
impaired the moral power required for such sympathy.
That is an axiom of modern experience. The guilty
cannot escape from himself, cannot empty himself. And
the incarnation was a moral act so supreme and complete
as to be possible only to a conscience at the pitch of the
perfectly holy. And the second answer is that what is
truly human is not sin. Sin is no factor of the true
humanity, but only a feature of empirical humanity
which is absolutely fatal to the true. What is truly
human is not sin, but the power to be tempted to sin.
It is not perdition but freedom. Because Christ was
true man he could be truly tempted; because he was
true God he could not truly sin; but he was not less
true man for that. Among all his potentialities that of
sin was not there ; because potentiality is only actuality

powerfully condensed; and had potential sin been there
its actuality would have been but a matter of time and
trial. But temptation was potential; and it became
actual in due course. He could be tempted because he
loved; he could not sin because he loved so deeply,
widely, infinitely, holily, because it was God he loved—
God more than man. Thus the only temptation with
real power for him was a temptation to good—to inferior
forms of good. It was not the temptation to forsake the
righteousness of God, but to seek it by other paths, less
moral and less patient paths, than God's highway of the
holy cross. It was not salvation that brought Christ
to the Cross. All Israel was set upon the faith of a
salvation in God's righteousness. The collision arose
upon God's way of righteousness. What more plausible
to a man of such power and of such ideas as Christ
than to organise and lead his zealot nation in an irresistible crusade against pagan empire for a new order of
society wherein should dwell the righteousness of God?
That was the Puritan dream. But even a parliamentarian
army was still an army; and a Cromwell ruled for God
by the sword—as many of us who are his admirers to-day
would seek the kingdom by the vote, that is, by our political tactics instead of by his military. It was what still
makes, and always has made, the chief temptation of his
Church—the reformation of society by every beneficent
means except the evangelical; by amelioration, by re-
organisation, by programmes, and policies, instead of by
the soul's new creation, and its total conversion from the
passion for justice to the faith of grace, from what makes
men just with each other to what makes them just with
God. It was the temptation to save men by rallying
their goodness without routing their evil, by re-organising

virtue instead of redeeming guilt. To fleer at the Church's anomalies and enormities needs no great insight or courage now; the lads do it. But it does need more than common insight, it needs more than shallow scorn, to realise that it is not there that the Church's peril lies; and that these palpable things are but the graver symptoms of a far subtler error in which many of the critics themselves are tied and bound. It is the error in a Church which preoccupies men with their rights rather than their mercies, with redress rather than redemption, with social change where it is men that must be changed if society is to be saved, with their brotherhood to each other when the thing lacking is sonship to God, with goodness rather than grace, with religion rather than faith. It is the error which leads men to think that we can have a new Church or Humanity upon any other condition than the renovation in the soul of the new covenant which Christ founded in his last hours, before the very Church was founded, and which is the Church's one foundation in his most precious blood.

So when it is asked, If He was so holy that he could not sin what becomes of that moral freedom which identifies him with man? the answer is that absolute holiness is the true freedom and the only divine freedom. Impeccable holiness is the only power by which the divinest things are finally done. A complete incarnation into a free humanity is possible only to the absolute holiness which created the freedom. And only a soul by its nature identified with God's holiest will could fully use or impart that freedom which is the ideal of a true humanity. And such a soul *must* do it.

I am well aware how supersubtle this must seem to

some : but it is not possible to breathe the air of a region
so high without some subtlety.   And without breathing
that air the Church stifles in the tasks of a world.   She
must come up here often to breathe, when her very
stalwarts are foreign to the saving secret, heavy with
spiritual sleep, and slow of heart to understand heavenly
things.

§   §   §

The difficulty of conceiving psychologically the kenotic
process in the divine consciousness is certainly an
impediment, but it is not an obstacle.   ' It is out of
reason ' is the complaint.   ' We cannot think together
the perfect God and the growing man in one person.'
No, we cannot think them together.   But also we cannot
realise them apart.   It is only by a paradox of thought
that we possess our own souls and their reality.   The
central things of the soul are thus alogical.   Life transcends thought.   Personality itself is thus alogical ; and it
forms the unity in which truths cohere with practical
effect which will not harmonise and co-operate, which
refuse to be systematised.   Faith is not rational in the
coherent, the scientific, the systematic sense of the word
rational.   It would be impossible to believe in a God at
all if we insisted on such rationality as His supreme
norm.   That insistence is the root of much atheism, at
least in regard to a personal God.   Personality and its
movements are alogical—especially on an infinite scale.
For instance, if there be an infinite personal God He is
self-caused.   But a self-caused being is as great a blow to
rational conception, and as deep a mystery, as the passage
of the Son from his eternal being to a life of limitation
and growth.   Yet the mystery of a self-caused Being
is indispensable to our belief in the divine origin of the

world. And certainly (to take another case) to personal
religion absolute Grace is as indispensable as our freedom
and responsibility. So essential for our faith in the
divine nature of Christ also may be the mystery of the
Kenosis, and the inconceivability of the self-dispowering
of the Eternal Son, and the self-retraction of his glory.

§   §   §

Most theories which attempt to deal with the Kenosis
have set themselves to answer the question, What did the
Son renounce in becoming man ? What attributes of
Godhead had to be surrendered for incarnation ? And the
replies have been various. Some have begun by a distinction between the relative and the immanent attributes
of God. They have said that the relative attributes are
those that were set up with the creation of a world, such
as omnipotence, omniscience, and the like, which would
have no meaning before a discrete creation was there;
while the immanent attributes are those ethical and
spiritual qualities, such as absolute love or holiness, without
which God would not be God at all. And such thinkers
have gone on to say that the Kenosis meant the renunciation of the former and the retention of the latter. Godhead in Christ parted with omniscience, and omnipotence,
as with omnipresence ; but it did not, and could not, part
with absolute holiness or infinite love. Other theories
have gone farther, and have seen in the Kenosis a renunciation of even such immanent attributes as a divine
self-consciousness and absolute will.

In regard to the former class of theories the criticism is
that even the relative attributes could not be parted with
entirely. At most they must be thought of as latent and
potential even were no created world there. They were
ready when creation arose. They are equally necessary

to Godhead with the immanent qualities which, again, cannot be wholly immanent, but must have a real relation to any world created by the Will of the absolute love.

In regard to the second class of theories, if the renunciation is carried so far as to part with a divine self-consciousness and will, it is not clear what is left in the way of identity or continuity at all. What is there, then, in common between the Eternal Son and the man Jesus? What remains of the divine nature when we extinguish the immanent ethical and personal qualities in any absolute sense?

§   §   §

To get over those difficulties we may perhaps take a happier course. Let us cease speaking of a nature as if it were an entity; of two natures as two independent entities; and let us think and speak of two modes of being, like quantitative and qualitative, or physical and moral. Instead of speaking of certain attributes as renounced may we not speak of a new mode of their being? The Son, by an act of love's omnipotence, set aside the style of a God, and took the style of a servant, the mental manner of a man, and the mode of moral action that marks human nature. (For morality, holiness, is surely not confined to the infinite mode alone.) He took the manner that marks a humanity not illustrious, not exceptional, but sheer and pure, where pomp has taken physic, and exposed itself to feel what wretches feel in life's awful storm. Take the attribute of omniscience, for instance. In its eternal form, it is an intuitive and simultaneous knowledge of all things; but when the Eternal enters time it becomes a discursive and successive knowledge, with the power to know all things only potential, and enlarging to become actual under the moral conditions that govern human growth and the extension of human knowledge. Here we have not so much the renunciation of attributes, nor their conscious possession and concealment, as the retraction of their mode of being from actual to potential. The stress falls on the mode of existence of these qualities, and not on their presence or absence. And the history of Christ's growth is then a history of moral redintegration, the history of his recovery, by gradual moral conquest, of the mode of being from which, by a tremendous moral act, he came. It is reconquest. He learned the taste of an acquired divinity who had eternally known it as his possession. He won by duty what was his own by right. As he grew in personal consciousness he became conscious of himself as the Eternal Son of God, who had dispowered himself to be the son of man by a compendious moral act whereby a God conscious of humanity became a man equally conscious of deity. And by a compendious moral act I mean a prevenient act including in principle all those moral sacrifices and victories which worked it out in an actual and historic life.

The attributes of God, like omniscience, are not destroyed when they are reduced to a potentiality. They are only concentrated. The self-reduction, or self-retraction, of God might be a better phrase than the self-emptying. And it is only thus, indeed, that growth is made possible, and evolution started on its career. No evolution is possible on other terms, none unless the goal is in the start. All we have otherwise is only movement and variety. So far is growth, then, from being incompatible with, the infinite, eternal, and almighty that it is demanded by it. Evolution is a mode of the self-limiting power innate in a personal infinite. And only so is it possible. The conditions of time must lie within the possibilities of Eternity, the growth of man within the infinite mobility of the changeless God. *Finitum non capax infiniti* is the principle of Deism ; the principle of Christian theism is *infinitum capax finiti*. If the finite lies beyond the infinite and outside it then the infinite is reduced to be but a larger finite; the infinite can only remain so if it have the power of the finite as well.

§   §   §

These points deserve, and need, perhaps, closer attention. An attribute cannot be laid down, for it is only the Being himself in a certain angle and relation. But there are accidental relations, relations, for instance, contingent on human freedom, which determine the form in which the attribute exists. They determine its mode of being, according to the particular position in which the subject finds himself. Thus omniscience and the rest are not so much attributes as functions of attributes, or their modifications. Omnipotence means not that God should be able to do anything and everything that fancy may suggest ; but that, in working his will of love, God is, from his own free resource, equal to all it involves, and is really determined by nothing outside himself. Omnipresence, as absolute independence of space, means that God is not hampered by space, but can enter spatial relations without being tied by them, can exist in limits without being unfree, or ceasing to be God. And so on with omniscience and the rest. And the following illustration has been given from the spectrum. A dispersion into colours is not essential to sunlight, which is light without it. It was hailed and used as light before such a breaking up was known. Therefore the dispersion is not a quality or attribute of light. But it is

Y

potential in light all the same.   As soon as the prism is
there this relative property of light appears necessarily.
Suspend the relation, remove the prism, and the dispersion ceases.   So it is with the divine omniscience.   Omniscience is only a detailed aspect of God's absoluteness,
incidental to the existence of a creation.   Before the
prism of creation was actually there God was, and God
was light.   He had absolute and simultaneous intelligence as a necessary feature of his being.   But since he
created, the absolute intelligence of God in relation to the
world becomes in its form omniscience, which could only
cease with the removal of the world, but even then would
only retire into another absolute form.

God's knowledge, therefore, may be discrete in actual
(shall I say empirical?) omniscience, or it may be
retracted and concentrated into potentiality.   In the
Kenosis it is contended it did so retire.   This happens
in a measure even with ourselves.   I am not at every
moment in full consciousness of all the knowledge I
possess.   In ordinary life I know much that I am not
conscious of, that never occurs to me, that is as though it
were not, it is *in petto* and potential till some crisis arrive.
I do not become conscious of it till certain circumstances
arise, and a situation is created that changes it from
potential to actual and active.   Meantime, where is that
knowledge?   Does it exist?   Has it a real existence
before it emerge in that situation?   And so it may have
been when Christ at the world's crisis became man—not
a brilliant man, but true man, normal man. In the matter
of knowledge Christ, as God, Christ in his eternal form,
had an intuitive and simultaneous knowledge of all; but
when he put aside that eternal form of the Godhead, and
entered time, his knowledge became discursive, succes-

sive, and progressive. The omniscience (or the omnipotence) of God does not mean that it is incapable of limitation but rather that with more power than finitude has it is also more capable of limitation. Only it is self-limitation; He limits himself in the freedom of holiness for the purposes of His own end of infinite love. The divine omniscience, morally retracted and potential in Christ, developed by his exercise in a life-series of moral crises and victories; till, culminating in the cross and its consummatory victory, it emerged into actual consciousness and use in the Glorified, to whom all things were delivered of the Father, all power given in heaven and earth—when he was determined by the resurrection so as to be the Son of God with power. What he achieved was not the realisation of an old ideal but the redintegration of an old state, He became what he was, and not merely what it was in him possibly to be. He reconquered by moral conflict, under the conditions of human rebellion, a province, *even within himself*, which was always his by right. In finding the sheep that were lost he gradually finds the self, the mode of self, the consciousness, he had renounced. Even for himself the losing of his life was the regaining of it. The diminuendo of the Kenosis went on parallel with the crescendo of a vaster Plerosis. He died to live. And his post-resurrection power is other in form than that of his earthly life. The form of a servant gives place again to the form of God. There is a sentence of Milton, in a letter to Bigot, on his loss of sight which occurs to my mind. "It is not so much lost as revoked and retracted inward for the sharpening rather than the blunting of my mental edge."

§ § §

It is fruitless to discuss these matters if we come to their consideration with only physical or material ideas of what is meant by words like omnipotence. A friend once told me that her little boy posed her by discovering that there was one thing God could not do—he could not see the back of his own head. That is only an absurd case of the popular and childish order of difficulty which is the working capital of popular scepticism as well as of popular apologetic. It starts with the maxims of common sense to explore the region of eternal spirit and holy immutable morality. And the object of education is not to provide us with ready-made solutions to such crude questions, but to raise people to putting the proper questions and to get them into schools that will exercise them in good and evil. I am thinking, of course, chiefly of the higher education; and I mean the schooling in moral ideas, and in the methods appropriate to moral ideas, in modern times. It would mean worlds for our Christian faith, which brought such an inversion of moral values, if the ethic of Kant and its developments came to receive as much attention as the universities have given to the great pagan ethic of Aristotle. I mean such an escape from the physicists, biologists, and psychologists, however refined, as shall discipline the mind in the elements, at least, of ethical method, the genius of ethical ideas, and the sense of ethical terms; and shall make proper answers possible by enabling people to put the proper questions. The bulk of the questions with which the amateur critic poses faith, and the illiterate heretic delights the public, are as unanswerable as if it were asked—what is the difference between London Bridge and four o'clock?

§   §   §

With this in mind I would return to point out that God
is God not physically but morally, not by power but by
love.   That is the Christian revelation.   The nature of
Godhead is Holy Love.   There lies the region, the nature,
and the norm of its omnipotence.   It is no arbitrary or
casual omnipotence, which puts out power just for the
sake of doing it or showing it.   It can do, not everything
conceivable to freakish fancy, but everything that is
prescribed by Holy Love.   To a physical omnipotence
it is indifferent.   Such being its nature, its object with
Humanity is a kingdom of such holy love.   But, con-
sidering man's actual sinful state, this can only be effected
by redemption.   To this end the Son of God sympathetically renounces the glory of his Heavenly state.   He
does it for God's sake more than for man's, for love
of the Holy more even than of the sinner, to glorify the
Holy through the sinner, and to hallow His name.   And
nothing can hallow Holiness but Holiness, nothing else
can satisfy it, nothing else can save.   God's holy name
must be saved that the sinner may be—and saved by an
all-holy peer.   And Christ does it by the holy way, by a
moral act of love, and not by a *tour de force*.   It is an
exercise of sanctity, and not an exertion of strength.
That is his satisfaction to God.   He presents God with
a perfectly holy Humanity.   He does it because he is
holy infinite love; he can do it because he is almighty
for that love.   It is not a love which might itself be
finite, only with a miraculous physical omnipresence;
but it is an almighty love in the sense that it is capable
of limiting itself, and, while an end, becoming also a
means, to an extent adequate to all love's infinite ends.
This self-renouncing, self-retracting act of the Son's will,
this reduction of Himself from the supreme end to be

the supreme means for the soul, is no negation of his nature ; it is the opposite, it is the last assertion of his nature as love. It is no negation of his freedom ; it is rather the freest energy of his whole will. He never willed anything so mightily and freely as the subjection, the renunciation of self-will to the holy requirement of God. It is the concentrated omnipotence of love, and not of mere power, that underlies his limited earthly existence. And it is incessant obedience. The whole detail of that earthly existence is the expression of the act of will by which, in his omnipotent love, he entered the world. " The act of a great spirit is to be always in action." All his decisions taken on earth, all his several volitions are integrated in the one foregone act that brought him to earth, the one premundane act of pregnant self-concentration for the carrying out of love's saving purpose with the world. It is a concentrated and seminal omnipotence we meet here, a concentration even of that self-concentration wherein the world was created and God became immanent in it. (If the Creator could not have become immanent in creation His infinity would have been curtailed by all the powers and dimensions of space. And if immanence could not pass by a new act into incarnation then God would have been lost in his world, and the world lost to God.

In love we were created and endowed with freedom by an act of God wherein he limited his own freedom by the area of ours. His omnipotence received a restriction— but it was from an exercise of His own loving power and freedom ; and an exercise of it greater than could be rivalled by all the freedom man received. The freedom that limits itself to create freedom is true omnipotence, as the love that can humble itself to save is truly almighty.

God in his vast act of creative love laid a limit upon himself to give room to the freeborn to live. He drew in his universal energy and causation to that extent. But any limit laid upon power by such love is an exercise of omnipotence. And when God in his creative love gave man freedom, it was a mightier exercise of His own free power than could be matched by all the power man might exert or fancy in the use of his freedom. So it was also with the new Creation. There was more omnipotence (if we can so speak) concentrated in the person of Christ than was spread in all creation. To appear and act as Redeemer, to be born, suffer, and die, was a mightier act of Godhead than lay in all the creation, preservation, and blessing of the world. It was only in the exercise of a perfect divine fulness (and therefore power) that Christ could empty and humble himself to the servant he became. As the humiliation grew so grew the exaltation of the power and person that achieved it. It was an act of such might that it was bound to break through the servant form, and take at last for all men's worship the lordly name.

Let us escape, then, from crude notions of finite and infinite, of weakness and omnipotence. (If the infinite God was so constituted that he could not live also as a finite man then he was not infinite.) There was a limitation to that extent on His power's infinity, and one which he Himself did not impose. But if He did live as finite man, then so far was it from being a limitation of His freedom (except externally and formally) that it was the greatest exercise of it. It was the greatest act of moral freedom ever done. The Godhead that freely made man was never so free as in becoming man. His self-limitation was so far from impairing his being that it became the mightiest act of it that we know. It was not limitation so much as concentration. Was Christ less mighty for his work when he was straitened till it should be accomplished? It was rather His intensest concentration for the carrying out of His final purpose with the world. It was the most condensed expression of holy love. It was holy love acting at a point once for all. And holy love (may I repeat) is the supreme category of the Almighty. It is the object for which all God's omnipotence exists. To achieve that object *is* His true omnipotence. How, then, could omnipotence be impaired by its own supreme act? Such divine immanence as is implied in Creation rises by a farther and mightier limitation to incarnation. But it is by a new creative act— not by prolonging the old process; not by a culmination in Christ of the soul of the world, not as the summit of God's identity with the world; but by a unique, crowning, and moral act of self-identification. Immanence cannot explain incarnation, which is a new departure of more moral nature. The incarnation is not God's identity with the world prolonged, but a new self-identification, which is yet older than the world. The self-limitation became more severe, but it also rose to a new and a mightier exertion of divine power. If one may use a figure from physics, the structure, the nature, of His action on the world changed under the increased pressure. By his own will God in Christ reduced his intelligence from being actual to being potential, within the kingdom of power or nature ; while from that potentiality, as Christ grew in grace, it developed and regained actual omniscience by living it back, by the moral way of the kingdom of Grace, till he left the world behind, to be determined as the Son of God in power.

§　§　§

It need hardly be pointed out how free such views leave us in regard to those ignorances and limitations in Christ which make so much more trouble to us than they did to the evangelists; those errors, in respect of the form of the future no less than the history of the past, which he shared with his time and race. If a young critic tells us that Christ was ignorant of many things which the modern schoolboy knows, we may wish the fact put more reverently, and less like a school-boy, but we have no vital interest in challenging it. If we are reminded that there were miracles, and even teachings, which were impossible to all his power and knowledge ("greater things than these") because he was, like most preachers, dependent on his audience, and could do nothing mighty amid unbelief—there is little to trouble us in that. If he did not know it was because he consented not to know. And whatever he did not know, at least he did know that which is the root, and key, and goal of all knowledge. He knew to its foundation that fear, and obedience, and communion of God which is the beginning of all wisdom that is not self-destructive. And whatever he could not do—and he could not invent printing—he could do the one thing needful for God, the one thing which changed our relations to God, the one thing needful to give man the power of doing at last what he was made for, and of achieving through His redemption, the eternal kingdom of God, in which telegrams and airships are forgotten among the potsherds of the earth. He did the central deed in which all man's great and final doing lies potential. He secured for ever the moral realm without which our engineers are but building sand and organising catastrophe. He did the work of God;

and he did it in the sense that his doing was God at His
supreme work.   It is here that we find our safe seat amid
the inevitable results of criticism.   And it is here we find
a far larger Saviour than the humane Jesus of mere
religious liberalism.   It is no way to deal with so great a
blessing as criticism arbitrarily to challenge or curb its
rights.   The way is to fix our faith beyond its reach.   It
is to return to the Epistles for the key of the Gospels, for
the evangelical secret, and the principle of the Highest
Criticism of all.   The judgment of the cross criticises all
criticism, and the finality of its felt salvation is the rock
impregnable.

§   §   §

To recapitulate.   The Church has always taught an
earthly renunciation on the part of Christ, which takes
its eternal value from the premundane renunciation
that made him Christ.   We have to make our renunciations in life alone; but he made his before life.
We have no choice as to our birth ; he had.   His will
to die was also his will to be born.   It is only by
such a moral *act*, and not in the course of some ideal
process, that we can think of his entry from a world
of power and glory upon the conditions of earthly life.
Only by a moral act could he incarnate himself in human
life, which is in its nature a grand act, choice, and venture,
which is moral at its core, moral in its issues, and moral
in its crown.   If it was a real and universal human life
he lived, that could only be by virtue of a moral act
which is at least on the scale of the race ; and if he was
to master the race his act must be on an even greater scale,
greater than the whole race's best, and as great as Holy
God.   The act that consented to become man was a
superhuman act, an act of God.   He did become crea-

turely.   He did not simply enter a creature prepared for
him.   When he was born human nature was not transformed by a special creation into some superhuman thing
for the spirit of God to enter—as a foreign palace might,
by great furnishing effort and outlay, be transformed into
an English home to honour a visit from our king.   Nor
were the two streams parallel while unmingled.   There
could not be two wills, or two consciousnesses, in the
same personality, by any psychological possibility now
credible.   We could not have in the same person both
knowledge and ignorance of the same thing.   If he did not
know it he was altogether ignorant of it.   But the ever-
during Sun in heaven was focussed in Christ—condensed
to burn the evil out of man.   The divine energy was
concentrated for the special work to be done.   The fulness of the Son's Godhead was still the essence of Christ.
That Godhead lost nothing in the saving act.   It took
the whole power of Godhead to save ; it was not the Son's
work alone ; far less then was it the work of any impaired
Son.   It was not the work of a God *minorum gentium,* as
the Arian Christ is.   It could not be the work of any
created being, however great.   The value of the soul
would slowly and surely sink if we believed it salvable by
any creature.   It would lower the soul that the most
High made for Himself were it saved by a second-class
God.   Such is the ethical effect on society of a false
theology.   The divine nature must belong to the universal
and final Redeemer, however its mode and action might be
conditioned by the work it had to do.   The divine
qualities were there ; though their action was at once
reduced, concentrated, intensified within the conditions
of the saving work.   The divine qualities were kept, but
only in the mode that salvation made necessary.   Jesus

did not know everything actually, empirically, but only what was needful for that work. But, as that is the central final work in human nature, the knowledge required for it contains the promise and potency of all knowledge. And, as to the exercise of power, he did what God alone could do in forgiving human sin, a salvation which is the nucleus and germ of all worthy power beside. His knowledge, his power, his presence were all adjusted to his vocation. His vocation was not to apply or exhibit omnipotence, but to effect the will of infinite love, and master all that set itself against that. And that divine vocation was only possible to one who had a divine *position*. The world's Redeemer must be the Son of God.

§   §   §

If we ask *how* Eternal Godhead could make the actual condition of human nature His own, we must answer, as I have already said, that we do not know. We cannot follow the steps of the process, or make a psychological sketch. There is something presumptuous in certain kenotic efforts to body forth just what the Son must have gone through in such an experience. God has done things for his own which it has not entered into the heart of man to conceive. It is the miracle behind all miracle. All detailed miracle was but its expression. It is the miracle of grace. And it can be realised (little as it can be conceived) only by the faith that grace creates, that answers grace, and works by love. Let us not be impatient of the secret. Love would not remain love if it had no impenetrable reserves. Love alone has any key to those renunciations which do not mean the suicide but the finding of the Soul.

LECTURE XII

THE PLEROSIS OR THE
SELF-FULFILMENT OF CHRIST

LECTURE XII

THE PLEROSIS OR THE SELF-FULFILMENT OF CHRIST

THE closeness of the Church's bond with Christ will always go hand in hand with its belief in his deity. And the more it realises his salvation the more it will know the roots of it to be in the great act of a Christ before the worlds. The whole faith of the Church has turned upon a conception of Christ which sees in him the act of God, and worships in him God's immediate revelation, God's personal guarantee of His holy saving love, and the eternal mediator of our communion with Him. Christ is much more than the personal realization of the idea of Humanity and the guarantee of its universal attainment. That is to say, in the Church's history a faith in the God in Christ underlay a faith in the man in him. The *disciples* indeed began with the divine prophetic man, in the order of knowledge; but with the *apostles and the Church* it was otherwise. They came to read him in the order of value, not from the man upwards but from the God downwards. That was after the great *finale* which made disciples into apostles and a group into a Church. What did this, what made apostles, and made a Church, was not the humane side

or function of Jesus, but the redeeming God in Jesus.
A Church and a theology must be inseparable always.
The saving faith that makes a Church lays hold of
Christ theologically, in his deity.   It does not view
him as the pledge of our human future, but as the
foundation of our new communion with a holy God who
will make Humanity's future just what his Kingdom
demands.   Living faith knows nothing of an undogmatic
Christ.   An undogmatic Christ is the advertisement of a
dying faith.   Christ's permanent relation to the world is
dependent on something that can only be dogmatically
expressed—on his eternal relation to the Father.   His
effect in ensuring its final destiny depends on his eternal
relation to the Father, on his sonship before the world
was.   He is the final Saviour of men, and the surety of
man's future, only as the Eternal Son of God.   No
created agent of God could give us that certainty of the
Kingdom of God which faith must have for the Kingdom's sake.   It must come in a constant and living
mediator who is no mere medium; in a historic person
who is not a mere historic link between the ages; in the
only begotten Son who declares the Father from His
bosom, and who *is* the revelation he *brings*.   For only
God can reveal God.   And the King of God's Kingdom
must be God.

Hence, if faith be not saving faith but only sympathetic; if it be but an illumination, or an inspiration,
and not a new creation ; if it be a spiritual culture and
not a spiritual conversion; if it is first concerned to be
liberal and not evangelical, progressive and not positive,
not regenerative; then there is no foundation and no
future for any belief in the Godhead of Christ, however we
may play with old terms.

§   §   §

Such a belief is an experience which breaks into two
orders of inquiry. It opens up questions about the
threefold nature of God, or a Trinity as deep as
Godhead, and questions about Christ's historic person—
how the humanity of Jesus is related to his Godhead,
how the nature of his personality fits his function
as the direct visitation of God. It is this latter
question, the Christological rather than the Trinitarian
question, that is of such lively interest to-day. But
any belief in either a Trinity or an Incarnation can
only flow from a final experience of grace by the sinful
soul. And it belongs solely to a Church which confesses
the sin of the world only because it confesses still more
humbly and gladly the absolute holiness of the Saviour.
The Godhead of Christ is an interest of religion before
it is an interest of theology. It is the spring of that
worship of Christ, which in the history of the Church
preceded and inspired thought about him. When we
worship Christ the living Lord and the organ of our
communion with God (as the Church has steadily done),
or when we give him absolute obedience as the King of
the Kingdom of God and the living guide of all history to
that consummation, then we give him a place that can be
held by no mere part of creation, and no mere unit of
history. Is the Kingdom of God the consummation of
creation? Then surely the Saviour and King of the
Kingdom must be one with the Creator of creation.
The world which was made for such a Christ must have
been made by him. The largest conception of creation is
much more than cosmic in range ; it is also redemptive
in power. It thinks of the cosmos as the arena or the
base of God's salvation. The ground plan of creation—

z

what is it if it be not found in the final plan of salvation?
Has creation any ground plan else? Plenty of process,
but what plan, what goal? The goal to which the whole
creation moves—is it not that Eternal Redemption?
Does it not all wait and work to the manifestation of the
Sons of God? The whole cosmos is great with the re-
deemed Kingdom. But if so, surely then the Kingdom's
Saviour and King is Creation's Maker and Humanity's
God. Christ as the soul's living Lord must be the
Eternal Son.

I know that this is a logic more spiritual than rational.
The problem is not philosophic. It is certainly not to
find a reasoned adjustment of the finite and the infinite
of an absolute and created life. Nor is it a question of
deifying Humanity, as the Church's earlier creeds were
apt to construe it, and the positivist mind tends to
construe it still. The question is this—when we begin
with the Gospel, when we begin with God's holy and
loving will for the world in Christ—how are we to secure
its realization in man? How are we to establish in man
as a race Christ's mutual, personal, and loving communion with such a God? That is something which no
prophet was ever able to do. Prophetism was a failure
for such a Kingdom; it could not establish a national,
to say nothing of a racial, communion with God; how
could a Christ merely prophetic succeed? Did Christ
succeed by that part of his life which was chiefly
prophetic—the part prior to his death? The result
of his life and teaching was that they all forsook him
and fled; but the result of his cross, resurrection, and glory
was to rally them and create the Church in which he
dwells. Is not the creation of God's Kingdom a task
beyond the power of any instrument, any creature? Is

it not God's own work? Whoever did it must be God
himself. Godhead must directly perform and sustain
the great act that set up such communion. God must
do it in person. Only one who incarnated God's holiest
will as His son alone did could produce and establish in
men for ever the due response to that will—the response
of their whole and holy selves. Holiness alone answers
holiness; and only the Holy God could make men holy;
it could be done by no emissary of His. We cannot be
sanctified by commission or deputy. No intimation of
Himself by God (through the holiest of creatures)
could effect such an end. His *news* of Himself must rise
to His *sacrifice* of Himself; His self-sacrifice must further
be his self-vindication as holy; and from that it
must go on rising to His *self-communication*. The Father
who *spoke* by his prophets must *come* to save in the Son
and must *occupy* in the Spirit. He offers, gives, Himself
in the Son and conveys Himself in the Spirit. He
who is the end of all, humbles himself to be the
means, that he may win all. God in Christ asserts
Himself in his absolute freedom (" I, even I, am
he "); He limits Himself for His creature's freedom
("that blotteth out thy transgressions "); and bestows
Himself to make that freedom communion (" For I am
with thee, saith the Lord, to save thee "). It is all one
holy love and grace, in this Eternal threefold action,
both within God and upon man. Only on this Trinitarian conception of God can we think of such a salvation
as ours. Only so can we think of Christ as God with us.
But then also we must follow on to ask how such a
Christ is related to this eternal and invisible God.

§   §   §

We have no call to-day to prove the real manhood

of Jesus. For that is universally owned; and it is all that many can own. Things were otherwise in New Testament times, when it was freely held that the manhood was phantasmal and unreal. It is against such a notion that the writings of John are directed, and especially his Epistles—a fact which makes them somewhat irrelevant when used against the Socinian position in our own time. They were directed on people who were more ready to admit the divinity of Christ than his humanity. And with such people we have at the moment little to do.

Nor are we always called to convince people of the uniqueness of the man Jesus. That is, in some sense, freely owned by most who consider the matter seriously at all. Everything turns on what is meant by unique, whether he is unique in degree or in kind, whether it is the difference between the created and the increate. I have more than once pointed out that what is denied to-day is not a superior revelation in Christ but the absolute finality of that revelation. What we have to stand by is that finality—not of course in the sense that evolution has come to an end, but in the sense that all evolution is now *within* God's final word and not *up to* it. It is unfolding the Christ and not producing him. Christ is God's seventh and last day in which we now forever live and labour in rest. That is to say, the divine revelation is final but the human religion which answers it is not final. The word is final, but the response is progressive. The finality is as to the kind of God revealed and not as to the compass, which always enlarges upon us as culture enlarges our grasp. It is a question of the explication of God's last gift of Himself. And what we have chiefly to keep in view is the sort of uniqueness in

the man Jesus which is required for the final and personal gift of Godhead in him.

Now for such a purpose a Christ merely kenotic is inadequate. We have already seen that all revelation is
God's self-determination. For any real revelation we must
have a loving self-determination of God with a view to
His self-assertion and self-communication; and this
self-determination must take effect in some manner of
self-divestment. We have examined the kenotic, or self-
emptying theories of such an act, and we have found
them either more helpful or less. But whether we take
a kenotic theory or not, we must have some doctrine
of God's self-divestment, or His reduction to our
human case. Yet, if we go no farther than that,
it only carries us half-way, it only leads us to the
spectacle of a humbled God, and not to the experience of a redeeming and royal God. For redemption we need someting more positive. It is a
defect in kenotic theories, however sound, that they turn
only on one side of the experience of Christ, viz., his
descent and humiliation. It is a defect because that
renunciatory element is negative after all; and to dwell
on it, as modern views of Christ do, is to end in a
Christian ethic somewhat weak, and tending to ascetic
and self-occupied piety. For we can be very self-occupied
with self-denial; it is the feminine fallacy in ethics. We
must keep in view, and keep uppermost, the more positive
process, the effective, ascending, and mastering process
which went alongside of the renunciation in Christ, nay,
was interwoven with it, as its ruling coefficient. I mean
that, besides the subjective renunciation, we must note
the growth, the exaltation, of his objective achievement,
culminating in the perfecting at once of his soul and our

salvation in the cross, resurrection, and glory. I should not decline to speak carefully of a progressive incarnation. We must have some view, which may be kenotic indeed, but must also be more positive than kenoticism alone.

§   §   §

Now, the whole Christology of the Church, I keep saying, has been its effort to conceive by thought the reality it lived on in its faith of Christ's saving work and presence for good and all. For the most part, we have seen, the Church has tried to solve the problem by the doctrine of two distinct natures inseparably coexisting in the person of Jesus. Sometimes, indeed, it has gone so far as to speak of two personalities coexisting within that single historic life. But no creed (we have seen) has ever been able to do more on such a basis than to place the two natures or persons alongside each other, to say that each must be believed as a postulate of Christian faith and experience, and to repel attacks or heresies which threatened to destroy either, or to enhance the one at the expense of the other. No systematic reconciliation, far less a psychological, has ever yet been effected. And the attempts at adjustment have always have tended to impair one side or other of the antinomy. One nature lost a piece of itself to the other, and so really lost its indiscerptible self; or else one was swallowed up by the other. Either an injury was done to the nature of human personality, by ignoring its necessary law of growth and making Jesus a mechanical prodigy of abstract revelation, without a moral interior (as in Byzantinism) ; or damage was done to the unity and changelessness of the triune God (as in Arianism, or in some extreme kenotic theories).

§   §   §

Most of those theories were fastened on the Church
in the interests, indeed, of a true redemption, but at a
time when the theology of redemption, was apt to be
conceived in terms of substance rather than subject, of
metaphysic rather than ethic, of things rather than persons.   The terms were, however finely material, yet too
material to be duly personal and ethical.   The object of
redemption in the creed-making age was less to forgive
man than to immortalise him, less to convert him than
to deify him.   It was not a work of grace in the sense of
mercy, in the sense of destroying mortal guilt, but in the
sense of destroying a fatal disease.   Grace was the infusion of an incorruptible divine nature or substance into
corruptible human nature.   It was antiseptic.   It was
the inoculation of the one nature by the other, and the
consequent gift of ἀφθαρσία rather than forgiveness and
communion.   It gave life rather than moral peace.   It
was not the restoration of unclouded personal relations
so much as the deification of human nature by trans-
fusion of the divine.   It was more a communication of
properties than a communion of hearts and wills.   And
it is easy to see the result of such a theory in the Roman
doctrine of the sacraments, the kind of virtue they convey,
and the ethic with which they may co-exist.

But we have come to a time in the growth of Christian
moral culture when personal relations and personal
movements count for much more than the relations of
the most rare and etherial substances.   The conscience
has come to be the *locus* of faith, especially since the
Reformation turned grace from subsidy, or antidote, to
mercy.   It is a question of the holy conscience of God in
relation to the guilty conscience of man.   We are concerned with a relation of wills, of the holy will and the

unholy. Redemption is moral regeneration, and not mere cure, not mere rescue from an entail of spiritual disease and death. We are not to blame for a mere disease, but redemption is rescue from what does leave us culpable. Sin is more than a disease; and it is curable by no magical infusion, but only by moral action on the part of God; wherein person deals with person, and soul with soul, in a mutual act of Grace and Faith. Faith is man's greatest moral act, as Grace is God's. It becomes the serious acceptance of God's mercy and not the reception of Christ's body. Regeneration is the result of faith and not of baptism. Death is banished by new living. Such faith is what makes Christianity; and its experience is the material of all theology. Thus religion, salvation, gives the law to theology, and not theology to salvation. This is especially the case with Christology. Forgive me if I repeat so often that the principle from which we must set out to understand the person of Christ is the soteriological principle. Any metaphysic must follow that and not precede it; it must be a metaphysic of history and not of being, of soul and not of substance, of the moral soul and not the noetic substance, of ethic and not of thought—and especially of the Christian ethic condensed in faith as the new life. All Christology must rest on a moral salvation, spiritually and personally realised. And any metaphysic involved must be the metaphysic of redemption, which is only the superlative of a metaphysic of ethics. We believe and therefore we speak. We believe and then we think. We explore the New Creation. It is from the experience of Christ's salvation that the Church proceeds to the interpretation of the Saviour's person.

§   §   §

Starting, then, from the canon that the Incarnate is immediately known to us only as the Saviour, it might be better, it might save us much confusion and collision, if we were less concerned to speak or think of the two natures within the life of Christ, as we have long ceased to think of two persons, or two consciousnesses. Neither does justice to the interest of salvation. As that interest is the interest of personal communion, and not of human deification, *it might be better to describe the union of God and man in Christ as the mutual involution of two personal movements raised to the whole scale of the human soul and the divine.*

§   §   §

This is what I would venture (with more heart than hope) to expound.

There is a certain fascination at present in the idea of Christ as the apex of that spiritual evolution which emerges to a divine height in man. He is viewed as the consummation of a grand spiritual process construed on scientific lines, as if all the series, from the nebula to man, were a vast pneumatic biology. And doubtless if the human process in history were simply one of teeming movement onward and upward, there would be no difficulty but much propriety in speaking of Christ as the divine blossom of the race, or its "heaven-kissing hill." But then I have more than once said that if such evolution were the law and scheme of life, its crown and bloom must be at the close of the series, and not in the far past. We could have no Christ till we had evolved into the Kingdom of God. But the historic Christ is there to act on man and save him, and not simply to consummate him. He is there to bring about man's consummation and not simply exhibit it. He is not a product

not product
but source,

of man's spiritual evolution but its grand source.   If ever we attain to Christ it is by Christ.   The King makes the Kingdom and not the Kingdom the King.

Moreover we have seen that moral experience and the psychology of faith will not let us think of man's spiritual history as a process of simple progress, even on the wide whole. (See Lecture V.) There is much more than that allows for, more that is mystic, resolute, dogmatic, more of a passion, a collision, and a tragedy in life; in life, note, and not only in some lives. Man does not simply unfold to God but God descends and enters man. With this invasion religion has much more to do than with evolution. The immanent consciousness of the divine becomes positive religion only when the leap, the choice, the resolve of faith treats it as the upheaval of a transcendent reality.

For what is the verdict of religious psychology? How does it interpret the spiritual experience of the race as shown in its supreme form of faith? Life and progress, especially on the religious plane, show that at least a two-fold movement goes to make up the spirituality in human history, two movements whose opposite directions produce much friction. And I do not allude by that to the twofold process within history, wherein degeneration is at constant war with development, decay with life, and lapse with progress. That might all go on on what I would call the horizontal plane of movement—the onward movement and the backward. But I allude rather to the vertical action, so to say, in which man is constantly seeking unto a God and God is constantly passing into man. Christianity is a religion of depth before it is a religion of breadth. It spreads to all souls because it pierces the whole soul. It is so catholic because so radical, so liberal because so searching. Its God the heaven of heavens cannot contain; and he does not shrink from descending into hell. Its kingdom does not grow up through the ground like the grass; it descends out of heaven from God. Its prayer that ascends there is moved by a spirit which comes down from there. Man's word to God is interlocked with God's word to man. To conceive history as the field of those two movements on the upright plane of spirit—the upward movement of man's quest for God, and the downward of God's conquest of man—is far more congenial to the mystery, grandeur, and tragedy of the soul than the simple, evolutionary, and culminating process on the level plane of Time alone. We grow laterally every way, so to speak, and not only on a plane. The soul dilates into its circumambient eternity, as it were; it does not merely proceed. The city of God is foursquare every way. So that we have this advantage, that, while we allow its place to the progressive process which fascinates so many, we yet supplement it with another which gives history a far more massive interest, a more vivid, dramatic, and crucial interest, a far more moral interest than an ordered process can yield. We grow in substance and power, and not merely in range and vision. One would like to do justice to the evolutionary idea, the progressive idea; but one would like still more to do justice to the redemptive idea, the regenerative, the deepening idea. For Christ came to do more to deepen men than to broaden them. He came as the fulness and not simply as the ideal, the form to be filled. He came as a life, and not simply as a line of life.

These movements are both at work in the growth of the God-led historic soul as prayer and answer, as evolution and inspiration. Religiously (*i.e.* supremely) they are the two movements that make the world, if we interpret it from its spiritual height.   And they give us the categories in which God and man meet.   They meet in action rather than in being; and the unity of being is just such as is required for mutual action and communion.   God and man meet in humanity, not as two entities or natures which coexist, but as two movements in mutual interplay, mutual struggle, and reciprocal communion.   On the one hand we have an initiative, creative, productive action, clear and sure, on the part of eternal and absolute God; on the other we have the seeking, receptive, appropriative action of groping, erring, growing man.   God finds a man who did not find Him, man finds a God who did find Him.   We have the self-complete God who cannot grow, in whom all things are already, Yea and Amen; and we have the inchoate man who must grow, and stumbles as he grows; and we have movement in each. We have on the one hand the perfect God who cannot grow; and yet, as the *living* God, he has in his changeless nature an eternal movement which He implanted as growth in the creature He made in his image.   And on the other hand we have this waxing man, who only grows into the personality that communes with God.   He grows through the moral exercise of that passion for the Absolute and Eternal which is so much more than God's return upon Himself because He does not return void but laden with free souls for His sheaves.   We have these two movements permeating the whole life of historic humanity, and founding its spiritual psychology.   If we leave Christ out of view for the moment, we recognise such a strife, such a " Lord's controversy," not in Israel only but in the great psychology of the race.   All spiritual existence is action.   History is action, and reciprocal action. It is commerce, and even conflict, with the transcendent. Its sense of God is not that of subjective immanence but of living contact with a living spiritual reality. A true psychology of religion leaves you at the last face to face with a choice and a venture; not an experience in the sense of an impression, but, more actively, in the sense of a *decision*; the decision, namely, that what we feel facing us, urging us, dominating us, is not an illusion but the presence and action of a transcendent reality. That is the sure venture of faith. The divine thing in the soul is not a mystic subjectivity but objective truth acting upon us at closest quarters, as a finer, fuller soul in soul.

The vast issue in our personal Humanity, therefore, is not the still conjunction of two natures in the soul, but the crisis of two permanent and fundamental movements in it; it is not the union of two entities but the action of two powers, one passing one way and one another. If the whole drama of the soul of man could be compressed into one narrow neck and one strait gate, that is what we should have—the tremendous friction (so to say) of these two currents within a personal experience, And if we could widen that neck at one part, what we should have would be a whirlpool* in which the two currents become mutually and crucially involved, forming a centre of perfect rest.

§ § §

Rudely speaking, that may be used as an image of what we have in Christ. At his central place we have what we might call the node at which the two movements, being compressed, meet, rotate, and cast a fine

---

* What the old theologians would have called a περιχώρησις

column to heaven. The calm is the calm of intense victory. If life be a comedy to those that think, and a tragedy to those that feel, it is a victory to those who believe. But, however it may fare with our imagery, in Christ, we have two things, the two grand actions of spiritual being, in final peace and eternal power. We have the whole perfect action of Godhead concentrated through one factor or hypostasis within it * and directed manward both to create and redeem ; and we have also the growing moral appropriation by man's soul moving Godward of that action as its own, as its initial divine nature and content. In Christ's life and work we have that divine mobility† in which the living Son eternally was—we have, that coming historically, and psychologically, and ethically to be. He came to be what he always vitally was, by what I have called a process of moral redintegration. He moved by his history *to* a supernal world that he moved *in* by his nature. We have that divine Son, by whose agency the world of souls was made, not now creating another soul for his purpose, but himself becoming such a soul. Surely, as I have said, if he had it in him to make souls in the divine image it was in him to become one. On the one side we have a personality, originally existing under those spiritual and discarnate conditions (for which our individualist ideas of person are so inadequate and misleading) —we have that personality taking the form and conditions of a corporeal life, in order to be the arena and the organ of God's revelation and man's redemption. (You may observe that what we are dealing with is not a contrast

---

* By what theologians used to call an *apotelesma* in the Son.

† I ask leave to use the word mobility to express that uncaused self-contained vitality, that changeless change, in God which is the ground of the manward movement of which I speak.

of finite and infinite natures, but of corporeal and discarnate spirituality or personality.) And, on the other
side, we have him growing in this corporeal personality,
this increate but creaturely life. We have his eternal
person living under the conditions of corporeal personality;
we have his divine mobility, therefore, translated into
human growth. We have together within one historic life
the gradual descent and the growing ascent, by a moral
process in each case. We have them on a world scale,
an eternal scale, the scale and manner of spiritual being
in so far as experience tells us of spiritual being. And we
have them in the unity of one historic person, to show
that, however inadequate earthly personality is to
heavenly, they are not incompatible, and they are capable
of the supreme mutual act of love and grace. In the
person of Christ we have the crisis and sacrament of
divine and human love. Do not let us speak here of
impossible contradictions in logic. Let us rather
remember here again that the reconciliation of such
rational antinomies as God's sovereignty and man's
freedom only takes place in the unity of one active
person which has equal need of both for full personal
effect.　　　　§　　§　　§

Christ thus embodies the two movements of spiritual
reality in which man and God meet. Such movements are at bottom acts. For the world is not so
much the abode of God as the act of God; and man's
function in the world is not so much to settle immanently
into it, even into its growth, as to overcome it, subdue it,
and find himself for a transcendently active God in it.
In either case the movement is a vast act, and the goal is
a personal communion of acts. On either side the
personality is put into a dual act and consummated there.

So much must be allowed to the idea of immanence; which is a very fertile idea if it is construed ethically as action, and not ontologically as mere presence or mere movement; if it is viewed as the personal action within the world of a Person who needs other persons and their free acts for the communion which in Christ He found absolute and eternal.

Creation is only maintained by the standing act of the one God in his grace; who is, therefore, duly answered only by a whole devoted life as the standing act of man in his faith. God is active in his work as its incessant creator, just as in His kingdom He is incessant redeemer; and man, too, subsists in action, and becomes what his action makes him; and he attains the kingdom by the constant act of faith which integrates him into the act of grace. Life, history, at its highest may be figured as a wire traversed in opposite directions by these two great spiritual currents, movements or acts.

§   §   §

Let us mark still more carefully their co-existence in Christ.

First, we have man's movement to God, or man's action on God, either in the way of aspiration and prayer, or in the way of acquiring from God moral personality.

It should here be remembered that human personality is not a ready-made thing, but it has to grow by moral exercise, and chiefly, in the kingdom of God, by prayer. The living soul has to grow into moral personality. And this should not be ignored in connection with the moral psychology of Christ. He no more than we came into the world with a completed personality—which would be not so much a miracle but a magic and a prodigy.

What he brought with him (if some repetition be

pardoned in a series of lectures) was such a soul as was bound morally (and not by a fated necessity) to grow, under his life's vocation, to the personality that was the complete and final revelation of God, the agent of man's redemption, and the *locus* of man's communion with God. A soul of Godhead is the necessary postulate of the redeeming personality; it is the necessary foundation for the growth of that personality; and it is the necessary condition of the finality of his work. It was a personality that differed from all others by finding its growth to lie in the unaided and sinless appropriation of that which it already was. The *potuit non peccare* rests (but in no fated or mechanical way) on the *non potuit peccare*. The ground of his inability to sin did not lie in the immunity, and almost necessity, of a nature or rank, but in the moral entail, the moral reverberation, of his great, initial, and inclusive act eternal in the heavens. His renunciations on earth had behind them all the power of that compendious renunciation by which he came to earth; even as his earthly acts of individual forgiveness, before he came to the universal forgiveness of Calvary, had behind them that cross which he took up when the Lamb was slain before the foundation of the world. His relation to God was immediate from the first, and perfect; but that did not give him any immunity from the moral law that we must earn our greatest legacies, and appropriate by toil and conflict our best gifts. We have to *serve* ourselves, heirs to the greatness of our fathers. *Non potuit peccare*, nevertheless. The intimacy of his connection with Humanity was in that respect but qualified. Yet to his own experience the moral conflict was entirely real, because his self-emptying included an oblivion of that impossibility of sin. As consciousness arose he was unwittingly pro-

A A

tected from those deflections incident to inexperience which would have damaged his moral judgment and development when maturity came. And this was only possible if he had, to begin with, a unique, central, and powerful relation to the being of God apart from his own earthly decisions. So that his growth was growth *in* what he was, and not simply *to* what he might be. It was not acquiring what he had not, but appropriating and realising what he had. It was coming to his own unique self. I have already said that I am alive to the criticism to which such a position has been exposed, in that it seems to take him out of a real moral conflict like our own. And the answer, you have noted, is three-fold. First, that our Redeemer must save us by his difference from us, however the salvation get home by his parity with us. He saves because he is God and not man. Second, the reality of his conflict is secured by his kenotic ignorance of his inability to sin. And third, his unique relation to God was a relation to a free God and not to a mechanical or physical fate, or to an invincible bias to good.

§   §   §

The second movement is God's movement to man.

In this connection we note, *first*, that God by his nature does so move.

He is no Deistic God. His changeless nature is not stock-stiff and apart. It has an absolute mobility. It has in it the power and secret of all change, all out-going, without going out of Himself. It is part of his *self-assertion* as the absolute God that he should *determine Himself* into *communicating Himself*. He moves, he was not moved, to give Himself in revelation to man. But was man, then, eternal in God, if in His gift to man He

do not go out of Himself in this act ?   That cannot be ;
for man is His creature and the creature is not eternal.
But He went out always to His increate Son, in whom
and through whom all creation is and all Humanity ; in
and through whom alone we have the revelation and
actual gift of Himself ; who was coming, and not merely
prophesied, in the Old Testament, and in a less degree
in other faiths.

Second, He moves to save.

The coming of Christ in the long course of history is
the coming of God the Redeemer.   Man's hunger for
deliverance is the greatest movement in all the soul's life
except one—God's passion to save, and his ceaseless
action in saving.   It is here alone that we grasp God's
real presence and rest on it for ever.   Valuable as
speculative versions of the Incarnation may be, we only
really have it and believe in it when we sit inside it, by
the saving action which sets us in Christ, and assures us
of the incredible fact that we are included by God's
strange grace in the same love wherewith he loves his
only begotten Son.   We are sure of the Incarnation only
as those who taste the benefit of Christ's death in union
with him.

§   §   §

What we have in Christ, therefore, is more than the
co-existence of two natures, or even their interpenetration.   We have within this single increate person the
mutual involution of the two personal acts or movements
supreme in spiritual being, the one distinctive of man,
the other distinctive of God ; the one actively productive
from the side of Eternal God, the other actively receptive
from the side of growing man ; the one being the pointing,
in a corporeal person, of God's long action in entering

history, the other the pointing of man's moral growth in the growing appropriation by Jesus of his divine content as he becomes a fuller organ for God's full action on man. The two supreme movements of spiritual being, redemption and religion, are revealed as being so personal that they can take harmonious, complete, and final effect within one historic person, increate but corporeal.

We seem, viewing it in this light, to have something that comes nearer to our experience, something we can verify, and something, therefore, that is of more religious value to us, than if we speak too much about a conjunction of natures. That is not within our experience; and therein it shares with such theories as a metaphysical Trinity, or the adjustment of mercy and justice in God, a certain spiritual impotence as it works to its results.

§   §   §

When we set to consider the nature of God's union with man in Christ we must give proper effect to each side. In the first place nothing must be done to imperil the absoluteness, the freedom, of God, His creative initiative on grounds entirely within Himself. Accordingly, the union in a corporeal Christ can only be an exalted form of God's relation to those finite conditions which underlay the existence of a created world, and made it at the same time a finished world. That is to say, it was a relation that had its roots in Eternity, a relation within the absolute God, an immanence of the world in the Transcendent, of the corporeal personality in the spiritual.

But, in the second place, nothing must be done to impair the reality of human life, the conditions of its finitude, the necessity of growth within the course of time. It does not begin as a finished article. It begins with certain possibilities, with a destiny engrained in the protoplast; but it only passes from a destiny into a perfection through a career.

But, having given due effect to each side, how can we have those apparent contradictions united in one historic personality—absolute God and relative man, absolute finality and growing attainment, absolute Grace and growth in Grace, the victory won and yet the victory to be won, the Kingdom come and the Kingdom coming? How are we to adjust the contradiction between the absolute and the evolutionary in this concrete and crucial case? On the threshold of such inquiry let me remind you once more that it is only in the alogical unity of a person for whose action and growth they are necessary that we find the harmony of several antinomies that defy rational adjustment.

§   §   §

We may take a step by remembering the form in which the union is expressed. It is not in a monumental person but in an active, not in a quiescent personality, statuesque and ideal, but in one who exists in a vast movement and is consummated in a crucial act. The union means that this act or movement is twofold. In a sense, but in no monistic sense, we have one nature, in two modes of action; for moral reality must be in heaven what it is on earth. It is a polar movement, the reconciliation of two directions, two tendencies, and not the fusion of two quantities, and certainly not of two forces. It is wills that are concerned; and wills are not forces so much as elective and directive powers over forces. If will be a force, it is a force that differs from all others in choosing them, aiming them, coordinating, and concentrating them. It lays the guns, so to say.

As the union of wills we have in Christ, therefore, the union of two moral movements or directions, and not merely of two forces or things; and we have their reconciliation and not merely their confluence, their mutual living involution and not simply their inert conjunction. Much that may seem obscure would vanish if we could but cease to think in terms of material substance or force, however fine, and learn to think in terms of personal subjects and their kind of union; if our minds gave up handling quantities in these high matters and took up kinds. It is the long and engrained habit of thinking in masses or entities that makes so unfamiliar and dark the higher habit of thinking in acts.

§   §   §

And the next step we take is to note that it is a union whose object is above all religious. It is not to provide us with a scheme of things, or a ground of ethic. It is to save. It is to restore. It is to restore the soul's communion with God. It is to regain true religion by a new birth. The nature of the union must be given us by the nature of the purpose to be served and the work to be done. The canon for the Incarnation, I have said, is soteriological. It is the work of Christ that gives us the key to the nature of Christ. It is the experience of faith in his work that alone opens to us the person and the deity of Christ as the creator of the new life with God. And difference of experience here, the difference between saving and sympathetic faith, covers a difference in the type of religion, which a few generations always reveal as really another religion. What we have to ask about Christ then, is this, what account of him is demanded by that work, that new creation of us, that real bringing of us to God, not simply in nearness but in likeness? We are to think about Christ whatever is required to explain the most certain thing in the soul's experience— namely, that he has given it the new life of God and mercy, and saved it from the old life of guilt, self, and the world. We ask what is required in one who not only opens communications but restores to such as we are real and complete communion with God, one who does not pass us on but keeps us in himself, to keep us in God? What is required in one who is himself our reconciliation and our holiness before God ; one who is God's holiness in human form; who unites the receptivity which is religion with the creativeness which is revelation; in whom revelation and religion are completely one on the whole historic scale? The union of God and man in Christ was of the nature required by that saving work, and not by the idea of a paragon Godman. It is the union in one kenotic person of God's distinctive action and man's. We have God as a Trinity, *i.e.* as a personal God who, without going out of Himself, can move, love, communicate, in a perfectly spontaneous way, with-out being moved by any power outside, who has in His holy self both the ground and object of his outgoing love. And we have man as a person, but as a creaturely person, with a twofold disposition—first, to receive rather than to create, and second by this receptivity to grow as a person, from the living soul in which he begins, to its own latent quality and destiny. Is it quite impossible* to unite in

* Here let us once more remember that, when we speak of the possible or impossible, we are not appealing to the licence of a psychology merely scientific or phenomenal, but to a sympathetic and spiritual psychology ; to a psychology which comes not by the detached observation of religion as a historic fact, but either experiences religion in that per-sonal and mystic feature which makes it faith, or at least pursues with sympathetic imagination the spiritual process of those who are the classics of the evangelical experience as the summit of religion. Troeltsch is perhaps the greatest of our authorities on the psychology of religion ; and he has done valuable service in the stand he has made on this point.

one person—not omnipotence and feebleness; that is impossible—but the absolute outgoing love of God and the perfect but growing reception of it by man? Is it impossible to have, in one saving man, perfect revelation and perfect religion perfectly interpenetrating? Is it impossible to have, in one mighty person, salvation already guaranteed and salvation in course of being wrought? Did he not himself preach of a kingdom that was coming because it was come? Is it impossible to have in that person's very constitution a salvation which is only worked out by his own appropriation of the deep content of his own saving soul? His was a soul framed for saving, so to say, as the others were framed for being saved; and when he came to himself it was to a Saviour, he came, as we come to ourselves as his saints. His growth in grace was the history of the world's moral crisis, it was, in the same act, the growth of our salvation; for the atoning cross was the principle and the achievement of his whole moral life. But it was the working out of a salvation which was already there, in virtue of the great renunciation whereby the Creator of souls came in fashion as a soul he made. In a sense, we were saved by Christ before he was born; and he was born because we were thus saved. Could the agent of creation in Godhead not appear among the persons he created? Could the Creator Son not become a creaturely soul, however increate?

§   §   §

What we have, then, is this. The union of God and man in Christ is so far like the Creation. On the one side it is a finished work of God, on the other it is a progressive work of man. It is a finished work of God in so far as this; the exceptional, the increate person

of the historic Jesus, as the kenotic incarnation of
the eternal Son by his own act and movement, contained the Godhead in its whole fulness of holy love.
So that that person by his holy constitution, whether
he knew it at every moment or not, guaranteed
the perfect consummation of salvation in the ever
perfect sinlessness of the Saviour. But the union has
another side—the appropriative ascent and the progressive deepening of the man Jesus in this sinless
life and holy work; his enlarging sense of the work
to be done, his rising sense of the power to do it, and
his expanding sanctity in the doing of it. We may
speak of a progressive incarnation within his life, if we
give it a kenotic basis. He grew in the grace in which
he always was, and in the knowledge of it. As his
personal history enlarged and ripened by every experience, and as he was always found equal to each moral
crisis, the latent Godhead became more and more
mighty as his life's interior, and asserted itself with the
more power as the personality grew in depth and scope.
Every step he victoriously took into the dark and
hostile land was an ascending movement also of the
Godhead which was his base. This ascent into Hell
went on, from His temptation to His tomb, in gathering
power. Alongside his growing humiliation to the conditions of evil moved his growing exaltation to holy
power. Alongside the Kenosis and its negations there
went a corresponding Plerosis, without which the
Kenosis is a one-sided idea. *Er starb und wurde.* The
more he laid down his personal life the more he gained
his divine soul. The more his divine soul renounced his
immunities the more he acquired of glory. The more he
discarded his privilege the more he appropriated his

dignity.   The less he thought of prerogative the more he grew in power.   More and more, as he laid by what he eternally was, he came to be what he began by being. The eternal son learned by suffering the sonship he had never forgotten.   And this was the positive process of the long act of our salvation.   Our redemption was the achieving also of his old incarnation.   The growing involution of those two movements of descent and ascent was the procession also of the reconciliation of God and the world.   Then the consummation came, and it was all secured where it could never be undone.   But it must be for ever unfolded for what it is, and not to what it might be made to become.

Thus the sinless growth of Christ's character is in the very act growth also of his objective achievement for us. It is the moral process of man's salvation, and the gradual act of God.   Christ's perfect progress to perfection, his finished style of achieving his finished work, is only the obverse and detail of God's act of our redemption, already absolute in His holy love and His holy Son.   His self-sanctification was ours also.   Christ worked out the Salvation he was.   It was only in history and its conditions that he could realise all that was superhistoric within him.   He was exercised unto the godliness he brought with him.   The deepening of his faithfulness was the emergence of his deity.   He was not acquiring deity, he was unfolding it.   And in his lowest limits his divinest mastery shows.

§   §   §

When we are asked, then, what we mean by the God-head of Christ we may begin by disowning certain things which we do not mean.   We do not mean that the whole Godhead and its omnipotence was packed, as

it were, into conditions of space and time in that historic person (though the whole Godhead was involved in him and his work). We do not mean that " the baby Jesus was the Lord of Hosts," except in some sense that would take much explaining. We do not mean that Jesus himself ever so felt. Nor need we mean that at every moment of his life he had an equal sense of what he was. Nor do we even mean that at any moment of his humiliation he necessarily had the full sense of all he was. But we do mean that as the Eternal Son he was the complete and final action of the holy and gracious love of God our Saviour; that his holy Humanity went up always as an absolute satisfaction and joy to God; that God saw in him the travail of His Own Soul and was satisfied; that in Christ's historic person God offered himself in his saving fulness to and for mankind with the omnipotence required for his saving work.

§   §   §

And when we are asked what we mean by the manhood of such a Christ, we do not mean some stalwart dignity with which he faced and owned God in self-respecting godliness. The "manliness of Christ," like his " bravery," is an unpleasant phrase. Nor do we mean an elemental force and passion which linked the natural side of his personality to the world with the fervour of a Titan's blood—as if but for the grace of God he could have been an antedated Mirabeau. We mean much more than his intimate and sympathetic humanness. For the essence of Humanity is conscience. It is man's moral relation to a holy God. And Christ's manhood, therefore, consists in the moral reality of his experience, his conflict, and his growth. It means his true ethical personality growing in an actual historic situation. It means that he counted in the public of his age, and really inhabited its spiritual *milieu*. It means that he filled a mighty place in the social situation of his land and time, and that the immediate reference of all he said and did was to that situation, however vast, and even infinite, the total horizon was, the total bearing of his action or speech. And above all it means that his action arose ethically out of what he was, that his carriage expressed his soul, that his vocation rested on his position, that his receptivity is the greatest human activity, that he was, first and foremost, the ever receptive Son of the holy Father, and that he only did the things which were shown him of God. His manhood was in his perfectly active receptivity. His subordination was no inferiority. His obedience was his divinest achievement. And out of that obedience grew his vast creative, commanding, and even coercive, effect upon the world. His kingly rule is but the upper side of his filial sacrifice, of the obedience which put him *by* man's side while he was *on* God's. His human person was not the most illustrious of the many spiritual and providential personalities that had appeared on earth from God. It was in its nature exceptional and miraculous. It was a new departure—more above other men than the first man was above the nature from which he rose ; yet as truly of man as man is of nature. He was all men's creator in a true man's life. And his *identity* with Humanity lies not in prolonging, as it were, to the sky the rarest matter of the race, but in his own voluntary act of *self-identification* with it. His identity with man lay in no mere continuity of substance, nor even in participating in personality, but in his assumption of man's *conditions* of personality, and his renunciation of

God's. It lay in his active acceptance of the human
and sin-laden conditions of communion with God in such
victorious and sinless way as to make that communion
possible and real for every other personal soul. And
amid all that we recognise in him of human conditions
and human growth, even his growth in the consciousness
of what he was, we shall be most careful to note that any
growth in his sense of his Godhead was not the growth
or acquisition of that Godhead itself.

What man has in common with God, altogether, is
not the kind of identity which is claimed in various
theories of continuity and immanence. The immanence
of God is indeed the true unity of Creation; but it is not
the principle of the communion of God and man. It is
too little ethical for that. Man's identity with God is
formally, personality; and, materially, it is a mutual
spiritual act possible only to persons. It consists in the
personal nature, and especially the personal action, which
alone make communion possible. So much of parity
there is, else communion were impossible. On each side
is a spiritual person. But in the case of Christ, and in
view of his work to restore communion, the personality
was no created gift, but the Creator himself in a bodily
eclipse instead of heavenly glory. The soul's Redeemer
was the soul's Creator, divested of everything but the
holy love in which he created, and raised by the deep
and long renunciation to a power in which lies the
salvation for ever and ever of the whole created race and
world. Man is indeed incomparable with God, but
incompatible he is not. And in Christ the compatibility
becomes full communion. In Christ the living God is,
to the extent he lives, the giving God. In Christ we
were neither made nor saved to eke out some lack in

God, nor to meet some hunger in his being; but of his fulness have we all received. And we are here as the fulness and overflow of his creative love, to his praise and glory in our faith's receptive and sympathetic love.

God in Christ is the maker of his own revelation. It was God himself that came to us in Christ; it was nothing about God, even about his eternal essence or his excellent glory. It is God that is our salvation, and not the truth about God. And what Christ came to do was not to convince us even that God is love, but to be with us and in us as the loving God forever and ever. He came not to preach the living God but to be God our life; yes, not to preach even the loving God but to be the love that God forever is.

In Mr. Glover's fine book recently published on *The Conflict of Religions within the Roman Empire* (Methuen, 7s. 6d.) he has naturally much to say on the historic figure and effect of Jesus Christ—so much that it involves more beyond concerning his person that he does not say. Mr. Glover gathers up his belief about Jesus in the following compressed sentence. "Jesus of Nazareth does stand in the centre of human history; he has brought God and man into a new relation; and he is the personal concern of every one of us." That is really a tremendous thing to be able to say, as the conclusion of a true historian. It has the note if not the fulness of the true Christian faith. And it offers a welcome contrast to much of the religiosity of slashing litterateurs who are iconoclasts destitute of the historic sense, as well as of moral delicacy, and the inward light, and whose moral ideal is not the loyal but the rebel. But it is a conclusion that carries us farther than the writer goes, farther, of course, than he may say he was entitled to go by the

scope and compass of his book. At any rate it carries
the mind into a region which we may call metaphysic or
not but which is certainly metempyric, and compels
conclusions much beyond those of moral æsthetic or
religious impressionism. It may be quite true that
Christianity was early captured by Greek and other
metaphysics, and that their bond remains upon Christian
thought to this day. It may be that some who take a
position as decided as Mr. Glover's towards Christ as
" One who brought God and man into a new relation,
and who is the personal concern of each one of us," are
yet unable to use with entire heartiness the language
of the current creeds about the conditions in Christ's
person which underlie such a function and place. But
what is the real explanation of that capture of Christianity by the metaphysic of the early centuries ? Is it
not here, that the work of Christ, the position of Christ
—his work and place as Mr. Glover states it, his
redeeming, reconciling work as the early Church experienced it—that these are not intelligible to faith's own
thought without some metaphysic. A metaphysic of
some kind is bound up with a Christ of this kind.
Without some metaphysic you have not a base for that
mystic adoration of Christ which is so much more than
divine ethic, and which a whole class of churches has
lost. It is impossible to believe in one who changed
the whole relation between the race and God without a
metaphysic of the relation between that one and God.
It is impossible to think of Christ as the personal concern
of every person without a relation between his person
and every other which it is not an absurdity to conceive
in the theological way which makes Christ the agent of
their creation. Such a relation between Christ and other

men carries us, as soon as we reflect and ask about it, into a Christ supra-historic, supra-human, and premundane. Some metaphysic of personality is inevitable—except to such minds as have a native nescience, a positive endowment as negative poles in all that region. Only it must not be a metaphysic of mere thought, brought up to faith and imposed on it—injected as it were into its tissue as a preservative which hardens it, or, if not hardening it, then soaking it in an inspissated gloom. It must be a metaphysic of faith itself. It must be some form of the post-kantian metaphysic of ethic ; a metaphysic of the ethic which culminates in God's supreme moral act of redemption and in man's supreme moral act of faith. It is on such lines that a modern Christology must be shaped—slowly as the rebuilding may come. A faith in metaphysic is one thing, and the metaphysic of faith is another. The former dominated too much the theology and the religion of the past; to the latter belongs the future. It belongs to the metaphysic which is demanded by the psychology of the distinctive experience of faith. It is only the Christ of the reconciled conscience that promises us a Messiah of the intelligible world. It is only the Christ of the New Creation that can be the Christ of a complete *Weltanschauung*, and wear the crown of a new world wherein dwelleth the righteousness of a holy God.

§   §   §

I hope, in these too compressed and tense but not unmeaning words of mine, that the Lord in some measure has been transfigured before us. I hope the atmosphere has been luminous even if every thought is not lucid, and that it has been good to be here even if not knowing all we said. The glory of the Lord is something more than lucid when it breaks out upon waiting, watching, praying, bemazed men. And there is laid upon us, as we go down from the Mount, the command of silence in the form of an incapacity for due speech. We cannot see for the glory of that light, and what we do see is as yet beyond a man to utter. Still I trust we have felt some of the depth of that Glory which with unveiled faces we shall one day behold, and rejoicing in it shall be made like it. Let us, as we descend, go down with a secret which we cannot perhaps expound but which we cherish, and smile to each other like silent lovers in a crowd, and thus in a true Church of faith-adepts overcome the world. Let us go down to know that there is nothing in all the raging valley—neither the devilry of the world nor the impotence of the Church—that can destroy our confidence, quench our power, or derange our peace. Let us go down to know that the meanest or the most terrible things of life now move beneath the eternal mastery and triumphant composure of an almighty Saviour and a final salvation which is assured in heavenly places in Jesus Christ our Lord.

§ § §

And now may he who so emptied himself that he was filled with all the fulness of God dwell fully in us; may he raise, rule, and perfect us in all holiness; to the end that, bowing before him with every knee both in heaven and upon earth, and ever more calling Him Holy, Holy, Holy Lord, we may be, in Him, to the praise and glory of the Father's Grace Who made us acceptable in the Eternal Son, world without end. Amen.

B B

Finished Oct. 30-11